The End of Days

MATTHEW HARPER

The End of Days

African American Religion and Politics in the Age of Emancipation

The University of North Carolina Press *Chapel Hill*

This book was published with the assistance of the Z. Smith Reynolds Fund of the University of North Carolina Press.

Set in Arno Pro by Westchester Publishing Services
Manufactured in the United States of America

The University of North Carolina Press has been a member of the Green Press Initiative since 2003.

Library of Congress Cataloging-in-Publication Data
Names: Harper, Matthew, author.
Title: The end of days : African American religion and politics
 in the age of emancipation / Matthew Harper.
Description: Chapel Hill : University of North Carolina Press, 2016. |
 Includes bibliographical references and index.
Identifiers: LCCN 2015049992 | ISBN 9781469629360 (cloth : alk. paper) |
 ISBN 9781469629377 (ebook)
Subjects: LCSH: African Americans—Southern States—Religion. |
 African Americans—Southern States—History. | African Americans—
 Southern States—Social conditions. | Freedmen—Southern States—
 Social conditions. | Reconstruction (U.S. history, 1865–1877)
Classification: LCC BR563.N4 H357 2016 | DDC 277.5/08108996073—dc23
 LC record available at http://lccn.loc.gov/2015049992

Jacket illustration: African American soldiers mustered out at Little Rock, Arkansas, by Alfred R. Waud, from *Harper's Weekly*, May 19, 1866 (courtesy of the Library of Congress, LC-DIG-ppmsca-21005).

Sections of the Introduction and chapter 1 were originally published as "Emancipation and African American Millennialism" in *Apocalypse and the Millennium in the American Civil War Era,* edited by Ben Wright and Zachary W. Dresser, Baton Rouge: Louisiana State University Press, 2013.

To Elizabeth Keim Harper

Contents

Illustrations

Acknowledgments

One of the abiding myths of American individualism is that we pull our-selves up by our own bootstraps. But, truth be told, I am only standing—if I'm standing—because folks keep giving me a hand up. A whole community of people helped me write this book. I became a historian because I liked people and found them curious. As an extrovert, I have not always looked forward to hours in the archives alone. Lucky for me, the research and writ-ing were a social process, from start to finish.

This project began when Grant Wacker pointed me toward old issues of the *Star of Zion*. As the project shape-shifted through the years, teams of fellow readers and researchers pointed me in new directions. Those in my writing groups read many early drafts. Seth Dowland, Sarah Johnson, Brantley Gas-away, Elesha Coffman, and Jacquelyn Whitt: I could not have written this book without your help. I am happy to acknowledge my intellectual debt to Fitz Brundage, who had the uncanny ability to say what I wanted to say but could not; Donald Mathews, who kept asking big questions; Laurie Maffly-Kipp, who managed to be both a sympathetic and a skeptical reader; J. Cameron Carter, who would not even let me buy him a cup of coffee for his wisdom; and Reginald Hildebrand, whose criticism changed my analysis during at least two important moments in the book's development. Heather Williams, Stephen Kantrowitz, Jacquelyn Dowd Hall, John Giggie, Craig Werner, Skip Stout, and Charles Irons offered encouragement about the project when I sorely needed it. For the same reason, I owe thanks to my colleagues at Mercer University and the friendly folks at Calvin Summer Seminars. Over the four good years I had at the University of Central Arkansas, my colleagues readily lent help. Kenneth Barnes, Story Matkin-Rawn, Lorien Foote, and David Welky read chapters and proposals. Michael Rosenow and Jeff Whittingham served as writing partners, making the process more collegial and a good deal more fun. In the final stages, the good people at UNC Press have been great to work with, especially Chuck Grench, Jay Mazzocchi, Jad Adkins, and the anonymous readers whose keen comments substantially improved the book.

Librarians—it too often goes without saying—are a historian's best friends. I want to thank the many archivists and librarians who helped along the way, especially Nicholas Graham, Eileen McGrath, Jason Tomberlin, and the entire staff at the North Carolina Collection, UNC Chapel Hill; Linda Simmons-Henry at St. Augustine's College; Phyllis Galloway at Livingstone College; Monika Rhue at Johnson C. Smith University; Jane Johnson at the Public Library of Charlotte and Mecklenburg County; Bill Kreuger at the Iowa Masonic Library; Ellen Hampton Filgo at Baylor University; Timothy Purkiss at Torreyson Library, UCA; and the staff at UNC's Davis Library, Calvin College's Hekman Library, and Mercer University's Tarver Library. Thank you for making my life easier.

If I am ever tempted to take sole credit for my work, I need only remember that I did it with other people's money. Year-long fellowships from the Louisville Institute and the Christian Scholars Foundation/Emerging Scholars Network and a summer grant from the University Research Council at the University of Central Arkansas cleared my schedule and filled my pantry as I wrote and revised. I received financial support to travel from library to library: the Off-Campus Research Fellowship and grants from William B. Umstead Endowment, the Center for the Study of the American South, and the Mowry Fund at the University of North Carolina. During my research travel, several strangers took me in. Diane and Andy Pettifor offered me a room, good food, and transportation around town, at no charge, despite never having met me before; and at Belmont Abbey in Belmont, North Carolina, the Benedictine monks' call to hospitality extended even to penniless historians on archival trips. They might have thought they were entertaining angels unawares, but it was I who was in the company of angels.

For my sake, family and friends became cheerleaders, counselors, proofreaders, babysitters, errand-runners—whatever it took to help me finish. Countless friends let me use them as sounding boards or readers. I have room to name only some of them: Hilary Green, Todd Granger, Benjamin Sammons, Rosalie Genova, Emily Brewer, Wallace Daniel, and Andrea Williams. My parents, Jeff and Patty Harper, what haven't they done for me? Jim and Barbara Keim, Shirley Sennhauser, Nancy Pennington, and Stefan and Kelly Booy offered moral support and childcare when I needed them the most. Lillian and Charity both arrived after this project began. When the book competed with them for my attention, they usually won, and I thank them for that. Finally, I dedicate this work to Elizabeth, because she always believed this book was worth writing, even when it meant sacrifice on her part. And she, more than anyone, has made the years of research and writing happy ones.

Introduction
His Plan for Them Was Clear

Foolish talk, all of this you say, of course; and that is because no American now
believes in his religion. Its facts are mere symbolism; its revelation vague
generalities; its ethics a matter of carefully balanced gain. But to most of the four
million black folk emancipated by civil war, God was real. They knew him. They
had met him personally in many a wild orgy, or in the black stillness of the
night. His plan for them was clear; they were to suffer and be degraded, and
then afterwards by divine edict, raised to manhood and power; and so on
January 1, 1863, He made them free.

—W. E. B. Du Bois, *Black Reconstruction*, 1935

Edwin Jones lived in unsettling and uncertain times. He became active in
politics amid the largest social and economic revolution in American history, and he and his fellow black Southerners were at the heart of it. In the
midst of Civil War, slaves had walked off plantations, many of them into
Union Army lines. In doing so, they remade the world. Their insurrection
and military service helped dismantle the Confederacy. By the end of the
war, the largest slaveholding nation on earth had freed all of its four million
slaves. At the time, slaves constituted the largest capital investment in the
United States, worth more than all other forms of capital, with the exception of the land itself. This economic revolution was accompanied by a
violent political one, as Edwin Jones well knew. Former slaves and former
slaveholders struggled for political power in Southern states, using armed
militias and vigilante forces on the ground, as conservatives and radicals
tried to oversee the revolution from Capitol Hill.

The economic and political battles were intense when Jones addressed a
mixed-race audience in North Carolina in 1867, two years after emancipation but before black men secured the right to vote. Things could hardly
have been more uncertain. Jones, however, reflected none of this uncertainty. He told the crowd "that the negro was about to get his equal rights,"
including the right to vote. As evidence, Jones cited "references to the II and
IV chapters of Joshua" which, he explained, offered a "full accomplishment

of the principles and destiny of the race." At this point, the white magistrate who recorded the speech may well have wondered, why was Jones so confident about equal rights? There was movement in Congress toward the idea of universal manhood suffrage, but, as Jones spoke, the fate of black men's voting rights was far from settled. The magistrate might have also asked why Jones's political speech suddenly switched to the Book of Joshua. More confusing was the passage itself. The second and fourth chapters of Joshua offered no prophecy and said nothing of "destiny," much less of African American destiny. What did this Old Testament account, which described the siege of Jericho and the crossing of the Jordan River by ancient Hebrews, have to say about black politics after the Civil War?[1]

Jones was doing what many African American politicians, clergymen, and ordinary freed people did in the decades following emancipation. He wrote black experience into a biblical story, in this case, the siege of Jericho and the crossing of the Jordan River. Jones knew that the second and fourth chapters of Joshua recounted an ancient event in the early national history of Israel; but he also claimed that the passage described the emancipation of Southern slaves and their fight for citizenship rights. Black Protestants saw biblical stories like these not as distant history that offered only moral lessons, but as living, ongoing stories that spoke directly to African American experience. Jones's speech then was a public declaration that African Americans, and not white Southerners, were God's favored people. Because the biblical stories were, in a meaningful way, about *them*, black Protestants could use the narratives to predict their own future and not just recount the ancient Hebrew past.

And that's just what he did: Jones interpreted biblical narratives to predict the future. He spoke of "the destiny of the race" with confidence, as if he knew what was coming. He believed God had specific plans for the race's future. And the future he forecast was a better one: "the negro was about to get his equal rights." Jones's two theological moves—(1) writing black experience into religious narratives, and (2) confidently prophesying a better future for the race—were commonplace among black Protestant leaders in the postemancipation South. And, as Jones did, they applied that theology directly to the political issues at hand.

In the decades that followed, Southern politics remained volatile, particularly for African Americans whose prospects too often fell into the hands of the legislators, landlords, and mobs who most opposed their freedom. Black Southerners engaged in critical, heated debates with whites and among themselves. At the center of those political debates were conversations very much like Edwin Jones's speech. What was God's grand plan for the race and human history? How did the current political crisis fit into that plan? Black Southerners spoke of their destiny and their vision of the end times. They littered their debates with biblical and theological references. It would be hard for historians of Reconstruction and Jim Crow to ignore the ubiquitous theological references in black-authored documents. The section titles, chapter titles, and epigraphs in their scholarly work repeat those references—words like Jubilee, Zion, the Valley of Dry Bones, and the New Jerusalem. Each of those references carried specific meaning, yet political historians rarely attempt to explain the theological concepts or biblical stories that those references mean to invoke. Had Jones invoked the book of Esther rather than the siege of Jericho, the implications for black political rights would have been quite different.

For Jones, black politics sprang from the pages of the Bible, but there were other sources for black political visions. In attempts to explain the political outlook of the freedpeople, historians have turned to proletarian consciousness, to the culture of political activism formed in slavery, or to black Southerners' grip on republican ideology and equality before the law.[2] These attempts have focused not so much on what happened politically to black Americans as on the political ideas and actions of African Americans themselves. Before emancipation, slaves followed local and national politics and knew their value as laborers. When they secured freedom, they shared their poor white neighbors' American dream of being yeoman farmers, owning the land they worked. They seized upon American constitutional principles of individual liberty and the consent of the governed. They took to the courts to defend their equality before the law. Yet Edwin Jones's speech and the politics of other black Southerners in the postemancipation period become understandable only if we also pay careful attention to how different theological ideas mattered on the nitty-gritty level of state and local politics.

For African American Protestants in Jones's day, the emancipation of four million slaves was the clearest evidence that God was at work in human history. Abolition represented the end of one age and the beginning of another. It also marked a dramatic intervention by God, one designed to alter the course of history and steer the world toward its glorious, God-appointed end. For decades, black Americans had prayed for and prophesied the coming of freedom. Some antebellum prophets predicted emancipation in ways that eerily matched the Civil War. When freedom finally came, it proved to them that God was on their side and had already begun a plan to vindicate and elevate the race. As Jones did, they returned to emancipation and biblical narratives to understand exactly what God had in store for the future.

Emancipation was *the* key moment in black Protestants' eschatology. *Eschatology*. If the word means anything to the general reader, it conjures up the image of someone walking the streets wearing a sandwich board that reads, "The End is Near." "Eschatology" literally means the study of the end times or the last days. But the sandwich-board prophet peddles a narrow and unrepresentative version of eschatology. To the specialized reader, it is the branch of formal Christian theology that deals with the final things: death, the second coming, Judgment Day, and the millennium.[3] The term encompasses both those who say the end is near and those who say it is far, far away. Eschatology surfaces in funeral sermons and anytime Christians speak of what is to come. Black theologian Gayraud Wilmore urges us to think of eschatology as the "understanding of ultimate realities that have to do with time, history, and human life."[4]

Eschatology describes black Protestants' attempts to locate themselves within God's plan for human history—past, present, and future. They wrote themselves into biblical and supernatural narratives. These narratives identified them with the past and foretold their future. As they located their experience within biblical stories and predicted their future, they spoke often of the destiny of the race, as well as traditional eschatological topics like the second coming of Christ or the millennium. Their eschatology included an understanding of the progress and decline of God's kingdom on earth and the destiny of peoples, nations, and races in God's plan for human history. Black leaders interpreted events of their era as turning points in biblical stories, in supernatural battles of good and evil, and in millennial prophecies.

To say that black Americans were focused on the end of days means two things. First, like white Americans, black Americans were interested in end-times theology, the end of days. Second and more important, they were concerned with the end, or purpose, of their days. What was the cosmic significance of black Southerners' everyday lives? In nineteenth-century black eschatology, what mattered most was the belief that God's design for human history—justice, peace, equality—would surely triumph over the plans of evildoers. Black Southerners repeatedly returned to the memory of emancipation, because there they viewed most clearly evidence that a realm of divine justice could descend upon a realm of earthly injustice. So, the defining feature of African American eschatology was hope—not the hope of wishful thinking but a firm belief that "the arc of the universe is long but it bends toward justice," as Martin Luther King Jr. would say a century later.[5] In the late nineteenth century, that hope had two prongs: first, an end to race prejudice, and second, a special role for the African race within Christian history. These two hopes, or strains of thought, sometimes went hand in hand; but at other times, they existed in tension with each other and fueled debate among black religious leaders. These debates existed within and between denominations and within and between local congregations.

The hope in an end to racism found biblical support in Acts 17:26: "God hath made of one blood all nations of men for to dwell on the face of the earth." This verse, black Protestants argued, supported their claim of the monogenetic origins of the human race and laid out God's intentions for all races to dwell together in harmony. Some saw evidence around them of the eroding of white racism. Others considered it black Americans' duty to Christianize the nation, and thus rid it of race prejudice. Expounders on this eschatological theme found further proof in John's vision in Revelation of "a great multitude, which no man could number, of all nations, and kindreds, and people, and tongues," all gathered around God's throne.[6]

The second and competing theme in black eschatology—belief in a special role or destiny for the race—drew heavily on Psalm 68:31: "Princes shall come out of Egypt; Ethiopia shall soon stretch forth her hands unto God." In this verse, black ministers interpreted Ethiopia and Egypt as the entire "Negro race." For some, it was a prophecy that those of African descent would turn from their "sin; idolatry—forgetfulness of God" and embrace Christianity. Many interpreted the passage as an imperative for black Americans to evangelize Africa, and others envisioned a new black African state to rival the powerful nations of the world. Many hopes stemmed from this oft-quoted verse in Psalm 68.[7]

Many nineteenth-century black Christians held comfortably in tandem the two themes within black eschatology—race destiny and an end to racism. Others, however, saw them in conflict. The belief in a special destiny for Africans and African Americans necessitated some sort of racial essentialism. Even though most black ministers affirmed the monogenetic origins of the human race, beliefs in race destiny implied that the races had distinctive aggregate character traits and peculiar God-ordained futures. Some black Protestants were uncomfortable with the race essentialism of their colleagues and shied away from proclaiming a separate black destiny. Other leaders thought it hopeless to reform America from the inside and staked their millennial hopes not on an end to racism in the United States but in solidarity with people of color around the world. The method behind black eschatology was remarkably regular. African American Christians wrote themselves into biblical narratives, found evidence of God's favor in current events, and predicted a triumphant future. The themes they emphasized and the conclusions they made, however, at times diverged widely.[8]

Not all African American political leaders concerned themselves with eschatology. Even though Protestant thinking permeated black political discourse, the two were not coterminous. And white Protestants, too, were concerned with the providential and eschatological meaning of human events. Nearly all Americans in the nineteenth century assumed that they were part of a large God-directed drama; war, drought, and revivals moved human history toward its appointed end. If white Americans did not relive biblical stories as black Americans did, they were nonetheless committed to interpreting major events as part of God's sacred historical design.[9]

Nineteenth-century African American eschatological thought, however, defied the theological categories of white Protestantism. When analyzing eschatology, scholars normally zoom in on millennial beliefs, and they categorize them as premillennial, postmillennial, and amillennial. These categories refer to the dating of the second coming of Christ vis-à-vis his prophesied 1,000-year reign of peace. Premillennialists believed Jesus would return to earth before the millennium. Archetypal premillenialists, the Millerites, climbed hilltops on October 22, 1844, because they expected Jesus's dramatic return. Other premillennialists were less certain about the date but shared the Millerites' conviction that the Second Coming was imminent. Some, like dispensational premillennialists who gained popularity in the twentieth century, spelled out clearly how the apocalypse would unfold: first, a dramatic return of Jesus Christ to rapture the faithful into heaven; then a seven-year period of tribulation when Satan would be unleashed on the world; then another return of Jesus Christ, this time as a victor riding on a white horse to defeat Satan and inaugurate the millennium.[10] Whether they believed Jesus was coming next Tuesday or after a seven-year tribulation, premillennialists expected a sharp break between the present and the future. As Timothy Weber put it, they "lived on the edge of eternity only one second from a divine in-breaking."[11]

Postmillennialism, the dominant strain of eschatology among late nineteenth- and early twentieth-century white Protestants, led followers not to mountaintops but to soup kitchens and settlement houses. These white

Protestants expected the second coming of Christ to follow an earthly millennium. Earlier this belief found expression in notions of manifest destiny, that God had preordained American prosperity and expansion.[12] But by the 1880s and 1890s, Northern white Protestants interpreted the millennial reign of Jesus described in the Revelation to St. John figuratively as the world's destiny to achieve peace and justice through the progress and perfecting of human institutions. The earthly work of the church would usher in a golden age, the millennium, after which Jesus would return.[13] So, they put their energy into bringing about the millennium through social reform, working in sanitation efforts, education, temperance, and orphanages. Unlike premillennialists, they saw continuity between the present and the future.

A third option, amillennialism, uncommon among American Protestant thinkers, eschewed debates over the timing of the millennium. Amillennialists rejected the belief in a literal millennium. Rather, they understood the book of Revelation's prophecy symbolically as referring to Christ's rule in their own day and not to the apocalypse or some future golden age. The millennium, they argued, had arrived at Jesus's first coming in Palestine and would end with his second coming at the end of human history. Amillennialists, like Lutheran and Dutch Reformed immigrants, were not looking for the millennium in city slums or on hilltops. The millennium, they believed, was in the church or in the hearts of believers.

Black Protestants agreed on the millennium no more than white Protestants did.[14] African American eschatology was not a strand of thought, but rather a common framework that encompassed different, conflicting strands of thought. Most black Protestants held views of the end times that did not fall neatly into the categories of white millennialism. Rather, they blended elements from premillennialism, postmillennialism, and amillennialism. For example, African Methodist Episcopal Zion (AME Zion) bishop James Walker Hood, whose formal writings were amillennialist, in other venues gave dire warnings of an imminent day of judgment akin to those of premillennialists. In his addresses to other ministers and congregations, Hood routinely connected the earthly work of God's people with a future golden age, clearly a postmillennial way of thinking. Black theologians, pastors, and lay people simply did not feel confined by existing eschatological categories. Black Protestants spent more time in debates over what the millennium would be than when it would come.

Some of the difficulty in categorizing black millennialism lay in black Protestants' peculiar mix of hope and sorrow. Unlike many premillennialists,

African American Christians almost never despaired over the future of the world. One North Carolina Baptist, Rev. C. J. W. Fisher, admitted that the "world appears so corrupt that Christians sometimes think it is going over into the hands of the devil." But Fisher told his audience that appearances could be deceiving and that Christianity, not the devil, was gaining power in the world.[15] Fisher and his colleagues did not easily retreat into an other-worldly passivity. Rather, they fully expected to be vindicated and see progress in their own day. This hope in earthly progress differed significantly, however, from the postmillennialism of white reformers. First, they had already experienced a sharp break in history, the sudden breaking in of God at emancipation. Second, black Protestants tempered their hope with a good deal of sorrow. They sang mournful slave spirituals and lamented the persistent oppression that marred their experience of freedom. Black churchgoers held more sober assessments of human nature than did most white postmillennialists, even as they remained convinced that in the end God would make all things right.

For this reason, many black Protestants make a better comparison with seventeenth-century Puritans. New England Puritans were, one could argue, postmillennialists. They believed in earthly progress; they named their children Increase and Truth Shall Prevayl; they dated Christ's return after the millennium. Yet a firm belief in human depravity tempered their optimism. God himself, not human progress, would inaugurate a *literal* millennium with favor upon his chosen people, the New Israel. Puritans, especially those that immigrated to America, were prone to believe themselves the heirs of Israel's promise. Their journey to the New World mirrored the arrival of Israel in the Promised Land. Black Americans, too, believed that God, in a decisive moment of history, would usher in a new era, and show special favor to a specific people. But for them, as Albert Raboteau has argued, "the Christian imagery is reversed." Crossing the Atlantic, for African American Christians, was not the start of the millennium but the beginning of tribulation. Raboteau continues: "This is, as Vincent Harding remarked, one of the abiding and tragic ironies of our history: the nation's claim to be the New Israel was contradicted by the Old Israel still enslaved in her midst."[16] African Americans' belief in the destiny of their race to rise from slavery to prosperity ran counter to white American nationalism and eschatology.

They were as concerned with stories of the past as they were with visions of the future. Black Americans saw themselves in the biblical accounts of Israel and the early church. According to twentieth-century black theologian James Cone, the reading of biblical stories enabled black people to be "taken from the present to the past and then thrust back into their contemporary history with divine power to transform the sociopolitical context." That is, in many African American religious traditions, the people do more than retell stories. They relive them. Black Protestants, in the words of Cone, "break the barriers of time and space as they walk and talk with Jesus in Palestine."[17] Slave spirituals expressed this living experience of the past:

> Were you there when they crucified my Lord?
> Were you there when they crucified my Lord?
> Oh! Sometimes it causes me to tremble, tremble, tremble.
> Were you there when they crucified my Lord?

In this song, the singers ask one another if they have witnessed the crucifixion. The question assumes that it would have been possible for nineteenth-century Americans to have actually been there. The song collapses all the distance of time and space, such that African Americans in the nineteenth century might find themselves outside Jerusalem early in the first century. The lyrics offer a typological reading of scripture, something American Protestants beginning with the New England Puritans had done. In such readings, biblical passages not only chronicled an original event but also symbolically described other events in history or even the future. For example, on the literal level, the story of the prophet Jonah concerns his three-day stay in the belly of a great fish, but in a Christian typological reading, the story's real meaning is about Jesus's three-day stay in the tomb. The typological interpretation conflates the stories of Jonah and Jesus and sees both in the one passage. Black Protestants often employed multiple typological readings of a single text. They certainly understood, for example, that Jesus's crucifixion happened in a particular place and time. Yet through spiritual practices and typological interpretations, they were able to place themselves within the story. They understand the pages of scripture to be speaking about their own experience.

Biblical stories offered them ways to narrate their own story. Part of the calculated suffering African slaves experienced in the Americas was the loss of communication, being displaced to a land where they could be not be understood nor understand. Even though some Africans arrived with others who spoke their language, most slave communities had no common language to rival that of their captors. The transatlantic slave trade and the confines of chattel slavery left slaves as strangers in a strange land—in great suffering and without the language to tell their own story. Traders and owners, however, were not entirely successful in the effort to deny slaves a language. Slaves responded by recasting their home cultures in a new environment.[18] And they also made use of new languages and cultures to tell their story. They arrived in a world saturated with biblical imagery, narratives, and symbols. For them, as Vincent Wimbush has described, the Bible became a "language-world."

> With this "language" they began to wax eloquent not only with the
> white slavers and not only among themselves, but also *about* themselves,
> about the ways in which they understood their situation in America—as
> slaves, as freed persons, as disenfranchised persons, as a people. For the
> great majority of African Americans the Bible has historically func-
> tioned not merely to reflect or legitimize piety (narrowly understood),
> but as a language-world full of stories—of heroes and heroines, of heroic
> peoples and their pathos and victory, sorrow and joy, sojourn and
> fulfillment. In short, the Bible became a "world" into which African
> Americans could retreat, a "world" they could identify with, draw
> strength from, and in fact manipulate for self-affirmation.[19]

The "language-world" of the Bible offered black Americans many stories to choose from, each affording them an identity as God's favored and afflicted people. Southern slaves' identification with the Hebrews in Egypt, Moses, and the Exodus is well known.[20] Raboteau notices that slaves' religious vision of their own Exodus was prescient. "Black Christians," he writes, "warned antebellum America (in terms strikingly prophetic of the Civil War) that it stood in peril of divine judgment unless it quickly repented the sin of slavery." That black Americans, like ancient Hebrews, had experienced a dramatic emancipation, served only to confirm their belief that African Americans were God's chosen people.[21]

Black identification with Israel went beyond the story of Exodus. Literary scholar Christopher Hobson identifies four prophetic traditions in African American theology. The Exodus-Deuteronomy tradition stressed the Israelites' and African Americans' status as God's chosen people whose special covenant relationship with God came with certain blessings and curses; the Isaiah-Ezekiel strand of prophecy emphasized God's restoration after a period of exile or suffering; those in the Jeremiah tradition declared God's coming judgment for sin and forecast disaster; and the Daniel-Revelation tradition, more explicitly eschatological, expected the apocalyptic collapse of earthly kingdoms and the coming of a new kingdom of peace and justice. These categories belong to Hobson's analysis, not to any actual factions among African American contemporaries, but they help us see that black Protestants made heavy use of the entire Old Testament and not of Exodus only.[22]

Edwin Jones wrote black experience into the siege of Jericho and the crossing of the Jordan River. His 1867 speech reminded his audience that God's provision for the Hebrews went beyond their freedom from bondage. In the book of Joshua, God miraculously aids his people in battle as they conquer a land peopled with strong foes. The walls of the well-fortified city Jericho, in the words of the slave spiritual, came tumbling down. If God freed black Americans, Jones reasoned, he would also continue to give them what they needed—the franchise and federal protection, for example—to defeat their better armed enemies. Similarly, black Americans routinely appropriated the Day of Jubilee, a feature of Israel's Levitical law, as their own struggle for freedom and economic justice. Black Protestants at times understood themselves in exile, identifying with the Israelites' suffering in Assyrian or Babylonian captivity. The Old Testament prophets and New Testament church history gave black leaders numerous other narratives within which to situate their people's experience. As Allen Dwight Callahan has noted, the Bible "is replete with upsets that flout the rules of power, privilege, and prestige." The Bible champions the underdogs, the barren women, the younger sons, and the disinherited. Is it any wonder that "modernity's most thoroughly humiliated people" have turned again and again to its stories?[23]

The biblical challenge to power and privilege intensifies in the New Testament gospels. Black Americans identified with the life, death, and resurrection of Jesus Christ because his suffering and triumph over death spoke deeply to their own experience. Christian theologians for a long time have understood Jesus to be an embodiment, or type, of Israel and vice versa. That is, they believed, the Old Testament promises about Israel the nation found fulfillment in Jesus the person, and Jesus's life summarized the history of the people of Israel. As described in the Gospels, Jesus mirrors major figures like Moses, David, and Elijah and the nation as a whole. New Testament writers chose Old Testament imagery to identify Jesus as a symbol or culmination of the nation's history.[24] Given the close relationship between Israel the nation and Jesus the person in Christian theology and New Testament writings, it was not hard for black Protestants to identify with both Israel and Jesus. It was this belief in Jesus as fulfillment of Israel that set up black theologians to say "Jesus is black." Because the people of Israel, embodied in Jesus, became the outcast and the oppressed of society, Cone argued, Jesus (or Israel) in any contemporary situation remains the outcast and oppressed of society. So, in Cone's words, "Jesus is black."[25] That controversial claim first surfaced in twentieth-century black theology. However, nineteenth-century black Americans' identification with Jesus was strong enough that Cone could claim his ideas had a history. Their identification with Jesus Christ, though historians pay it less attention, rivaled their identification with the Hebrews of the Exodus. And in both cases, black believers claimed for the race a peculiar mission or destiny.

The End of Days is concerned with the story that African Americans told about themselves—their past and their destiny—and the effect that story had on black politics in particular places in the postemancipation South. W. E. B. Du Bois, the leading African American scholar and activist of the early twentieth century wrote, "The American Negro has always felt an intense personal interest in discussions as to the origins and destinies of races."[26] This was certainly the case for the postemancipation generation of black Americans. In the latter half of the nineteenth century, black Americans published dozens of race histories, communal narratives that chronicled biblical and world history, with attention to the development of their race and the destiny that awaited them. Collective race history was so important to African Americans that sociologist C. Eric Lincoln called it the "soul" of black religion. That "soul" came from black Christians' ability to define themselves on their own terms, as another scholar noted: "It is blacks giving meaning to the world, past, present, and future. Not on the official (read 'white' 'academic') but rather as *they* interpret their corporate story."[27]

Reliving and retelling the past empowered black believers to resist the oppression of their own day. It had real-world application. Cone explained its relevance to twentieth-century black religion: "Through the experience of moving back and forth between the first and twentieth centuries, the Bible is transformed from just a report of what the disciples believed about Jesus to black people's personal story of God's will to liberate the oppressed in the contemporary context."[28] We can similarly characterize nineteenth-century black Christianity. By placing their experience in the stories of Old Testament Israel or of Jesus, black Protestants resisted the dominant narratives of their day that worked to subjugate African Americans. They found more than inspiration or motivation in these stories. The narratives offered political strategies that shaped African American history, not just African Americans' understanding of their history.

Aspects of black eschatology may seem otherworldly; believers expected their lives to be changed by a sudden supernatural act. But eschatological visions allowed believers to imagine a new social order in this world. For African American Christians, the next world was not a disconnected and spiritualized afterlife with no bearing on this world. Instead, the next world included an eschatological vision of peace and justice that many expected to break in on the here and now. Eschatology was political.[29]

The emphasis on the real-world urgency and political significance of these ideas may seem odd to those well versed in theology, especially given the fact that in Western Christian theology, as German theologian Jürgen Moltmann lamented, eschatology became "a loosely attached appendix that wandered off into obscure irrelevancies." Because theologians talked about the second coming and the millennium as events tacked onto the end of time, coming from somewhere outside human history, it was possible for many Christians to segregate their eschatological beliefs from the rest of their religious lives. Although Moltmann did not believe in an imminent second coming or a sudden rapture, he protested against the definition of eschatology as the study of the distant future. "Eschatology," he argued, "means the doctrine of Christian hope ... From first to last, and not merely in the epilogue." Believers should not relegate hope to some distant age but let hope "suffuse everything here" and now.[30] Cone noted that black people talked about this kind of Christian hope long before Moltmann and his German colleagues did.[31] For nineteenth-century black Protestants, eschatology was not just about distant events. It held the power to transform the present. Their views on emancipation and the end times set the terms for political debates on a wide range of issues: racial independence, party politics in Reconstruction, land ownership and tenancy, migration out of the South, moral reform, Populism, Jim Crowism, and disfranchisement.

Though few historians have written about black eschatology per se, they have approached the concept from different angles. Their approaches offer different points of entrance into a discussion of divine history and human history in African American thought. They have analyzed African American identification with the Exodus story, black millennial thought, the religious origins of black nationalism, African American prophecy, and two literary genres—the communal narrative and the jeremiad.[32] These varied approaches have worked well to explain the contours of black religious thought, but they have been less concerned with events on the ground. As Michele Mitchell has shown, African Americans' prominent debates and anxieties over "racial destiny" mattered for missions to Africa, moral reform, full inclusion as American citizens, and black separatist movements.[33] We must ask, how did particular theological ideas shape African Americans' conversations and decisions in particular political moments?

Because so much of nineteenth-century politics took place on the level of individual counties and states, it makes sense to bring a discussion of theology down to earth by focusing on the politics of one Southern state. North Carolina boasted four of the earliest black religious colleges and the longest-running black religious newspaper in the South. African Americans in North Carolina did not necessarily discuss theology and politics more often than other black Southerners did; but when they did, a number of black institutions were there to keep a record. And black North Carolinians by their own admission benefited from a greater degree of political freedom than did African Americans elsewhere in the South. Their wider array of political choices offers us more examples of how black Protestants worked out their theology on the ground.

The conversations among black Protestants in North Carolina involved African Americans from across the South and the nation. North Carolina served as a nexus between rural and urban, Northern and Southern black religion. The state's nationally known black leaders were well connected with both the northeastern hubs of black urban religion as well as with the large population of black agricultural workers who gathered in rural churches. They remained engaged in national and international issues. So, this book cannot and does not focus on North Carolina to the exclusion of the rest of the region. While including the discourse of nationally prominent black leaders, *The End of Days* highlights the conversations of local leaders for whom local issues seemed most pressing.

Who were black Protestant leaders?[34] Many came from the ranks of the ordained clergy. African American ministers took the helm of black religious institutions—schools, churches, and newspapers. And they were well represented among black officeholders and convention delegates. Ministers lived in the worlds of theology and politics, and made significant contributions to both. But they were hardly the only ones to inhabit both worlds. Edwin Jones, for example, was not a minister. Neither was the longstanding editor of the state's most important black newspaper. These lay African American leaders drew deeply from black Protestantism and were highly involved in the state's politics. Even though they were not clergy, they merged politics and theology as often as did their clerical colleagues. When I refer to black Protestant leaders, I mean to include ministers and laypeople alike.

That group of leaders was largely but not entirely male. Toward the end of the nineteenth century, some black churches in North Carolina began advancing arguments for women's ordination. One North Carolina bishop made waves by ordaining the first female deacon and elder in any Methodist church. But African American clergy remained almost exclusively male. Furthermore, women's lack of basic political rights in the nineteenth-century South, along with social norms that limited women's access to the public sphere, ensured that men outnumbered women in almost every place where black Protestant leaders spoke on behalf of the race. That did not mean that women kept quiet about state politics and church affairs. Black women's very active public presence is North Carolina has been well documented by others. African American women formed organizations to advocate particular policies like prohibition, penned women's columns in newspapers, and publically issued directives to black men. Claiming a majority of those who sat in the pews, black women organized themselves into women's missionary associations and auxiliaries. They lobbied for and won greater leadership roles within black churches. Though they were excluded from most of the conversations I study, women appear in this book as they do in the source material: as missionaries, temperance advocates, migrants, and church members.[35]

As a group, black Protestant leaders had significantly more education and money than the average black Southerner. But individually, they varied widely by education and class. The most outspoken leaders—newspaper editors, college presidents—held postgraduate degrees; yet even some of these leaders began life as slaves or sharecroppers. And they certainly remained in conversation with other working-class African Americans who filled both the pew and the pulpit. Most of the black Protestant leaders, be they well-educated bishops, rural ministers, female missionaries, or stump speakers like Edwin Jones, never wrote a book or theological treatise. Theological debates took place among poor farmers and elite clergy alike. Debates over politics surfaced nearly everywhere black Southerners gathered: in church conventions, the legislature, Masonic halls, public festivals, schools, and meetings of disgruntled sharecroppers.

When they engaged in political debates, they returned to eschatology, not merely to draw strength and inspiration but also to advocate for one action over another. That is, their eschatology not only helped African Americans understand events; it caused events. So, *The End of Days* tells the story of black Southerners' work to define and defend their freedom in the forty years following emancipation. From the midst of the Civil War, black Southerners understood themselves to be living in the end of days, at a climax in God's plan for human history. They fled plantations and joined Union forces. Black Northerners, too, sensed the import of the time and sent missionaries south in the midst of the conflict. Together they fought for control over majority-black congregations and church buildings. They worked to expand black power in wartime and Reconstruction governments. As they struggled through a violent political environment, they returned to a hopeful, prophetic eschatology to direct their own political strategies. The rapid changes during Reconstruction seemed to confirm black Southerners' belief that emancipation had inaugurated a new millennial era. But when Reconstruction collapsed in the 1870s and black prospects looked dim, African American clergymen and politicians searched for biblical narratives that could reconcile the promise of emancipation with the disappointment at hand. From emancipation on, ordinary black Southerners fought to own land and have economic security. Nearly all envisioned a future where black Southerners were landholders. But should they migrate to a faraway land, as did the Hebrews in the Exodus narrative? Or should they demand the land they had worked, as did landless Israelites on the Day of Jubilee?

In the years between Reconstruction and the Jim Crow era, African Americans waged battle after battle to protect black freedom. Along the way, they had cause to critically reflect on their status as God's favored people. Just as the Israelite prophets did, black Protestant leaders issued jeremiads, dire warnings to the faithful that they faced God's chastisement if they wavered from their calling. Many leaders interpreted political setbacks as evidence not that black Americans had been deluded in expecting a glorious destiny but that God was chastising his people to prepare them for that destiny. Even as white supremacists triumphed in the 1890s, disfranchising black voters, segregating transportation, and terrorizing black populations, African American Protestants returned to emancipation—to the religious meanings they gave emancipation—in order to understand their plight. With the arrival of Jim Crow, black Southerners once again had to reconcile their hopes forged at emancipation with the brutal realities on the ground. As David Wills has argued, if emancipation had not in fact alleviated black suffering, then African Americans' "story would have to be retold if it were not to lapse into meaninglessness."[36]

As freedoms eroded in the 1890s, black Protestant leaders increasingly turned to Christ's crucifixion to make sense of what looked like defeat. When they experienced loss, they closely identified with Jesus's death and especially his sense of abandonment on the cross. They chose more mournful biblical stories than those they had relived in the 1860s. Yet even at the turn of the century, emancipation loomed large in the sacred historical design. In fact, emancipation became so significant in African Americans' eschatology that it enabled many to predict better times ahead even as conditions deteriorated in the late nineteenth century. After the Civil War, African Americans lived not in Reconstruction, Redemption, or the Jim Crow era, but in the age of emancipation.[37] The divine act of emancipation spoke louder than any subsequent event; that is, in black Christian theology, freedom was always more significant than lynching, disfranchisement, or segregation. The strand of Southern history that narrates the end of the nineteenth century as declension, from a radical experiment in racial equality to the dark night of Jim Crow, would have been a story unrecognizable to black Protestant leaders. By highlighting the way black Protestants understood their own history—as both human and divine—this book tells a story that hopefully they would recognize as their own.

CHAPTER ONE

A Nation Born in a Day

On February 22, 1865, the 4th and the 37th U.S. Colored Troops, among others, occupied the port city of Wilmington, North Carolina. As the soldiers marched through the streets, they sang, "Christ died to make men holy, let us die to make men free." Slaves and free blacks lined the streets to cheer, dance, and celebrate.[1] One African American woman spotted her son among the soldiers. Young men who had left home as slaves now returned as liberators. Their presence meant the end of slavery. As one observer recalled, "[Union Army] horsemen were dashing in hot haste through all the streets picking up the Confederate stragglers who had fallen behind."[2] White civilians stood aghast as black soldiers secured the city. For local whites, the control of Wilmington by armed black men was apocalyptic, a dooms-day. One elderly white man heard a "shouting mass of ex-slaves" marching beside the lines of black Union soldiers, and, in disgust, he called out, "Blow Gabriel, blow, for God's sake blow."[3] He thought the world was ending, and he wanted it over quickly.

For local blacks, too, this day held eschatological meaning, though in a much different sense. Emancipation was the key moment in African American eschatology. That eschatology was on display the following Sunday when local African Americans gathered, as they usually did, for a sunrise prayer meeting at the Methodist church on Front Street. The church, a congregation of the Methodist Episcopal Church, South (ME South), had white and black members; it had a white pastor, even though the 800 black members easily outnumbered the 200 white members. Many of the church's services were biracial with segregated seating, but the sunrise prayer service, a longstanding tradition, was attended only by the church's African American members. On that Sunday, it was no ordinary prayer service. "The whole congregation was wild with excitement," observed the church's white pastor, "with shouts, groans, amens, and unseemly demonstrations." A black leader named Charles chose the scripture lesson from the ninth Psalm: "Thou hast rebuked the heathen, thou hast destroyed the wicked, thou hast put out their name for ever and ever." Charles told the people to "study over this morning lesson on this the day of Jubilee." After the scrip-

Company E, 4th U.S. Colored Infantry, 1865. Members of the 4th U.S. Colored Infantry helped capture Ft. Fisher and secure Wilmington in January and February of 1865. Photograph by William Morris Smith. Library of Congress.

ture reading, a black U.S. Army chaplain, Rev. William H. Hunter, stood up to speak. Born a slave in North Carolina, Hunter was freed at an early age and moved to New York. He later attended Wilberforce University and was ordained an African Methodist Episcopal (AME) minister. Chaplain Hunter had arrived with his regiment only days before, and he brought with him news that the world now looked very different. When he spoke, an observer noted Hunter stretching "himself to his full size and displaying to the best advantage for a profound impression his fine uniform." He proclaimed, "One week ago you were all slaves; now you are all free." The congregation responded with "uproarious screamings." Hunter continued, "Thank God the armies of the Lord and Gideon has triumphed and the Rebels have been driven back in confusion and scattered like chaff before the wind."[4] The emancipation of Southern slaves clearly held theological meaning for black believers, for both local Southerners like Charles and missionaries from Northern denominations like Hunter.

In the prayer service, leaders referenced multiple biblical accounts: the Day of Jubilee, the Exodus story, Gideon's victory, and the Psalms of David. Yet not one at that sunrise meeting made reference to the apocalypse, the millennium, or the second coming of Christ. So we could hardly consider the meeting an example of millennialism in the narrow sense. But the worshippers at the prayer service interpreted emancipation in light of God's plan for human history. They placed their experience within a sacred historical design that offered a glimpse of the future. Black Protestants' theology of emancipation had immediate ramifications on the ground, in their experience of emancipation, in their movement out of white-controlled churches, and in their early political organizing.

Freedom, Prophesied and Interpreted

Years and decades before, many free blacks and slaves clearly prophesied the end of slavery; and when emancipation came, they greeted it as prophecy fulfilled. They anticipated emancipation as a divinely inspired event, an apocalyptic event when God would break in on human history. Like other American Protestants, black Protestants believed in a providential God, a being actively at work in human affairs, showing favor to some and displeasure to others. As Albert Raboteau put it, they believed in a "God of History, a God who lifted up and cast down nations and peoples, a God whose sovereign will was directing all things toward an ultimate end, drawing good out of evil."[5] This belief in Providence led nineteenth-century Protestants—white and black—to look for divine meanings in all earthly affairs. This was especially true for major events like war, natural disaster, or national politics.[6]

For black Protestants, however, emancipation would be a providential event of a different order and magnitude. Rev. Morgan Latta, born a slave south of Raleigh, recalled the reaction to emancipation on his and neighboring plantations: "I heard the shouts all over the plantations, 'We are free!' 'Free from slavery!' 'God has heard our prayers. We have been praying for twenty-five or thirty years that we should be free, and God has answered our prayers at His own appointed time; He has bursted the bonds of slavery and set us all free.' "[7] Slaves across the region spoke of an appointed end to their bondage. One recalled the words of Old Solomon, a slave tortured when his master discovered his hidden stash of Bibles and hymnals. Solomon was not worried about the abuse he suffered: "He said it would not always be so—that slavery was to come to an end, for the Bible said so—that there would then be no more whippings and fightings, but the lion and the lamb would lie down together, and all would be love."[8] Slaves clearly anticipated an end to slavery and saw emancipation as an answer to prayer and a sign of the millennium.

In fact, American slaves had prophesied the end of slavery for some time. The most famous of black prophets to anticipate emancipation was David Walker, whose 1829 antislavery pamphlet panicked planters across the South. Walker was born free at the end of the eighteenth century, the son of a slave father and a free black mother. Though we know little about Walker's life, it seems clear that he grew up in Wilmington, attending a Methodist meeting house, one with black elders and an independent black prayer service. He moved around, stopping in Charleston before settling in Boston as a seller of used clothes. From there, he penned the most incendiary antislavery tract ever written. Walker drew upon the antislavery theology of Wilmington's black Methodists, to be sure. Clearly, he had absorbed their belief in a Providential God. Walker told slaveholders that "God rules in the armies of heaven and among the inhabitants of the earth." He was confident that God would right the wrongs of slavery, as he said, on "this side of eternity." He seemed to expect it to come even sooner. He wrote, "Every dog must have its day, the American's is coming to an end."[9] His prophecy was for a violent judgment to end slavery in this life and presumably within the lifetime of his readers.

Walker wrote that God, "being a just and holy Being will at one day appear fully in behalf of the oppressed." Walker predicted that God's intervention would take the form of civil war. He wrote, "although the destruction of the oppressors God may not effect by the oppressed, yet the Lord our God will bring other destructions upon them—for not unfrequently will he cause them to rise up one against another, to be split and divided, and to oppress each other, and sometimes to open hostilities with sword in hand."[10] Here, Walker's vision of apocalyptic justice sounded eerily like the Civil War.

In Walker's prophecy, all Americans, and not just Southerners or slaveholders, would suffer God's wrath. He pointedly attacked the racial prejudice of Northerners, noting "pride and prejudice" reigned "even here in Boston." Because all (white) Americans tolerated slaveholding, the entire nation would face judgment. "The God of armies and of justice rules in heaven and in earth," Walker preached, "and *the whole American people* shall see and know it yet."[11] The destruction Walker forecast was not sectional but national. He seemed to imagine a conflict, one of "pride, prejudice, avarice, and blood," that would "before long prove the final ruin of this happy republic."[12] Albert Raboteau surely had Walker in mind when he wrote that it was antebellum black Christians who first warned that God would send war to punish the nation and that ultimately their interpretation would find its way into Abraham Lincoln's second Inaugural Address: "Yet, if God wills that [the war] continue, until all the wealth piled by the bond-men's two hundred and fifty years of unrequited toil shall be sunk, and until every drop of blood drawn with the lash, shall be paid by another drawn by the sword, as was said three thousand years ago, so still it must be said 'the judgments of the Lord, are true and righteous altogether.'"[13]

Apocalyptic prophecies like Walker's often accompanied slave insurrections. Nat Turner, whose 1831 revolt was the deadliest in antebellum America, seemed clearly to be a prophet cast in Walker's mold. He thought the end of slavery and the second coming of Christ were both imminent. His revolt clearly linked radical Christianity, a millennial vision, and the end of slavery. In the aborted insurrection in Charleston in 1822, Denmark Vesey and Jack Pritchard preached a radical Christianity, and authorities shut down the AME Church, considering it a subversive group. In Virginia and North Carolina, insurrection scares were associated with slaves who had been converted during the Great Revival of 1800.[14]

The connection between radical Christian visions and insurrections goes back even further. A 1759 insurrection scare in South Carolina centered on a free black man named Philip John who disappeared into the woods and then told his wife "God Almighty had been with him in the Woods." The governor of South Carolina wrote that "[John attempted] to Stir up Sedition among the Negroes, by telling them he had seen a Vision in which it was reveal'd to him that in the Month of September the white People shou'd be all under ground, that the Sword shou'd go through the Land, and it shou'd shine with their blood, that there should be no more white King's Governors or great Men but the Negros shou'd live happily and have Laws of their own."[15] Like Turner, John's apocalyptic vision included a precise timing and the end to all slavery.

In 1775, rumors spread among slaves who were evangelized by John Burnett in St. Bartholomew Parish in South Carolina: there were stories "about a book that predicted a revolutionary transformation of the world, one in which blacks would be 'equally entitled to the good things of life, in common with the whites.'" One of the slave leaders had said "that the old king had received a book from our Lord, by which he was to alter the world, (meaning to set the negroes free), but his not doing so, was now gone to hell and in punishment; that the young king, meaning our present one, came up with the book, and was about to alter the world, and set the negroes free."[16] The slaves prophesied that God would intervene dramatically in history but through the actions of the King. Considering Virginia's royal governor's promise to emancipate loyalist slaves later that year, the South Carolina slaves' vision was not farfetched. As Eugene Genovese has argued, slaves in the American South "never gave up their expectation of deliverance and did not expect it to be handed to them without effort of their own."[17] The link between radical, millennial Christianity and slave insurrections bears this out. When deliverance finally came during the Civil War, slaves understood it to be both an act of God's deliverance and the work of their own hands. In Wilmington, Chaplain Hunter thanked God for freeing slaves, even though men from his own regiment had taken the city.

Northern free black clergy wrote about the Civil War as divine punishment for slavery. "The God of the Universe is a just God," wrote a minister in 1862, "and he is pouring out his wrath upon the country in political dissension, rebellion and cruel war: to avenge for the many wrongs inflicted upon an oppressed and helpless race." They expected freedom to come from the war, and described that expectation in millennial terms, a "future glory" to soon follow the present tribulation: "ere long the bright sun of our destiny will break forth from behind the dark cloud of oppression and adversity."[18] The Emancipation Proclamation confirmed their expectations. When Northern whites grumbled against the proclamation, one minister retorted, "It is the Lord's doings, and who shall hinder it?" Emancipation was prophecy fulfilled, another preached: "The time has come; it is written by the prophet Jeremiah."[19] Emancipation-era black ministers, David Walker, and countless slaves believed in a divinely orchestrated history; they prophesied a coming day of judgment, where God would punish wrongdoers. Clearly, their warnings were a kind of eschatology.

When emancipation did come, some slaves saw it as the coming of the millennium. The 9th New Jersey Regiment helped secure eastern North Carolina in 1862 and early 1863. After one victory, a Union officer wrote, "The slaves alone seemed rejoiced at our coming, and look up our victorious banners as signs of the approaching millennium."[20] When the 27th Massachusetts Regiment landed in northeastern North Carolina, an elderly slave woman greeted the troops with dancing. She told them, "Bless the Lord, Massa! I've been praying for you these forty years! I thought you never coming at all!

But you come at last! Bless the Lord."[21] Black soldiers, too, saw slaves' deliverance as a millennial or eschatological moment. "They believe that now is the time appointed by God for their deliverance," wrote Major General David Hunter.[22] Sergeant Norman B. Sterrett of the 39th U.S. Colored Infantry wrote on New Year's Day 1865 that the end of slavery was both a reenactment of Israel's conquest of the Canaanite peoples and the much-awaited coming of the kingdom of Christ: "And this year, yes, this present new year, He will mount His chariot of power, and will draw His sword of vengeance and will ride from Dan to Beersheba, and will drive out the Hittites, the Canaanites, and the Jebusites, viz, the rebels, the slaveholders and the copperheads and the cry shall be, from the highest mountain to the lowest valley, that this world is to become the kingdom of our God and of his Christ, for slavery is abolished forever."[23] Sterrett's interpretation of the war as both the fulfillment of prophecy and a reenactment of the Hebrew past was apparently commonplace. Colonel Thomas Wentworth Higginson, commanding officer of the First South Carolina Volunteers (colored), said his men "based their whole walk and conversation on the ancient Israelites."[24] Black Union Army chaplains and noncommissioned black preachers fostered a particular theology among African American soldiers, one that gave the war and emancipation profound eschatological meaning.[25]

When Chaplain Hunter and other black troops finally came to David Walker's hometown of Wilmington, those gathered at the Front Street Methodist prayer meeting—likely the same congregation of David Walker's childhood—were ready to give emancipation many layers of theological meaning. The congregation's white pastor Rev. L. S. Burkhead tried to explain what he heard. Burkhead jealously guarded his pulpit and in his own writing appears suspect of and at times hostile to any teaching in the church other than his own. He was deeply suspicious of Chaplain Hunter, who had had the audacity to take the seat "usually vacated for the pastor" on his first Sunday in Wilmington. Burkhead openly mocked the working theology of his black parishioners. Yet despite its mocking tone, Burkhead's description of the theology of emancipation that gripped black Protestants in Wilmington reveals a great deal. That theology, as Burkhead admitted, was expansive and powerful enough to change African Americans' attitudes and behaviors and to instill in them "bright visions" of some glorious future for the race. In that theology, emancipation came to mean many things: an act of Providence, an answer to prayer, a fulfillment of prophecy, a reenactment of biblical stories, and a sign of good things—in some cases, the millennium—to come.

The theology Burkhead encountered among his own church members could be found across the South and the nation, but it was especially representative of black Methodists, who by this time had developed a distinctive theology of liberation. The AME and AME Zion churches had seminaries, printing presses, and hierarchies independent of white Protestants. They were best positioned to advocate emancipation, to disseminate ideas of racial equality and black independence, and to leave a record of the same. Even black Methodists widely differed. In their relationships with white Methodists, some chose to soften the blow black independence dealt Southern society by accepting varying forms of white paternalism. Others did not. Yet, as one scholar has argued, their Wesleyan theology, with its emphasis on holiness and Christian perfection, emboldened black Methodists to imagine wholesale social reform. Most Black Protestants held radical beliefs on antislavery and racial equality, but it is not surprising that the most pointed examples from the period come from black Methodists.[26]

The Wilmington Methodists, like many other black Southerners, wrote their experience of emancipation into biblical stories. By placing themselves inside stories of the past, black Protestants were able to offer interpretations of the present and predictions of the future that differed from those offered by their oppressors. Southern slaves identified with the Hebrews' Exodus from Egypt, as many scholars have documented.[27] Freed slaves saw themselves in the Old Testament story of the Hebrews' flight from Egypt. After four hundred years of bondage, the Hebrews followed Moses out of Egypt into the Sinai desert. As they fled, God caused Moses to part the Red Sea to provide an escape from the Egyptian army. After the Israelites passed through on dry land, the waters returned to drown Pharaoh's soldiers. Black Southerners relived this story in their own experience of freedom from slavery as occasioned by the military defeat of their enemies. Rev. Burkhead explained his black congregation's excitement: "They had just crossed the 'Red Sea' dry-shod. In their estimation Pharaoh's hosts had been engulfed in ruin— gone down in a sea of blood! Hence they rejoiced with exceeding rejoicing."[28] The fact that black Americans, like ancient Hebrews, had experienced a dramatic emancipation, served only to confirm their belief that Africans or African Americans were God's chosen people and would relive the Exodus story.[29]

Black identification with Israel went beyond the story of Exodus. In the sunrise meeting at Front Street Methodist Church, Chaplain Hunter called the Union forces the army "of Gideon," and Charles, the lay leader, quoted from Psalm 9. In both cases, these leaders identified emancipation with the military exploits of Israel, just as Sergeant Sterrett had done on New Year's Day. Two years later, black political leaders in eastern North Carolina used the military conquest of Canaan as evidence that African Americans would gain suffrage and political power.[30]

Similarly, black Americans routinely appropriated the Day of Jubilee, a feature of Israel's Levitical law, as their own struggle for land and economic justice. The leader at the sunrise prayer meeting called the Sunday following the capture of Wilmington "the day of Jubilee." Rev. Burkhead noted that many black worshippers referred to emancipation as "their great jubilee."[31] Levitical law commanded ancient Israel to celebrate every fiftieth year as Jubilee. That year began with priests' trumpets announcing a Day of Atonement, a day when all slaves were freed, all debts were forgiven, and all the property that the wealthy had amassed was returned to its original owners. The practice of Jubilee no doubt would bring significant upheaval to social and economic order. Black Americans greeted the social and economic upheaval of emancipation as their own long-awaited Jubilee.

Black Protestants at times understood themselves in exile, in Assyrian, Babylonian, or Persian captivity. They appropriated stories of Jewish preservation during exile and prophesied an end to exile and a return to glory. Months after the sunrise prayer meeting, black residents of Wilmington prepared to elect representatives for the state's first Freedmen's Convention. The organizers for the Wilmington meeting published this call in the papers: "Freedmen of North Carolina, Arouse!! . . . These are the times foretold by the Prophets, 'when a Nation shall be born in a day' . . . The time has arrived when we can strike one blow to secure those rights of Freemen that have been so long withheld from us."[32] This call appropriated Isaiah's prophecy in which the Lord asks a rhetorical question: "Can a nation be born in a day?" The obvious answer (that such a project would take years) the Lord casts aside, and announces plans to bring Israel back from exile and restore the nation in a day. The prophecy of building a nation in a day came accompanied with a promise from God. The passage from Isaiah reads, " 'Shall I bring to the birth, and not cause to bring forth?' saith the LORD."[33] The organizers of Wilmington's mass meeting claimed Isaiah's prophecy for themselves; they planned to build a nation in a day, to leap immediately from emancipation to political action. In emancipation, God had brought the race to the moment of birth. As the prophecy promised, God would not fail to finish the job. One Democratic newspaper editor in Tennessee reported that African Americans referred to slavery as "Paul's time," but called Reconstruction "Isaiah's time." Presumably, former slaves knew the Apostle Paul from his admonition to slaves to obey their masters. They remembered Isaiah for his mission to "proclaim liberty to the captives," but perhaps also for Isaiah's prophecy of a return from exile. In either case, African Americans saw themselves in the prophecies of Isaiah.[34]

Placing themselves within biblical stories allowed black Protestants to chart their future. They could appropriate the plot of biblical narratives—reliving the plight of enslaved Israelites, for instance—and take comfort in the well-known resolution that lay ahead. Burkhead noted black worshippers' confidence in the future. By seeing emancipation as an event in these ancient biblical stories, African Americans at Front Street Methodist "now looked ahead with protruding eyes and swelling hearts to the dazzling lights of their coming glories." Burkhead mocked them for the quick jump from reading ancient stories to imagining a glorious future. That future included full participation in the body politic on terms of equality and "fine churches and residences . . . and plenty to eat and drink and wear." Their visions of the future differed, but almost all included acquisition of land, education, and political power, things which Burkhead found both laughable and dangerous.[35]

Almost immediately after emancipation, African Americans in Wilmington discarded entrenched forms of deference and submission. An hour or so after the sunrise service, Burkhead gathered lay leaders of the church to discuss the "never-to-be-forgotten sunrise prayer-meeting" he had just witnessed. As they met, Burkhead could still hear "the shouting and general demonstrations of joy at the jubilee . . . along the streets in the vicinity of Front Street Church." The celebrations continued throughout the day. During the regular morning service, when Burkhead led a service for the white church members, the congregation heard the noises of celebration outside. That afternoon, Burkhead preached before the church's black members, and he picked a somber passage of scripture in a vain attempt to calm the passions of the congregation. The worshippers were so excited, he wrote, that "an impassioned appeal would have almost thrown them into convulsions; at least they would have raised an uproar."[36]

In the days and weeks that followed that "tumultuously jubilant" Sunday, Burkhead noticed profound changes in the city's black population. "On all the streets of our City might be seen the exhibitions of the spirit of the newly acquired boon of freedom," he wrote. African Americans had for some time outnumbered whites in Wilmington, but with their newly acquired freedom, they seemed to increase in number. Burkhead observed, "The whole city seems to be alive with 'Africans.'" Some rural blacks made their way into the city when they heard news of the Union occupation. But longstanding residents made their presence known in new and bold ways. They flagrantly violated rules of deference to whites. Black women, for example, no longer ceded the sidewalk to white women. Burkhead complained, "They sing and shout; and preach and pray; and drink and swear; and fiddle and dance; and laugh and yell—'Ye-ah, ye-ah, the bottom rail on the top at last!'" The sudden change in the behavior of African Americans, whom white Southerners thought they knew well, mystified Burkhead and others. He was shocked to observe how quickly his black parishioners' experience of emancipation, with its "pure 'anti-slavery gospel' dashed with the radical spirit of political intrigue," had begun "to unsettle all their former principles and ideas of subordination."[37]

Religious Independence

Burkhead himself soon witnessed that lack of subordination within his own church, as he struggled to maintain control not only of his black parishioners but also of the building itself. All across the South, black Protestants declared their independence from white-controlled churches. It was one of their very first acts as freedpeople. By the early 1870s, a shrinking minority of black churchgoers remained in white-led churches. The separation was sudden, dramatic, and, to many, completely unanticipated. White Southerners experienced shock and confusion as they watched black church members leave in droves.[38] To black Southerners, however, the move came as no surprise. Their desire to separate from white churches extended back into the antebellum period.[39] They anticipated their departure as an important, even eschatological, event.

In recounting the history of black Baptists in North Carolina, nineteenth-century Baptist preacher J. A. Whitted used a curious phrase: "When the time came for a separation." With these words, Whitted implied that the movement out of white churches was an inevitable one, as if the establishment of independent black churches followed a preordained script. Whitted described the separation of black and white Protestants in the 1860s and 1870s, like emancipation itself, as a divinely appointed moment, one foretold by prophets. According to his account, "The prayer which [our] fathers prayed was 'Grant the day Lord when we may worship God under

Bishop James Walker Hood, 1895.
Hood came to North Carolina as a
missionary in 1863, held public office
during Reconstruction, and became
the most prominent black churchman
in the state. Image: J. W. Hood, *One
Hundred Years of the African Methodist
Episcopal Zion Church* (New York:
A.M.E. Zion Book Concern, 1895).
North Carolina Collection, Wilson
Special Collections Library,
UNC–Chapel Hill.

our own vine and fig tree,' and this prayer meant to them a separation from
the white churches." Whitted's reference to vines and fig trees was not his
own word-image; nineteenth-century black churchgoers frequently made
this biblical allusion to describe racial and religious independence. The image comes from Old Testament prophecies of the "last days," when God
would judge the nations, restore Israel to its glory, and show favor to the
oppressed. The prophet Micah told of "these last days": "they shall sit every
man under his vine and under his fig tree; and none shall make them afraid:
for the mouth of the LORD of hosts hath spoken it."[40]

Like Whitted, AME Zion bishop James Walker Hood invested the separation from white churches with eschatological meaning. In 1863, Hood, a
Northern free black preacher, left a comfortable pulpit in Connecticut and
took a train south to North Carolina in the middle of intense fighting. Delayed by a shifting war front and frozen rivers, Hood arrived in January 1864,
and immediately began planting churches right behind the troops. His
missionary efforts often took place fewer than fifteen miles behind the front-
lines. In Washington, North Carolina, he and his congregation twice had to
retreat as Confederate forces advanced, only to resume missionary activities
when Union forces regained control of the town. Such plucky tactics did
not go without reward. In 1864 when he arrived in North Carolina, Hood
was the only member of the AME Zion Church in the state. Less than ten
years later, he presided over 366 churches in North Carolina with upward of

20,000 members.[41] Hood was not alone. Hundreds of missionaries from Northern denominations organized independent congregations of freed-people during and after the war. It was a boon for Northern church plants in the South, but Southern whites had trouble understanding the mass exodus from their churches. In fact, Burkhead soon found Hood at the doorstep of his parsonage in Wilmington, and Burkhead praised Hood's "practical spirit." But there was no secret as to why Hood was in Wilmington: he was planting independent black churches.

Hood described the establishment of independent black churches—both the move by black Southerners in the 1860s and 1870s and the move by black Northerners earlier in the century—as the telos of the race's entire history, ancient and modern. All of God's prophecies and providential dealings with the "Negro race," in Hood's account, anticipated the race's ultimate purpose: "the Negro Church."[42] The success of racially independent churches served as both the sign of the new era and the vehicle for attaining the progress predicted for that era. In both Hood's and Whitted's denominational histories, the extensive church building efforts flowed out of black Protestants' eschatology; black Protestants imagined a glorious future on the heels of emancipation. The separation from white churches was one of the first and most significant of the changes that freedom brought. Black church leaders considered the change a sign of "a new epoch" in history, a foretaste of "millennial glory."[43]

Not all black Protestants equated emancipation with the independent black church movement. In fact, a minority of black Southerners chose to remain in white-controlled congregations even when they had opportunity to leave. Hood wrote as if the race moved out of white churches in one unified block. In contrast, Whitted's history of black Baptists in the state praised individuals who because of affection "refused to go out from their white brethren" even though the time for separation had come. Hood's and Whitted's denominations lived out their religious independence in very different ways. Independent black Methodists (the AME and AME Zion churches) jealously guarded their racial autonomy and eyed close relationships with white Protestants suspiciously. Black Baptists and Presbyterians in the state, while maintaining their racial independence, nevertheless valued their churches' efforts to remove racial barriers between white and black Protestants. Even some Methodists pursued ways to remain united with white Southerners even as they formed all-black congregations. Yet for those who left white churches, religious independence marked the end of days—that is, a new divinely appointed era, one foretold in scripture and inaugurated by emancipation.[44]

The new era nearly cost Burkhead his pulpit. Before the city fell to Union forces, he recalled, the African American lay leaders of the church agreed to submit to his authority. Shortly after emancipation, however, they petitioned for control not only over the church's black members but also of the church property. As black members outnumbered whites in Front Street Methodist, black leaders argued that the will of the majority should prevail. And their will, the leaders told the military authorities, was to affiliate with the AME Church.

A similar struggle happened earlier in New Bern, North Carolina. There, at the onset of the war, black Methodists of Andrews Chapel gathered to hear sermons from a white preacher in the ME South. That minister abandoned his pulpit when Union forces took control of the city in 1862. With the church's white congregants "having nearly all gone into rebeldom," an African American traveler from Pennsylvania noted, the black members simply came down from the balcony and claimed the church as theirs.[45] For Andrews Chapel and other ME South churches whose clergy had fled in support of the Confederacy, military authorities ceded jurisdiction to Northern Methodist Episcopal Church (ME) bishops. ME Bishop Osman Baker then appointed J. E. Round, a white Methodist minister, to take charge of the African American congregation that met at Andrews Chapel. At first, it seemed the congregation would soon affiliate with the majority-white Northern denomination. However, a white Congregationalist began to win the hearts of many of the congregants, and, in late 1863, the two white ministers competed for control of the black church.[46]

The competition became more intense one day in early 1864 when Hood and two AME ministers arrived in town. Hood recounted that "it soon became evident . . . so far as the colored people were concerned, the two white men were not considered. The contest was between the two colored organizations." The congregation wanted racial independence. Hood, the two AME ministers, and the two white ministers continued to compete for the loyalty of the congregation. After an open debate between Hood and the AME ministers, the congregation elected to affiliate with the AME Zion denomination.[47]

The congregants' vote triggered another controversy. Did the congregation's choice of pastor trump the ME Church's official appointment? Round maintained that he had authority over the congregation by virtue of Bishop

Baker's appointment, which was backed, theoretically, by the U.S. War Department. Moreover, Chaplain Horace James, superintendent of Negro affairs in North Carolina, gave his approval to Round. Hood and Round then sent arguments to Secretary of War E. M. Stanton. General Benjamin Butler forwarded his recommendation with the ministers' arguments: "So far as I am informed both Hood and Round are regularly ordained ministers, and are both men of good character. The point at issue is, shall a congregation of colored people . . . have the right to elect their own pastor, or are they compelled to have a pastor forced upon them by Bishop Baker's delegate?" While the congregation waited for the official word, Hood paid a visit to the office of the secretary of war in Washington, D.C. Two months later, the congregation received Secretary Stanton's terse reply: "The congregation worshiping in the Andrews Chapel are permitted to select their own pastor."[48]

Secretary Stanton's statement established an important legal precedent. Although civil courts had yet to decide ownership of church buildings, churches like Andrews Chapel were at least temporarily in the hands of the black churchgoers who occupied them. One contemporary estimated the value of Andrews Chapel at $70,000. According to black Presbyterian minister J. C. Gibbs, Andrews Chapel members made a compelling case for ownership of the church building. White Southern Methodists seceded from the Methodist Episcopal Church, seceded from the Union, and "ran off with the rebel army," the remaining black members explained. They argued "that rebels have no rights that loyal men are bound to respect."[49] Just seven years before, the U.S. Supreme Court had ruled that people of color had "no rights which the white man is bound to respect." The congregation then demanded a dramatic reversal of power in a short period of time. They were living in a new era. Even though the black members of Andrews Chapel were under white authority only months before, they now boldly articulated arguments for exclusive control of the church.

In Wilmington, black members of Front Street Methodist made similar arguments for their own autonomy. They pointed to evidence in the edifice itself. The inscription on their church's cornerstone read, "In Memory of the Rev. William Meredith, Founder of the African Church, in Wilmington, N. C."[50] African American leaders argued that the inscription guaranteed that the building was intended, as they told military authorities, "for the use of the African race from age to age."[51] Lay black leaders and Chaplain Hunter presented petitions to the military authorities in Wilmington claiming that they represented a majority of the congregation and should have the right to select their own pastor and to use the church building. For over a year, Burkhead and white officials in the ME South fought legal battles to retain their control over the pulpit and the property. Military officials arbitrated the dispute by declaring that the African American congregation had use of the building one-half of each day. Chaplain Hunter assumed the church's pastorate on Sunday, March 5, wearing his army uniform as he preached.[52] The African American lay leaders of Front Street Methodist considered their racial independence cause for celebration. Control over the church was "a gift of God through our Lord Jesus Christ which no man can buy or sell from us," they wrote.[53] They understood their religious and racial independence as a divine act. In 1866, white Methodist leaders appealed the earlier decision to Andrew Johnson's administration, and complete control of the property reverted to the ME South. The black congregants then marched a few blocks north to build the city's first AME Church.[54]

They lost the building but gained their independence. The story played out all across the South, as black Northern denominations grew rapidly with the addition of Southern churches. Nannie Alexander, the (white) wife of a white Presbyterian minister in Charlotte, North Carolina, recorded her memory of the upheaval that emancipation wrought on church organizations in the area. Black members of biracial churches of all denominations began to walk out. As a committed Presbyterian, she worried that independent black Methodists, because of their racial independence and autonomy, would win over African Americans from her own denomination. She bemoaned that "when the war was ended in 1865, the Freedmen nearly all ceased to attend services in the churches in which they were brought up, but gathered in large crowds to open air meetings conducted by men of their own race [the AME Zion Church]." Black Presbyterians, she feared, were being lured away by "uneducated, sensational, and unsafe leaders"—by independent black Methodists.[55] Alexander's fear that black Presbyterians would abandon their denominational identity in order to affiliate with a racially independent church was realized in part. Many black Presbyterians switched denominations rather than stay in white-controlled churches. An editorialist for the *Christian Recorder* considered the significant growth of the AME Church in 1865 as evidence that the church had entered "upon a new epoch, and is destined to illuminate her pathway by the dazzling splendor of millennial glory." The editorial boasted of church plants all across the country, especially in the South. "In Virginia and the Carolinas," the writer explained, "she [the AME Church] now follows in the war path of Grant,

Sherman and Sheridan, applying the Balm of Gilead to the wounded and dying soldier, and publishing salvation to the forsaken and heartbroken contraband."[56] The church organizers who oversaw this influx of black worshippers into Northern denominations ascribed eschatological significance to emancipation. Hood viewed the growth of black churches following emancipation as fulfillment of prophecy, a sign that black Americans were rising to meet an important destiny, and the first fruits of "the millennial glory of the Christian Church."[57]

African American millennial beliefs predicted significant church growth, but the same beliefs may have also caused the growth. Much of the postemancipation church growth came simply from black Southerners' leaving white churches. But their exodus alone cannot explain black church membership rolls. Many contemporaries observed a rather remarkable upsurge in conversions among freed slaves. Historian Daniel Fountain argues that the scholarly consensus on slave religion has overestimated the number of Christian slaves. Using a thorough survey of extant slave autobiographical material, Fountain claims that the majority of African Americans did not become Christians until after emancipation, a claim that many historians dispute. However reliable his methodology, one thing from Fountain's story is clear. A small but important core of African American Christians, slave and free, prayed for and prophesied freedom in ways that matched the conditions of wartime emancipation. When non-Christian slaves came to witness the fulfilled prophecies of their converted peers, they flocked to the church. The truth of black millennial claims garnered new converts to the faith. Fountain likely underestimates the strength of Christianity in slave communities, but historians cannot ignore the large number of conversions among the freedpeople. One scholar has recently dubbed the postemancipation period the "African American Great Awakening." These conversions were both evidence of the millennial importance of emancipation to believers and an outcome of those same millennial beliefs.[58]

The growth of independent black churches, Hood argued, was part of nation building. Hood believed that the race needed racially separate churches in order to establish itself as a distinct people. Independent black churches broke the ties of dependence and servitude that bound black Americans to whites. And churches became the arena wherein African Americans developed the skills of institution building, fundraising, and leadership. The independent black church movement formed the race, Hood argued, into a people—separate, distinct, and self-reliant. He preached, "The Negro Church has given the Negro the opportunity he needed; it has set before him an open door which no man can shut . . . All of this and more, much more, has God done for us [as] a people, as a Church."[59] Here Hood equated the race with Church, underscoring his belief that the formation of independent black churches marked the beginning of African Americans' history as a people or nation. In a sermon commemorating the first hundred years of his denomination, Hood equated black Christians with the Hebrews fleeing Egypt in Exodus and with the scattered Ethiopian people gathering in Jerusalem in Isaiah's prophecy. The act of leaving white churches (Exodus) and gathering in black churches (Isaiah) was a fulfillment of prophecy, an act that constituted black Americans as a race or nation.

Political Organizing

Not all shared Hood's reading of these passages, but black Southerners did understand emancipation and racial independence as the birth of a nation. This was evident in the 1865 Freedmen's Convention in North Carolina. As referenced above, the call for convention delegates in Wilmington headlined a quotation from Isaiah: "These are the times foretold by the Prophets, 'when a Nation shall be born in a day.' "[60] Organizers of the convention put a premium on racial independence. Throughout North Carolina cities, small towns, and rural counties freedpeople gathered in mass meetings to send delegates to the first Freedmen's Convention. It was the first step in the political organization of a recently emancipated people. It carried, according to the organizers, great political and eschatological import.

In September 1865, the delegates from Wilmington joined others from across the state at Raleigh's African Methodist Church. Of the 120 delegates, "the great majority of them were freedmen, not freemen," observed Sidney Andrews, a Boston journalist. The men were "not only North-Carolinians by birth, but slaves by growth," and the convention organizers wanted it known that this was a homegrown movement, not the machinations of outsiders. Contrary to these objectives, they elected Hood, a Northerner, as their president. Hood self-identified as a local, though he claimed less than two years' residence in the state. More important, the organizing committee stressed, and others reported, as Andrews did, that it was "really a Convention of colored men, not a colored men's Convention engineered by white men."[61]

Any appearance of being the puppets of other political actors would have undermined the convention's goal of writing equal rights into the North Carolina Constitution.

In his presidential address to the convention, Hood urged the delegates to find a balance between radical demands and patience. He mediated between factions that already existed. The delegates, he encouraged, should not feel afraid to say why they had assembled, "holding up the motto before God and men, 'Equal rights before the law.'" He told them to "assert always that we want three things": the right to testify, the right to serve on juries, and the right to vote. Such an agenda was radical enough that, Hood argued, it had to be accompanied with "faith, and patience and moderation," and without "harsh expressions ... about any line of policy."[62] Delegates to an 1867 convention of freedmen in Alabama had the same agenda, only they were willing to say publicly what the Raleigh delegates said only in the meeting: "we claim exactly the same rights, privileges, and immunities as are enjoyed by white men—we ask nothing more and will be content with nothing less."[63] In 1865, however, Hood's plea for moderation set the tone for the convention. Conveners debated about how patient to be in their demands for equal rights and how respectfully or deferentially such demands should be articulated.

Those debates had actually begun weeks before the delegates convened. Famous abolitionist Horace Greeley, in a public letter declining an invitation to the convention, urged the "colored people of North Carolina" to place this moment in an eschatological context. "Looking back at the momentous history," he wrote, "the stupendous transformation of the last five years, we must reverently say, 'This is the Lord's doing, and it is marvelous in our eyes.' Let us unwaveringly trust that the great work will be prosecuted to its legitimate and logical consummation." Greeley urged trust, accompanied by patience. So, even though Greeley supported black leaders' "righteous demand of enfranchisement," he cautioned, "this is not the work of a day, and we must learn to labor, and if need be to wait." Greeley reminded his readers of how long emancipation was in coming, how abolitionists had worked for it for nearly thirty years. He applied the lessons of the abolitionist movement to Reconstruction: "We may not win a full recognition of your rights directly; but the effort will never be abandoned until its success is assured."[64] The reality of emancipation argued that in God's timing patience did not preclude success.

Some black North Carolinians agreed with Greeley, telling him not to worry. Edward Brooks, editor of Raleigh's short-lived black newspaper the *Journal of Freedom*, assured Greeley, "No one who is acquainted with the character of the freedmen, can for a moment doubt that he will be hopeful, patient, and peaceful." Whereas Greeley's letter referred to the long abolitionist struggle as an example of hope and patience, Brooks cited instead the experience of slaves: "Years of unrequited toil and servitude, patiently and peacefully endured, hoping for the 'day of jubilee,' prove this."[65] Brooks and Greeley drew upon different pasts, white abolitionism and black slavery, but both recommended patience. Both pointed to emancipation as proof that God would ultimately grant them success.

Despite Brooks's statement that "Mr. Greeley need not be afraid," many at the 1865 Freedmen's Convention in Raleigh did not want to wait patiently for political equality. The call for delegates advertised that "a Nation shall be born in day," a message quite contrary to Greeley's slow and gradual approach. For some delegates, emancipation was proof that a dramatic revolution was underway; patience was not called for. Even Hood thought that patience had its limits. "We have waited long enough for our rights," he told a cheering audience." People used to say it was not the time to abolish slavery, and used to tell us to wait until the proper time arrived." By 1865, the time had come, and black Americans had little to wait for. Hood thought that African Americans should "gain all we want at once," even as he admitted that God's timing might be slower.[66]

Two delegates in particular had little tolerance for talk of waiting and moderation, and they seem to not have shared Hood's theological outlook. One was Abraham Galloway. Two years earlier, Edward Kinsley, a recruiting agent for the Union Army had called him "a man of more than ordinary ability, a coal black Negro," even though Galloway had inherited light skin and wavy hair from his white father. Galloway was born a slave near Wilmington, a few years after the death of David Walker. He escaped to Canada before helping others do the same. At the age of twenty-six, when Kinsley met him, Galloway had returned to his home state as a Union spy. His knowledge of local waterways proved helpful as the Union Army captured large parts of eastern North Carolina early in the war. It had not taken Kinsley long to realize that the thousands of slave refugees in New Bern looked to Galloway as a leader. As the same time that worshippers in New Bern's Andrews Chapel were fighting for religious independence, Galloway had his own plan to ensure the same for black soldiers. When Kinsley needed help recruiting for black regiments, Galloway arranged to meet him at midnight in a local abolitionist's home. There Kinsley was blindfolded and led to the attic, where he met Galloway with a revolver and a room full of black men. Galloway then extracted promises from Kinsley that the war would be for black liberation, not preservation of the Union, and that black soldiers would not be treated as pawns.[67]

Galloway must have brought that same kind of forthrightness to the 1865 Freedmen's Convention. There an observer characterized him as being "of exceedingly radical and Jacobinical spirit." He and John P. Sampson, accused of "somewhat wordy radicalism," would later serve as state legislators in the 1870s, and for the 1865 convention both tried to edit out deferential language from the official communications. They countered the moderate views of Fayetteville barber Isham Sweet and Greensboro carpenter and teacher John Randolph Jr., who though "radical in desire," according to Andrews, were in fact "conservative in action, longing for much, but content to make haste slowly."[68] It was a debate over timing and tact.

Outside the convention, radical whites encouraged the freedmen to make bolder claims for racial equality. Walker Pearce, a Northern white Republican recently relocated to New Bern, assured the delegates that their freedom was on firm footing: "The great question of your right to liberty, or otherwise citizenship, has already been affirmatively decided on the congressional forum and on the battlefield, and been ratified by the unanimous consent of Christendom." He told the delegates not to worry about securing the blessings of former slaveholders. According to Pearce, white rebels resisted black suffrage in order to postpone retribution: "whatever punishment a righteous Providence may see fit to inflict."[69] Pearce's understanding of Confederate defeat as divine judgment of evildoers was one that former slaves shared. Charles had made the same point in the Front Street Methodist prayer service. Although several of the delegates expressed gratitude for Pearce's sentiments, few repeated his words.

In the end, the moderates won. The committee that drafted the letter to the Constitutional Convention and state legislature included Isham Sweet and John Randolph, along with Rev. George Rue, the AME missionary whom Hood had competed with for allegiance of Andrews Chapel members not two years earlier. James H. Harris, a self-educated former slave who became the most important black Reconstruction politician in the state, chaired the committee and likely penned the communication himself. The document began with the utmost deference, qualifying every appeal with the words "humbly" or "reverently." The writers went further, admitting they "possess[ed] no power to control legislation in our behalf, and that we must depend wholly upon moral appeal to [your] hearts and consciences."[70] Democratic newspapers reported none of the document's demands but applauded its submissive posture. The convention, which unanimously approved the document, had tipped the balance in favor of securing good relations with white leaders.

The convention leaders' deferential tone was surely pragmatic. When political winds shifted two years later, black politicians would not be so conciliatory. But theology and pragmatism were not mutually exclusive. In fact, some made it clear that political equality was not contingent on bold action; it was foreordained. Their theology of emancipation gave them confidence in the success of their political agenda. In the meantime, black leaders saw room for pragmatism and prayer. In fact, the convention's communication argued from providentialism to secure "kindly ties" with North Carolina whites. To accomplish this, Harris downplayed the role that black Southerners played in securing their own freedom. Instead he wanted white Southerners to accept Confederate defeat as the act of God: "Though it was impossible for us to remain indifferent spectators of such a struggle, you will do us the justice to admit that we have . . . [acted] the part only as has been assigned us, and calmly awaiting upon Providence." Harris, in the spirit of conciliation, failed to mention that for many present at the convention "calmly awaiting" had involved wearing blue uniforms and carrying Springfield muskets. In the document, Harris asked the (white) readers, "Do you blame us that we have, in the meantime, prayed for the freedom of our race?" Because "God bestowed freedom," Harris reasoned, there was no reason why whites should feel animosity toward the freed people. Within the doors of the convention, a providential view of emancipation emboldened black demands for equal rights. Publicly, they hoped that same view would curtail white vitriol, however unlikely an effect that might have been.[71]

The 1865 Freedmen's Convention, as the first statewide caucus organized by black North Carolinians, holds several lessons for how African American leaders worked out their theology on the ground. Even though it was a nonsectarian political event, the convention gave Protestant Christianity a prominent place. The convention met in a church and elected a minister as president. A large number of the delegates were ministers, and delegates routinely appealed to other delegates' Christian beliefs and consciences. As their last act, the convention established the Equal Rights League to serve as the year-round institutional structure for black political organizing in the state. The league made provision for church organizations and societies to serve as auxiliaries, broadening the league's influence by using existing church infrastructure. Nonsectarian Protestantism quickly became the established religion of black politics.

Also, the delegates at the Freedmen's Convention expected reforms to align with a divine plan and within God's timing. In this view, God's ordained plan left room for human maneuvering, and many black leaders tried to walk in steps already laid out for them. Their political action could serve as God's way of instituting change or fulfilling prophecy. Hood believed that the Reconstruction-era political reforms fulfilled biblical prophecies. In his *Plan of the Apocalypse*, he wrote, "this symbol of a plentiful harvest [from Revelation 11:15] may refer to our own times . . . [it] seems to signify the next great period of prosperity, human progress, human liberty and human happiness. We are now having a great harvest of reforms of every kind."[72] That Hood himself had participated in these reforms did not diminish his claim that they were fulfillment of prophecy. Hood and his colleagues interpreted political actions, even their own actions, as the work of God.

Eschatology, then, provided a clear vision for the postemancipation political scene, even if concerns such as appeasing local whites limited or delayed it and even if a number of black politicians did not share the vision. Because of biblical stories, prophecies, and God's work in emancipation, black Southerners knew their future. Their confidence in the race's future allowed convention delegates to openly agitate for a righteous cause. No one present doubted that African Americans would secure suffrage and equality before the law. For some, the certainty of victory released them from a sense of urgency and commended a slower, more deferential path of reforms. For others, the dramatic intervention of God in emancipation had begun a new era where moderation and gradualism were no longer necessary. A shared eschatological outlook on emancipation did not translate into a uniform black posture during Reconstruction. Rather, it set the terms for debate. Black Protestants disagreed vehemently about political strategies; those disagreements were deeply shaped by a common theology of emancipation.

For both radicals and moderates, progress did not come fast enough after the convention. Both groups expressed disappointment with white responses to their communication. Most disturbingly, neither gubernatorial candidate in 1865 seemed ready to concede to black demands for citizenship rights. Black commentators lamented that both candidates held positions on race "virtually as they did previous to the war." "So," wrote editor Edward Brooks, "all charges that either party are for or against [equal rights] are mere bosh. To us it looks like a struggle for plunder and position, and we are like the old man who looked on while his wife fought the bear, remarking that he 'did'nt care a d—n which whipped.'"[73] African Americans remained outside a political process that ignored their demands to enter.

By 1868, however, the delegates saw at least partial fulfillment of their postemancipation expectations. Under Congressional Reconstruction, black men voted in elections for a new constitutional convention. North Carolina sent fifteen black delegates to a Republican-dominated state constitutional convention in Raleigh. Among them were Galloway, Harris, Sweet, and Hood. They faced constant harassment from a handful of conservative Democrats who refused to tolerate the black delegates' presence. After one conservative proposed revising the constitution to ensure that the white race not be degraded to the level of blacks, James Harris arose to give the hostile delegate a history lesson because he had "ignored the events of the past six years, or supposed that Grant had surrendered to Lee, or that the so-called Confederacy was a success." Harris's point was clear: recent history foretold a triumph for blacks and radicals. It was in vain that conservatives sought a victory. To make his point clearer, Harris drew an analogy between the current political strife and supernatural warfare: "When Lucifer had rebelled against Almighty God—had been vanquished and hurled over the battlements of Heaven—he too considered the laws unwise and unjust. But he had been forced to accept the situation."[74] The Republican majority erupted in laughter and applause. Harris laughed, too, it seemed, because his theological reading of emancipation opened for him a window onto the future. He laughed, we can assume, because, through that window, he saw God on his side.

The Memory of Emancipation

Over time, black Southerners turned again and again, as Harris did, to emancipation, and in recalling it, they reaffirmed the glorious future that awaited them. So, the importance of emancipation did not fade with time. Black communities commemorated the event each year in public celebrations across the state and the nation. These parades and festivals, with their marching militia units, floats, songs, and speeches, were meant, according to W. Fitzhugh Brundage, to "counter the dominant white version of the past." Black ministers, whose "powerful influence" often dictated the forms of the celebrations, "cast both the distant and recent past as scenes in a familiar spiritual drama." In their orations, ministers and other leaders looked back on emancipation as a divine act of redemption and many "anticipated . . . an even more profound, imminent, and millennial transformation in the status of black people."[75] These frequent commemorations ensured that emancipation's eschatological significance among black Protestants waxed rather than waned in the decades following the Civil War.

Those commemorations became hotly contested. During and immediately after the Civil War, blacks and whites held widely divergent views on emancipation. While the black congregation at Front Street Methodist interpreted emancipation as Jubilee, Exodus, and the sign of good things to come, Burkhead and his white parishioners considered the social upheaval "a tribulation" to be patiently endured. In the same month that Wilmington fell to Union forces, the *Religious Herald* in Richmond, Virginia, printed one white man's vision of an apocalyptic future where "heaven and earth might pass away, amid earthquakes and tempests, and thunderings and lightnings, and consuming fire." The writer saw the coming Confederate defeat as akin to Israel's captivity in Babylon. A white minister and officer in a Mississippi regiment, J. W. Sandell, saw similarities between the Civil War and the apocalyptic prophecies of Daniel. Decades later, Sandell published his thoughts, in which he declared that the U.S. government was the many-headed beast of Revelation.[76] White Southerners, too, were invested in eschatological remembrances of emancipation and the Civil War.

The white and black members of Front Street church shared much of the same theological worldview. They invested the past with providential meaning, and their theological expectations for the future gave them the ability to weather the present. But their radically different interpretations of emancipation left them unable to speak to one another.[77] And with the passage of time and regular commemorations, the white and black memories of emancipation became irreconcilable. Religious Southern whites mourned the Confederate defeat as God's chastisement of his beloved people while Southern blacks hailed it as God's long-delayed deliverance.[78]

These mutually exclusive memories of emancipation fueled political clashes, some of them violent. In Oxford, North Carolina, on January 1, 1874, the African American community gathered to celebrate emancipation. The day involved a parade led by black militiamen in full regalia through the town center. The marching of black soldiers to remember emancipation seemed appropriate, because for many slaves freedom came when the black soldiers did. It also reminded ex-Confederates of their recent military defeat, and the white community in Oxford balked. County officials rushed in to stop the parade. The black community subsequently brought suit, and the state's Supreme Court ruled that "the laws allow great latitude to do public demonstrations, whether political, social or moral."[79] The ability to publicly celebrate emancipation allowed black North Carolinians to continue to ascribe theological meaning to the historical event. Some black Protestants, however, thought the commemorations were excessive or hindered progress. AME minister James Handy, one of the early pastors of St. Stephens, Wilmington, complained of his community's constant retelling and commemoration of the past. "We must forget the past," he wrote in 1879, "live in the present, and remember that we are American citizens."[80] A historical memory of slavery and emancipation, to him, seemed to separate African Americans from the rest of the nation.

Others, like C. R. Harris, an AME Zion minister from North Carolina, thought regular commemorations were necessary for theological reasons. At the 1892 Agricultural and Industrial Fair in Alexandria, Virginia, Harris said, "This anniversary [of emancipation] deserves to be perpetuated as a memorial of the fervent zeal, indomitable energy, and sublime faith of the abolitionist, who, like Abraham of old, 'against hope believed in hope,' that the soil of America might be purged of the foul stain of human slavery." The memorial celebration would reinvigorate black Americans' hope for the future: "It will also remind us of that truth, so signally impressed by the lessons of the civil war, that God hears the cry of the oppressed, of whatever color or clime, and in due time comes to deliver them."[81] This religious confidence countered depressing news when it came; remembering emancipation lent weight to black claims that God was actively working on their behalf.

Within African American discourse, emancipation became a benchmark in time. Laurie Maffly-Kipp writes that late nineteenth-century race histories "hinged on the acts of civil war and emancipation as the harbingers of a worldwide spiritual and social transformation." In black Americans' retelling of world history, the "climax . . . came with the issuing of the Emancipation Proclamation." As early Medieval Christians (and eventually most of the world) marked time by the birth of Christ, African Americans marked time by emancipation. Within black communities, the years 1863–65 held a place akin the B.C./A.D. divide. African American writers reported events and race progress in relation to emancipation: "Ten years since emancipation" or "only thirty-five years after slavery," or "only a generation from slavery." Titles from African American literature, like Katherine Tillman's *Thirty Years of Freedom: A Drama in Four Acts* (1902) or her *Fifty Years of Freedom, or From Cabin to Congress: A Drama in Five Acts* (1910) and James Weldon Johnson's poem "Fifty Years" (1917) bear this out.[82] The memory of emancipation served black Americans' political ends. They reminded Americans of the central place black freedom played in the Civil War, and they wove their story into the nation's self-conception as free and democratic.

In emancipation, black Protestant leaders also wrote themselves into religious narratives. In 1865, they identified with stories of Exodus, divine judgment, military conquest, and Jubilee. Their experience of emancipation as a providential, prophetic, and even millennial event led to a theology that significantly informed their political action. Throughout the 1860s and 1870s, eschatological confidence emboldened and radicalized black politics even as it placed limits on that radicalism. Their theologies of emancipation, for black Northerners like Hood and black Southerners like the worshippers at Front Street Methodist, influenced the way African American leaders entered politics. Because of their eschatology, black Protestant leaders entered the age of emancipation with the confidence of prophets. They believed they knew the future and had God on their side. Reliving biblical stories emboldened them to accept nothing less than the outcome they expected—full political equality, for example—and afforded them the patience to move slowly and carefully.

CHAPTER TWO

Redemption and Exile

If some black Protestants expected emancipation to inaugurate an era where the fortunes of African Americans only steadily improved, then they faced a stumbling block just out of the gates. Radical Reconstruction had brought what many had prophesied; citizenship and voting rights for men followed on the heels of freedom. In 1868, African Americans helped rewrite the constitutions of every ex-Confederate state save one. These new constitutions seemed to solidify a new social order. Despite reports of rampant abuse from landlords and employers, black Southerners could at least rest in the knowledge that they and their white Republican allies controlled the legislature. But even this victory was short-lived.

In December 1870, Reconstruction seemed to be collapsing in North Carolina, and seventeen African American state legislators gathered in Raleigh to devise a political strategy to stop the impeachment of the Republican governor. They feared a complete political takeover by the state's Democrat party, more terror from the Ku Klux Klan, and new curtailments on black freedom. In the meeting, the lawmakers affixed their signatures to a short text, which they hoped would circulate among the state's black ministers and be read to their congregations. The circular they issued, "An Address to the Colored People of North Carolina," framed the political crisis within a biblical narrative—the story of Queen Esther from the Hebrew Bible. Esther's story told of life in exile and persecution in ancient Persia, and, as such, it differed sharply from the more familiar narratives of Exodus and the Promised Land. The Hebrews of Esther's time found a political voice and ways to protect themselves (with violence, if necessary) as an ethnic minority living in a hostile land. The Esther story, as retold by North Carolina's black legislators, made sense of black Southerners' new circumstances in the 1870s and even recommended particular strategies to avert those dangers.[1] Historians have cited the Esther circular for nearly a century to understand African American politics during Reconstruction. Some have ignored its religious nature altogether; others have cited it merely to show that religion was important. None have analyzed the religious content of the document, the

Esther story itself. The way legislators appropriated the narrative offered a new political vision for life in the post-Reconstruction South.

The plots and subplots within the Esther story, for example, allowed the legislators to present black North Carolinians as peaceful and pious citizens while making more subtle claims to the right of armed self-defense. Conservative white Southerners responded to the circular with alarm, because they understood its ambiguous messages and because they agreed that religious narratives held the power to legitimize or undermine political movements. Narratives, like the Esther story, also held power to structure and redirect political movements. As black Southerners turned to a diverse set of narratives to navigate the politics of Reconstruction, the Esther circular demonstrates just how significant those narratives could be in opening up new political visions. The Esther narrative was not the only or even most common biblical story black Southerners used to make sense of the collapse of Reconstruction. Some turned to Israel's forty years in the wilderness, calling the years after the 1870s a vast desert that stood between slavery in Egypt and the Promised Land in Canaan.[2] Others described the events as demon possession. Some black Protestants employed other exile narratives, like Daniel's. For example, one black writer described the Klan in Mississippi in 1872 as the cursed Chaldeans who feasted on plates stolen from the Jewish temple: "They see the hand-writing on the wall, and like Belshazzar they tremble and fear."[3] In their eschatology black Protestants used a variety of biblical narratives to find themselves within God's plan for human history, even when faced with defeat. Appropriations of stories like Esther's, then, help us to see how African Americans reconciled a hopeful eschatology with the painful realities of the 1870s. Some reconciled the two by migrating out of the South and seeking their destiny out West or in Liberia, as we will see in chapter 3. This chapter focuses on exile narratives, in particular the Esther circular, because a close and contextualized analysis of a document like this reveals its important political implications. This chapter also asks historians to think carefully about how we interpret religion and politics. Biblical narratives offered more than inspiration; they offered real political strategies. As black Protestants turned to different stories, they arrived at different ways forward.[4]

Black Southerners were not the only ones to frame the end of Reconstruction around religious narratives. The white Southerners who came to power at the end of Reconstruction called themselves "Redeemers," and their political victory, which came at the loss of African American political power, they called "Redemption." Recently, historians have argued that the religious connotations of the term "Redemption" were hardly accidental. As Daniel Stowell observed, conservative white Southerners could have chosen a secular political moniker for their action—such as the Restoration—but they used a religious term instead. The word "Redemption" called to mind the story of Jesus Christ's buying back or redeeming God's people with a blood sacrifice: the spilling of blood to rescue a land or a people from captivity. From 1869 to 1877, a diverse group of white Southerners believed themselves to be redeeming the South from Northern and African American political power, returning the region to "home rule." Their bloody overthrow of Reconstruction, they believed, held religious significance.[5]

For Redeemers, Confederate defeat threatened Southern identity and the values they attached to that identity. As Charles Reagan Wilson described it, "Fearing that crushing defeat might eradicate the identity forged in war, Southerners reasserted that identity with a vengeance." It was a "war of ideas," as one proponent of the Lost Cause said, and religious leaders waged battle by preaching that white Southerners were still God's chosen people. Redemption involved real weapons and real terror, but it was also a struggle on the level of ideas and narrative. The white Episcopal bishop of Alabama claimed that Northern radicalism was "a pestilent heresy." Presumably, to protect Christianity, Southerners had to root out radical Reconstruction though they had failed to defeat the Union Army.[6] Having lost a holy war, Southern Redeemers saw themselves as a remnant of Israel, whose task was to take back, or redeem, the land from foreigners and heretics.

Southern white Democrats, by imbedding their political actions in a narrative of redemption, gave an air of finality to their triumph. The rhetoric of redemption (buying back) implied that Reconstruction reforms were both temporary and unnatural and that "home rule" was the natural, resting place for the South. To conservative white Southerners, their defeat militarily and politically was not an "unmitigated calamity," as one white Southern Methodist explained in 1869. Confederate ideals would eventually have greater success. New Orleans Presbyterian minister Benjamin Palmer, a leading proslavery theologian, made a similar argument: "Can a cause be lost which has passed through such a baptism as ours? Principles never die, and if they seem to perish it is only to experience a resurrection in the future." Confederate defeat and radical Reconstruction were tribulations to endure; Redemption would restore order.[7] Black Protestants resisted the finality of "home rule," and produced their own religious narratives to imply the reverse:

that Reconstruction reforms were the beginning of a new era and that Redemption itself was temporary, a tribulation to be endured. For example, by
framing their actions in a narrative of exile, North Carolina's black legislators interpreted Democratic victories not as the end point of the story, but
rather as a midway point that would end with a return from exile. Black and
white Southerners employed competing religious narratives not only to interpret the end of Reconstruction in opposite ways but also to lay claim to
the South's future. Moreover, the narratives black Southerners chose revealed disagreements among themselves. While narratives like the wandering in the wilderness helped some black Protestants imagine autonomous
spaces or even black nationhood, other biblical stories like Esther's justified
federal intervention and armed self-defense for those living in exile.

A Demonic Plot

In North Carolina, as in other states in the Upper South, Reconstruction
was abbreviated. When the authors of the Esther circular met in December
1870, African American men had exercised their right to vote for only two
years. Under the 1868 state constitution, the newly enfranchised black population helped put Republicans in control of both houses of the General
Assembly, and black voters helped secure a second gubernatorial term for
Republican William Words Holden, a former Peace Party candidate. Black
residents began to see Holden as a guardian of their civil and political rights.
One church leader praised Holden for the favor his administration showed
to African Americans, calling him a "magnanimous executive."[8] When he faced
impeachment in 1870–71, the authors of the Esther circular spoke of Holden
as a protector.

Holden had not always been a friend to black North Carolinians. Although Holden wrested political power from the former slaveholding elite
and distributed it to white Republicans and others outside the planter class
in 1865, his plans to democratize the state sidestepped African Americans. In
the 1865 State Constitutional Convention, Holden ignored the petitions of
the freedmen. Despite repeated appeals from black caucuses across the
state, Holden did not support black delegates' right to attend the convention. By 1867, however, Holden changed course. He supported the inclusion
of black delegates to the state's Republican Party convention. In response,
James Harris, who authored the 1865 Freedmen's Convention communication, wrote a letter of support for Holden to Congress on behalf of the North

Carolina Equal Rights League, arguing that Holden helped protect the black population from disloyalists.[9] In 1868, when a biracial constitutional convention under Congressional Reconstruction enfranchised African Americans, Holden and leading black politicians like Harris quickly realized that neither African Americans nor white Republicans were likely to go far in North Carolina unless they yoked their oxen together. By the time of Holden's impeachment two years later, African Americans were among his staunchest supporters.[10]

The success of the new Republican majority, however, lasted for only one legislative term. From late 1868 to 1870, conservative Democrats turned to the Ku Klux Klan to help undermine the new radical Republican regime. The Klan launched a terror campaign throughout the state, concentrated in the central Piedmont, to intimidate black and white Republicans, to prevent African Americans from voting, and to disrupt black schools and churches. The terror began in Lenoir County in the eastern part of the state, where African Americans formed a majority. At first, a local branch of the Klan called the Constitutional Union Guard stole horses from African Americans, presumably to prevent them from farming independently. The violence turned political as the group began targeting Republicans, and, in retaliation, black residents set fire to the homes of known white terrorists. One state senator reported, "We cannot tell at night who will be living in the morning."[11] By late 1869, the center of the violence had moved west of Raleigh. There African Americans made up, on average, one-quarter of the population. Black and white Republicans together, then, had only a tenuous grip on local governments in the Piedmont. The Klan focused its attention on several Piedmont counties, and, as one local recalled, Klan members rode openly through city streets, "enquiring the whereabouts of the negroes and white radicals."[12] It is clear from the Esther circular issued the following year that African American communities feared for life and liberty. They described the Klan as a "band of Assassins" who "planned to saturate this state in the blood of the poor ... to prevent them from voting."[13] As the terror increased, the Republican Party indeed saw its numbers plummet in the state.

This kind of intimidation was common throughout the South. Conservative Democrats at first hoped to regain an electoral majority by economic pressure; black workers risked their employment by voting Republican. African Americans were dependent upon white landholders for their livelihood, but landowners were equally dependent upon black labor.[14] To effect permanent political change, conservatives turned to violence and physical intimidation, tactics that eventually worked to secure Democratic victories in every ex-Confederate state.

In the North Carolina Piedmont, as elsewhere, the escalation of violence not only threatened black life and liberty but also posed a problem for many black Protestants' eschatology. Black religious leaders had declared that emancipation was the beginning of an age of millennial glory. Black Protestants who experienced emancipation believed they were living in important days, watching the fulfillment of divine prophecies. They expected emancipation to precede a new era of racial justice, and the fast pace of Reconstruction reforms only confirmed their hopes. Certainly, a millennial hope had been the timbre of black political meetings in North Carolina, starting with the first Freedmen's Convention in 1865.

To be sure, many black Protestants had predicted trouble after emancipation. Even at the moment of emancipation, as former slaves read their experience into biblical stories, they saw rough patches ahead. One man among contraband slaves in Virginia in 1862 had confidence that what God began in emancipation, God would complete in a new era. But he warned that the completion may be far off. "What if we cannot see right off the green fields of Canaan, Moses could not. He could not even see how to cross the Red Sea."[15] By appropriating the Exodus story, the contraband slave was able to predict both a glorious future and a difficult road ahead. Herein lay the main difference between the optimistic eschatology of white postmillennialists and that of black Protestants. Postmillennialism assumed a rather steady swell of progress to usher in God's kingdom on earth. Black Protestants, in contrast, heavily relied on biblical stories to give a different shape to their hope. Things were getting better, but the storyline may not be so simple. Built into African American eschatological thought were narrative mechanisms that could make sense of major setbacks. As Reconstruction collapsed, those mechanisms were needed. The escalating violence of 1869 and 1870 demanded some sort of interpretation.

Harris, by then the state's leading black politician, offered such an interpretation in his impassioned speech on the House floor in January 1870. Harris had been born a slave near Raleigh but left the state when he earned his freedom in 1848. During the war, he helped recruit black soldiers for Union regiments and later returned to his home state. He worked as a schoolteacher and faithfully served the state's Union League. In 1866, his fellow black North Carolinians elected him chairman of the Freedmen's Convention. During his term in the North Carolina House in 1868–70, Harris stood out as the leading voice of black Republicans. His speech in January 1870, delivered ten months before Holden's impeachment, foreshadowed his colleagues' response in the Esther circular. In the speech, Harris made two seemingly contradictory points: (1) that the violence in the Piedmont was severe and alarming and needed urgently to be suppressed, and (2) that such violence was ultimately futile and would accomplish little. The former point spoke to the reality African Americans faced in the Piedmont. Harris urged his colleagues to respond quickly to avoid more tragedies in the center of the state. Harris's second point spoke to his own beliefs about the future: that emancipation had ushered in a new era of racial justice and equality and that Reconstruction reforms were destined to be strengthened, not repealed. Efforts to undermine those reforms, Harris believed, were in vain. How could Harris raise alarm about Klan activity while downplaying its significance? He turned to a helpful religious idiom. Harris framed the racial violence as the work of demons attacking God's plan. By calling the Redeemers and Klansmen demons, Harris made them seem dangerous, real enemies worth contending. Yet, because God's plans could not be thwarted even by demons or the devil himself, Harris maintained his belief in the futility of Klan violence to overturn Reconstruction.[16]

Two years earlier Harris had laughed at conservatives for their vain attempt at political victory. Now he remained baffled by his opponents' unwillingness to admit defeat. "Reconstruction is a fixed fact," he reminded his opponents on the floor of the North Carolina General Assembly. While conservative Southerners dismissed Reconstruction as a temporary setback, Harris argued for its permanence. He saw Reconstruction reforms, including black suffrage and racial equality, as the inevitable consequence of emancipation. But conservative Democrats never saw the reforms as inevitable or permanent. They resisted, Harris reasoned, not just Reconstruction reforms but God's plan for human history.[17] They were living in the age of emancipation. Whatever God intended for the new era, it most certainly would include black political power. God would not orchestrate such a dramatic event as emancipation without seeing it to completion by securing black citizenship rights.[18]

When Democrats continued to resist that plan, Harris called the Democratic Party the "machinery of the devil," again foreshadowing the language of the Esther circular. Harris gave examples of the kind of terror blacks faced from Democrats in Klan hoods. In Johnston County, a black minister "was dragged from his own house and severely and unmercifully whipped," and,

Harris reported, "the only objection against him was that he established in that County a negro school and a negro Church." In Statesville, North Carolina, a "party of disguised villains" nearly whipped an African American to death for "being in favor of negro schools." The same night, Harris reported, the Klan "for the purpose of gratifying their devilish spleen on another defenseless man," fired bird shot into a boy's face because his father wanted public schools for black children. Perhaps the most horrific case involved the family of Daniel Blue, an African American man in Moore County. Klan members, according to several witnesses, shot and killed Blue's daughters and pregnant wife. While Blue lay severely wounded but alive, one of the attackers killed his youngest child "by kicking its brains out with the heel of his boot."[19] With each example of atrocious violence, Harris referred to the Klan and its allies as "devils" or "demons."[20] His language showed that Redeemers were not the only ones to understand the time period through a religious metaphor.

But it was more than a metaphor. Black Protestants in North Carolina interpreted local conflicts during Redemption as supernatural battles, where the forces of heaven and hell took sides. Harris saw little separation between evil human acts and the forces of hell. As the Esther circular would demonstrate, the notion of supernatural warfare reached beyond metaphor for black leaders in North Carolina. When Harris said "demons," he meant it on at least two levels: as people capable of almost inhuman cruelty and as supernatural forces arrayed against God.

The supernatural battles that Harris described were also earthly ones. His speech on the House floor was literally a call to arms. Harris spoke in defense of the 1870 Militia Bill, a bill introduced by T. M. Shoffner, a state senator from Alamance County in the Piedmont, where the racial violence in the Piedmont seemed most concentrated. The bill gave Governor Holden authority to declare martial law and deploy militia units in any county he considered to be in a state of insurrection. Arguing for such a use of force, Harris told his opponents that black North Carolinians were prepared to fight the "devils in human flesh." He warned, "I have always counseled peace, but will say that if the Conservatives expect to drive the colored people into a support of their party by a system of intimidation, they will be mistaken." His warning sounded like a threat: "It cannot be expected that colored men will stand idly by and see men of their race hanged and shot in cold blood."[21] Harris made explicit what the organization of black militias after emancipation had implied: that although ex-slaves would not seek revenge for the violence they suffered in slavery they would not hesitate to defend themselves now. Harris's colleagues must have agreed: the Shoffner Act quickly passed both the House and the Senate.

Governor Holden's use of his new powers under the Shoffner Act became grounds for his impeachment, and set in motion the drama described later in the Esther circular. In 1870, racial violence intensified. Shoffner himself fled the state after the Klan began plans for his assassination. In Alamance County and neighboring Caswell County, leading Republican Party officials registered more black voters and won local elections. The Klan then began targeting top Republican officials. Late one night in February 1870, Klan members arrived on horses at the home of Wyatt Outlaw, a leading black Republican and educator in Graham, North Carolina. There the men beat Outlaw's elderly mother before leading Outlaw away, barefoot and bound. The next morning, Outlaw was found hanging from a tree on the Alamance County Courthouse lawn, with a note pinned to his dead body: "Beware, you guilty, both black and white." The coroner declared it a death at the hands of unknown persons, and the sheriff, himself a Klansman, never searched for Outlaw's murderers. A man professing to know the identity of the perpetrators was later found at the bottom of a nearby pond with a millstone tied around his neck.[22] Local Republicans asked Governor Holden and the U.S. Army for protection. On March 7, Holden declared Alamance County in a state of insurrection.[23]

Three months later, in Caswell County, the Klan took aim at John W. Stephens, a moderate white Republican who had been excommunicated from the local Methodist church for organizing and socializing with the county's black residents. In May 1870, the former sheriff invited Stephens to attend the county's Democratic convention at the courthouse. When Stephens arrived, local Democrats lured him into a vacant room in the courthouse, where three Klan members bound him, choked him, and stabbed him to death. After locking his body in a small room, the Klansmen rode away. Local law enforcement made no indictments. The dominance of the Klan in the county frustrated federal investigators. So many people had been complicit that it was impossible—until sixty-five years later—to pinpoint Stephens's actual murderers.[24] Caswell County's black state representative fled for his safety. On July 8, Holden declared the county in a state of insurrection. Five months later, the authors of the Esther circular remembered Holden's declaration as the dispersal of "a murderous host."[25] The problem only spread out across the Piedmont.

Outlaw's and Stephens's murders were but the most publicized acts of violence in Alamance and Caswell Counties. So, in July 1870, under the Shoffner Act, Holden called out the militia to suppress the insurrection. It was a tactic that had served Arkansas's Republican governor well the year before. The imposition of martial law and the timely arrests of suspected terrorists had significantly weakened the Arkansas Klan. So Holden asked Col. George W. Kirk to assemble militia companies from the white Republican strongholds in the western part of the state, while he put on alert black militia companies from the eastern counties. Kirk's troops arrested several prominent Democrats, among them a newspaper editor and former U.S. congressman, and held them as prisoners without charge, before a federal judge ordered their release. By September, things were more peaceful, but the Klan remained strong. Holden, without federal support, felt compelled to withdraw all militia units from the counties. In November, he declared the insurrection over, though little had changed on the ground.[26]

The governor's critics called the whole affair the Kirk-Holden War. Conservative newspapers reported on the advance of troops on vulnerable white populations in central North Carolina, though no blood was shed in the so-called war. When conservative Democrats gained a majority in the legislature in the fall elections, they used the governor's use of militia force as grounds to impeach him. Within weeks of taking office, the new legislators began impeachment proceedings. During and after the fall elections, African Americans in the state worried over their future. One U.S. Army official reported "a general feeling of uneasiness" among Raleigh's freedpeople. Rumors spread among black communities that the new legislature would reinstate black codes, curfews, and even slavery.[27] With a Democratic majority in the legislature and impeachment proceedings against the Republican governor, black North Carolinians feared that Reconstruction itself would soon collapse. Such a fate seemed hard to square with a hopeful eschatology. The bright futures that black believers forecast in 1865 seemed distant by 1870.

The Esther Circular

African American legislators responded to the impeachment proceedings with the Esther circular, a document that shed light on the other side of Redemption: how black leaders interpreted the end of Reconstruction in religious terms. The black lawmakers met in Raleigh, when the impeachment proceedings were underway. James Harris was not in the House at the time, having made an unsuccessful bid for the U.S. House of Representatives the month before. Among the black legislators who remained in the House, none had Harris's stature. Two important figures exemplified the diverse backgrounds of those African Americans who served in the House: George Mabson and Stewart Ellison. Mabson was the son of a slave mother and wealthy white father in Wilmington. In 1854, he left the state to get an education in Boston, where he remained until returning as part of the 5th Massachusetts Calvary. After the war, he resettled in Wilmington, where he became a Reconstruction officeholder and the state's first black lawyer.[28] Figures like Mabson had to work against their status as outsiders or Northerners. Surely he was a target of "a sensitive jealousy," as one observer at the 1865 Freedmen's Convention put it, "toward one or two delegates born in this State, but educated in the schools and under the influence of the North."[29] Ellison had stronger credentials as a local. He was born a slave in 1832 on the estate of an Episcopal minister in Washington, North Carolina. As a child, he was apprenticed to a free black mechanic and carpenter. After emancipation, he became a successful building contractor and grocer in Raleigh. Ellison served one of the longest tenure of any black state legislator: six sessions. He also was the vice president of the 1865 State Freedmen's Convention, the business manager of the *North Carolina Republican*, and Raleigh's first black elected city commissioner.[30] The differences among black political leaders in the state—region, education, lineage, occupation—did not preclude a nearly unanimous response to Holden's impeachment trial. Of the twenty black state representatives in 1870, seventeen signed the Esther circular.[31]

The circular compared the impeachment trial with the persecution of Mordecai in the Old Testament account of Esther. According to the biblical account, when the Hebrews lived in exile, Haman, a Persian official, became outraged because Mordecai, a prominent Jew, would not bow down before him. Haman devised ways to kill Mordecai and his fellow Jews. Haman secured an edict from the king calling for the massacre of all Jews and the plunder of their property. Mordecai's cousin Esther, who had kept her Hebrew nationality secret, gained the favor of the king and became one of his queens. While Haman built gallows to hang Mordecai, Esther proclaimed a three-day fast among the Jews. After the fast, the king heard Esther's plea for safety for all of her people, and Haman was hanged on the gallows he built for Mordecai. "Indeed," the circular read, "there is some analogy between our case and that of the Jews at that time." In the comparison, not since Haman's time had there been such "wickedness" as "proposed by the dominant party in the present General Assembly." In the extended comparison, contemporary actors were cast different roles in the Esther story. Governor Holden, facing impeachment, was the persecuted Mordecai. If he fell into the hands of the Democrats, who played the part of Haman, "those whom he protected will be the next victims." The state's African Americans were the persecuted Jews, and the African American legislators themselves, as leaders of an oppressed minority, played the role of Queen Esther.[32]

The legislators explained the motives of their political opponents and warned their constituents of the imminent danger. They described the Democrats' resistance to Reconstruction reforms as former slaveholders' anger at losing "their slave property." They argued that Republicans were persecuted only because "we refuse to bow the knee to them [Democrats or former slaveholders]." A political takeover by conservative Democrats, they argued, would have disastrous consequences. They alerted the readers to a new "system of disfranchisement" and the repeal of the militia law. The close links between conservative leaders and the Ku Klux Klan worried black lawmakers that their opponents "propose[d] to let loose their murderous band upon us and thus secure a majority." Such was, in fact, their plan. The authors of the circular lamented, "When this is done, our liberties are at an end." The circular issued such a dire warning in order to "arouse [black citizens] to such action as may tend to avert" the impeachment of Holden and a complete Democratic takeover.[33]

The document described a political problem and offered a strategy that the authors expected to yield political change. But the action the circular's authors recommended was not the usual political response: no conventions, no committees, no canvasses or coalitions. Instead, their plan for political action, at least explicitly, was to pray and fast. "To avert the impending evil we see no power in the arm of flesh," the circular contended. "We feel that we have too long neglected to seek aid at that source that never fails . . . Justice will not sleep forever. If we call upon God he will hear and answer us." They appointed January 13, 1871 as the day for all black North Carolinians to take off work, to assemble in churches, and "to cry unto the Lord."[34] It was a different kind of political action than readers might have anticipated, given the tenor of the circular.

It is difficult to discern to what extent African Americans heeded the circular's call to fasting. If the state's black population did set aside January 13 to pray, their actions failed to catch the attention of local newspapers. The circular itself, though, did attract the eye of the press. White newspapers both feared and ridiculed the call for prayer and fasting. The editor of the Raleigh *Daily Sentinel*, the capital's leading Democrat paper, mocked, "We have no objections to the colored people praying for the Governor, and doing it on empty stomachs, if they like." Unlike the authors of the circular, the editor, it seemed, attributed little political efficacy to fasting. If African American leaders wanted to make life difficult for Democratic leaders like the *Sentinel*'s editor, the editor seemed little threatened by prayer and fasting.[35] Still, the editor and others expressed alarm, fear, and vitriol at the publication of the Esther circular.

Both the *Sentinel* and the *Tarboro Southerner* responded first by questioning the circular's authorship, accusing Governor Holden of composing the piece. White Democrats routinely claimed that black political actors were but puppets of white Republicans. They were unwilling to attribute political ideas and actions to black Southerners themselves. So, it is not surprising that the Democratic editors assumed that black legislators were Holden's passive pawns and that "nine tenths of the negroes of the State . . . will understand neither [the circular's] import nor its bearing."[36] In reality, no evidence pointed to Holden's authorship. If Holden were to reinterpret the Book of Esther, it is unlikely that he would assign himself the role of a helpless Mordecai depending upon a rescue from black Carolinians.

When the newspaper editors dispensed with the question of authorship, they outlined their principal problem with the circular: its blasphemy. One titled the circular "A Blasphemous Address." The other called it a "blasphemous allusion to scripture" and a "mischievous circular . . . cloaked in a disguise of piety."[37] White Democrats balked at the circular, not because it opposed Holden's impeachment, but because it did so with the help of Holy Writ. Had black legislators protested the impeachment on secular grounds, the editorials implied, they would have been guilty of no more than a pitiful loyalty to Holden. Their protracted use of a religious narrative, however, made the circular, as one editor put it, "of the devil."[38]

Why would Democrats balk at the circular's use of religious narrative? Why did they focus on the circular's "blasphemy" and not on its political analysis? Perhaps Democrats were merely invoking the white Southern doctrine of the "spiritual church." This teaching, honed in the years of opposition to evangelical abolitionism, prohibited churches from dabbling in politics. In reality, it allowed Southern churches to lend moral support behind the existing social order but did not permit them to foment revolution or to advocate radical reform.[39] Invoking the doctrine seemed ill fit for the Esther circular. Its authors were politicians, not clergymen, and Democratic politicians had routinely employed scripture and religious narrative for political purposes—to defend slavery, to explain their losses in the war, and, recently, to justify violent attacks on the Republican electorate. It seems more likely that Democrats critiqued the religion of the circular because they opposed it as a move to claim moral legitimacy. They knew that religious narratives were powerful weapons in the struggle to tell the state's political history. The use of the Esther narrative delegitimized Democrats' rise to power and prophesied the party's future failure. Because Democrats and Republicans employed different religious narratives to lend moral authority to their political moves, the newspaper editors charged the Esther circular not with bad policy but with blasphemy. A lot was at stake in the use of religious narratives.

Careful readers of the Bible saw something sinister at stake in the use of the Esther story. The conservative editor of the *Tarboro Southerner* warned that the circular purposed to "incit[e] the negroes to violence and outrage," and would lead to "strife, bloodshed, and anarchy."[40] For those unfamiliar with the ending of the Esther story, the editorials' fear of violence would seem to be far-fetched. How violent could prayer and fasting be? But both the newspaper editor and the circular's authors had in mind the rest of Esther's story. After the Persian king ordered the execution of Haman, the problems for the Jews did not end. Under Persian law, a royal order, such as the one Haman secured from the king ordering the massacre of the Jews, could not be repealed, not even by the ruler who issued it. So, when the king later favored Esther and her people, he could not reverse the binding edict calling for the genocide of the Jews. Instead, he issued a second edict authorizing the Jews to defend themselves: "Wherein the king granted the Jews which were in every city to gather themselves together, and to stand for their life, to destroy, to slay and to cause to perish, all the power of the people and province that would assault them, both little ones and women, and to take the spoil of them for a prey."[41] By evoking the Esther story, the black legislators subtly claimed a right to armed self-defense. The Esther circular sent an ambiguous message. It openly decried the "arm of the flesh" and advocated only prayer and fasting. But the circular also included veiled threats: if conservative Democrats continued to use violence to disfranchise African Americans, then the state's black population had the right of armed self-defense, or at least the military protection of others. The Esther circular did not narrate the Jews' acts of self-defense; it didn't have to. The authors could assume that their audience would know the story well, and, given the fearful reaction of some white newspaper editors, they assumed correctly. Just in case the document's other readers were less astute than the editor of the *Tarboro Southerner*, the authors left small reminders of the rest of Esther's story: "the laws of righteous retribution have not been repealed."[42]

It was a clear reference to what would happen if God did hear the cries of the oppressed. If the day of prayer and fasting worked, and miraculously the governor survived impeachment, then what next? The Esther story had an answer. African Americans, as a persecuted minority in a hostile land, would need the power to defend themselves. The Jews of Esther's day were able to have peace in Persia only (1) by holding political power—in their case by currying favor with the king—and (2) by being armed and organized, able to fend off future attacks. If the black legislators saw an analogy between Esther's day and their own, it was this: God may not in the short term bring about total victory or a return from exile. Instead, God may provide a way for hostile parties to find a truce. That truce necessitated black political power and armed self-defense.

The Esther story framed the entire document and is hard to ignore, though, as we will see later, historians have done just that. The Esther circular also alludes to another narrative, that of a demonic attack. By calling for prayer and fasting, the leaders alluded to Jesus's words in the Gospels. When his disciples were unable to cast out a demon from a man, Jesus replied, "This kind [of demon] cannot be driven out by anything but prayer and fasting."[43] Thus the circular's authors equated the Redeemers with demons. A year earlier, James Harris had also equated Redeemers with demons and devils. By advocating prayer and fasting in response to Redemption, the authors of the circular demonstrated that the language of demons was more than metaphor. African American leaders saw themselves, their opponents, and the forces of heaven and hell, as actors in spiritual wars and in earthly politics.[44]

Both narratives—Jewish persecution in Persia and demonic attack— seemed to reinforce a larger story: that emancipation marked the beginning of a new era of racial justice and equality. The story of Queen Esther bracketed the 1870 Democratic takeover as a temporary persecution that would end disastrously for the persecutors. Moreover, because the Esther story came from displaced communities during and after Jewish exile, the story spoke to a return home, a future time when Jews were not at the mercy of foreign kings. The story offered strategies for living peacefully in exile and held out hope for a better outcome in the more distant future. By taking the Esther story as their own, the legislators were claiming their current persecution to be short-lived and a better future to follow. In 1870, the Esther story may have seemed more fitting to appropriate than the Exodus narrative. Both stories described a devastating setback en route to a greater glory. But the forty years of wandering in the wilderness in Exodus came as a punishment for the Israelites' own sins, whereas the persecution in Esther's story came from a hostile and murderous enemy. The legislators in Raleigh thought the latter matched their circumstances. Demonic attacks seemed just as fitting. Similar to James Harris's point in 1869, the legislators in 1870 considered the impeachment proceedings as an alarming, dangerous threat, but nevertheless futile.

The Esther circular argued for permanence to the new era of emancipation and Reconstruction, casting the Klan violence, electoral losses, and impeachment trial as temporary setbacks. The black struggle against Redemption took place on the ground—in militia units, legislatures, schools, and farms—but it was also a struggle on the level of religious narrative. Who gets to tell the South's story? Was Reconstruction an aberration in the region's history, or was it the beginning of a new era? Was the collapse of Reconstruction a return to a more natural state, or did it mark a period of exile that only interrupted the region's destiny? Even three years after Holden's impeachment, black leaders in the state continued to believe the setbacks were only temporary. In 1874, the African American editor of the *Fayetteville Educator* listed the ongoing attacks on Republican Party officials and black communities. A black legislator had been shot in the streets; a local white judge had murdered a black man with impunity. But the editor told his readers not to despair: "Revolutions never turn backwards."[45] Despite the evidence around him, the editor remained convinced it was not the end of the story.

Interpreting the Circular

The story, however, is exactly what historians have missed. The Esther circular made its way into many histories of Reconstruction. In *Black Reconstruction* (1935), W. E. B. Du Bois quoted two paragraphs from the North Carolina circular to display the political motivations behind Holden's impeachment and to argue that black leaders were faithfully representing black interests in the struggle. Du Bois understood well the relationship between black interests and Holden's administration, and he considered the circular of some import. Curiously though, he chose not to mention or comment on the Esther story, and in his omission he failed to see the authors' claim to armed self-defense or vision for life in exile. Dunning School historian and conservative white Southerner Joseph Gregoire de Roulhac Hamilton acknowledged the document's use of a religious narrative and the call for fasting, but he too made no comment or analysis about the Esther story and quoted from the only two paragraphs in the circular that did not mention God, supernatural forces, or Esther. Hamilton and Du Bois offered diametrically opposed interpretations of the time period, but they both interpreted the document without analyzing its central biblical story.[46]

Modern historian Eric Foner used the circular to highlight the importance of religion. Foner mentioned the reference to Esther, Mordecai, and Haman as evidence that black leaders used the Bible to help constituents understand public events. The appearance of biblical references in political discourse gave credence to Foner's argument that "during Reconstruction, black Christianity inspired not inaction but political commitment." Surprisingly, Foner, too, failed to mention the purpose of the circular: a call to prayer and fasting. Perhaps he did so because it is not possible to determine if anyone actually heeded that call. Still, we must note that black leaders were using the Bible in this case not to encourage black voting or some other typical form of political commitment. They were asking for prayer. As Foner argued, black leaders were trying to help their followers understand political events, but not in the way he suggested. Black politicians wanted the people to see Reconstruction politics as a supernatural drama. Some scholars tend to treat religious language as a medium to convey the political messages that secular language, albeit less powerfully, could also transmit. The 1870 circular demonstrates the shortcomings of this kind of interpretation. Black religion did inspire political action, as Foner argued. But it also changed political action in such a way as to blur the categories of "inaction" and "political commitment." Where do we, as interpreters, place prayer and fasting?[47]

If prayer and fasting are political acts, as the authors of the Esther circular assumed, then we cannot describe the effect of religion on politics as "inaction" or "political commitment." Such categories assume that religion either drives believers into politics or drives them away. It ignores altogether the narratives that ordered their political actions and the beliefs that shaped and altered their political strategies. Instead, attention to the role of narrative sends us in a more fruitful direction.[48] Black leaders situated the political events of 1869–71 in a religious narrative not just to make sense of circumstances for themselves or their followers but also because they understood political events to be part of a larger spiritual drama. In that drama, fasting could prove as effective as militias. Everything about the Esther circular sets up the reader to expect a political solution. In fact, the authors said they were writing to arouse the black community into political action. And what they meant was prayer and fasting.

It is generally well acknowledged that religion was important to black politics in the nineteenth and twentieth centuries.[49] To argue that would be saying nothing new. When the best political historians of our day speak of the importance of black religion, many have tended to treat black religion as institutional (the organization structure and recruiting grounds for black grassroots politics); as inspirational (what got black Southerners motivated to enter politics); or as otherworldly (what distracted black Southerners from their woes in this world).[50]

Analyzing the Esther circular suggests we look at the intersection of religion and politics differently: as narratives that shaped political means and ends. Religious narratives, for white and black Southerners, gave meaning and order to their politics. Religious narratives competed to legitimize or marginalize political movements; and, of course, the content of those narratives mattered for the course of the political movements themselves. The Esther circular raised alarm among readers because it argued for black power in a time of white terror. It is not sufficient to interpret the document as evidence that religion was important. The content of the religious narrative was what mattered, not merely the fact that it was religious. Had the authors of the Esther circular framed their plight with a different narrative—say, the military conquest of Canaan, as black politicians did at other times—they could have invoked a political vision of dominance and success, one where Confederates were soundly defeated and the freed people and their allies ruled the day. That vision made sense to many in 1867 and 1868. But by 1870, black leaders in North Carolina were searching for other narratives. The Esther narrative offered them a way to imagine life as an ethnic minority in a hostile land. In the collapse of Reconstruction, Esther made better sense of black political circumstances than did the Exodus or the conquest of Canaan, to at least one group of black leaders. The narrative helped them imagine a future where African Americans might have a political voice, liberty, and self-protection, even if they remained a marginalized minority in a land controlled by others.

My point should not be understood as opposed to Foner's or Du Bois's projects. Both were committed, as I am, to understanding the politics of black freedom as central to Reconstruction; their goal, unlike mine, was not to understand black theology. The irony is that by zooming past the Esther story to focus on politics, they missed the political message of the circular. The biblical story justified the use of self-defense and the protection of a sovereign political power. In 1870, the same story could be used to advocate the employment of black militias and an appeal to more federal intervention— precisely the same strategy that Holden and the Republican legislature had employed earlier that year. The legislators' use of Esther demonstrated a wide-eyed assessment of the threats they faced, a belief in prayer as a political strategy, and an advocacy of the very things most likely to enrage elite whites: black militias and federal troops. Later in the decade, some black Southerners would find biblical reasons to give up Reconstruction politics in favor of migration or economic uplift, but not the authors of the Esther circular. Regrettably, too few sources exist to say how ordinary black North Carolinians responded to the Esther circular. As the work of seventeen legislators, the circular cannot serve as a thermometer of larger black political or religious thought. Yet the document can warn us against looking past the content of the religious story to focus instead on the politics.

In his influential 1994 essay "African-Americans, Exodus, and the American Israel," Albert Raboteau marveled at what black Americans had done with an "ancient story of the Near East." The Exodus story—complete with runaway slaves, plagues, drowning chariots, and wandering in the wilderness— inspired slave revolts, internal resistance to slavery, and a sustained critique of American messianic nationalism. African American interpreters produced countless songs, sermons, and speeches that drew deeply and in varied ways on the Exodus. Nearly every detail of the Exodus story is important to understand black Americans' religious and political ideas. And, as Raboteau writes, "No single symbol captures more clearly the distinctiveness of Afro-American Christianity than the symbol of Exodus." But it was not the only symbol. Exodus was but the main narrative in a set of narratives that shaped black religion and politics. Some stories like Exodus maintained the connection between African Americans and the nation of Israel. Other stories called for identification with Jesus Christ as a suffering servant or with distant tribes brought into Israel's story. The rich and creative work that black Americans have done with other ancient stories from the Near East often goes ignored by historians, who write as if the Exodus story was all that animated black Christianity. At times, stories like Esther's opened up political imaginations in ways that Exodus could not.[51]

All this is to say, we must analyze narratives and beliefs at the intersection of religion and politics, and this is no less true for the end of Reconstruction. Black Christianity did not simply fuel political action; religious ideas shaped and transformed black political ideas and actions. The Esther story was hardly the dominant paradigm guiding black political responses to Redemption. It was but one example of how biblical narrative shaped black political imaginations. Yet the story should focus our attention onto the content of religious narratives, if we want to understand the strategies and visions black politicians saw.

Daniel Stowell, in his religious history of Reconstruction, noted that black Southerners' "providential understanding of history . . . rendered the end of reconstruction all the more devastating."[52] Certainly, the collapse of Reconstruction must have dismayed those who believed that emancipation had inaugurated a new age, ordained by God, where African Americans would advance and race prejudice recede. Indeed, the tone of the Esther circular was dismal: "our liberties are at an end!" We might expect black Southerners then to respond either with drastic measures to meet the drastic times, or to despair and withdraw from politics. Some did, of course, despair; and others responded by migrating elsewhere. But other black Southerners continued their political agendas after Redemption and continued to date their progress, unhindered, from emancipation with yearly celebrations. Black Southerners found ways to make sense of their persecution and remained undeterred in their aims of political participation, land acquisition, and self-protection. The narrative structure of black eschatology goes a long way to explain why this was so.

CHAPTER THREE

Exodus and Jubilee

Exile narratives from Israel's past may have helped some African Americans imagine a place for themselves in the post-Reconstruction South, but for 1,500 sharecroppers in Lenoir County in eastern North Carolina, by 1877 living in exile had become too difficult to bear. In fact, as they planned an exodus, they referred to the South not as a land of exile but as a "House of Bondage," the same term Israelites used for Egypt. When the Israelites fled their captors, they entered a vast desert and grumbled at the lack of food and drinkable water. Some wanted to return to Egypt. The migrants from Lenoir County had cause to grumble as well. Their exodus failed in almost every way. In late 1879, many of them huddled together in a church building in Indiana, freezing, broke, and exhausted, wanting to return to North Carolina but unable to afford the return trip.[1] Few black Southerners thought of Indiana as the Promised Land, but the sharecroppers stranded there were not the only ones seeking their destiny in an exodus out of the South.

All across the South in the late 1870s, disgruntled African Americans organized migrations, to Kansas, farther west, or to Liberia in West Africa. Migrations were hardly new to black Southerners. Indeed, their history had been one of successive migrations. Slaves had migrated across the African continent, across the Atlantic in the Middle Passage, and often between destinations in the Americas before arriving in the American South. Former slaves had participated in colonization schemes in the early nineteenth century, leaving for Canada, Sierra Leone, and Liberia. In the decades before the Civil War, more than a million slaves left their homes in the Upper South for the new plantations of the Deep South. Dubbed "the second Middle Passage," it was larger than the first, forcibly relocating more slaves than had ever come to the United States during the Atlantic slave trade. After emancipation, black Americans traveled the country searching for lost relatives and higher wages. After Reconstruction, deteriorating political and economic circumstances prompted black Southerners to once again consider moving. Post-Reconstruction movements were but the next chapter in a long history of migration.[2] The sharecroppers from Lenoir County left in search of land; they had come to believe that, in God's plan for the race, they would become landowners after emancipation. By 1877, they had waited for land for more than twelve years.

Freedmen's Bureau agent James Sinclair noticed that expectation of land back in 1865 when he traveled among North Carolina's freedpeople. They eagerly expected to receive titles to confiscated lands of ex-Confederates. They believed that the property distribution would take place around Christmas Day 1865 or New Year's Day 1866. At a meeting in Lumberton, North Carolina, Sinclair tried to dissuade black farmers from their "extravagant ideas in relation to confiscated lands," with little success. He told them there would be no scheme to redistribute plantation owners' land among former slaves, but his audience remained convinced that "something very important [was] going to happen" around Christmas Day.[3] Black Southerners' "extravagant ideas" about property redistribution were widespread. Former Union Army officer Carl Schurz reported to Congress in late 1865, "In many localities I found an impression prevailing among the Negroes that some great change was going to take place about Christmas." Schurz continued, "They ardently desire to become freeholders. . . . In the independent possession of landed property they see the consummation of their deliverance."[4] In the minds of former slaves, with freedom came land.

The connection black Southerners made between land and freedom had two biblical precedents, Exodus and Jubilee. Black Protestants saw themselves in both of these stories; and in both stories, freed slaves acquire land. The role Exodus played in black American life has been well documented.[5] Exodus told the dramatic story of God's deliverance of the ancient Hebrews from slavery in Egypt. The narrative portrayed the power of Israel's God and the emancipation of God's people. It inaugurated the national period of Israel and showcased the Hebrews' long and troubled journey from Egypt, across a wilderness to Canaan, the land of their ancestors.[6]

The meaning of Jubilee is not as well known. Levitical law, which developed later in Israel's national history, called for Israelites to keep every fiftieth year holy as a Year of Jubilee. For forty-nine years, the people were allowed to buy and sell land and to obtain slaves from among the debtors or through warfare. During this timeframe, some families and tribes amassed large estates and many slaves, while many debtors lost their lands and indentured themselves or their children to pay their debts. But on the first day of the Year of Jubilee, priests sounded trumpets to announce the Day of Atonement when slaves were freed, debts were erased, and property was redistributed back to landless families and tribes. Jubilee leveled the playing field, in accordance with Levitical law: "The land shall not be sold permanently, for the land is Mine, [says the Lord]." The same held true for slave property. In short, the Year of Jubilee entailed freedom for slaves and property redistribution.[7]

Black Americans wrote themselves into both stories, and often conflated Exodus and Jubilee. Indeed, Exodus and Jubilee carried common meanings: freedom from slavery and acquisition of land. In both cases, freedom came dramatically—with Moses's parting of the Red Sea in Exodus and with the sounding of trumpets in Jubilee. Black Southerners' experience of emancipation as a dramatic and sudden event gave both stories a particular resonance. Exodus and Jubilee ran so parallel to black Southerners' experience because in both stories, a leader or the government announced the end of slavery, and slaves participated in their own dramatic emancipation. In both, landless slaves became property owners.[8]

Exodus and Jubilee, however, held important distinctions, especially for black Americans. Exodus described a large migration after emancipation to a land set aside for the newly freed. Jubilee, in contrast, restored to the landless a title to their homeland. These two very similar stories operated in tension for black Southerners—one arguing for colonization and migration, such as the ill-fated move to Indiana, the other for black land ownership in the state of their birth, much like the former slaves' expectation of property redistribution in 1865. The tension between Exodus and Jubilee became clear whenever black Americans debated the best way to get land: should they leave in search of better economic circumstances, or fight for opportunities to own land in their home state?

Exodus and Jubilee could both be appropriated literally and metaphorically. In the immediate postemancipation period, many African Americans expected Jubilee's Day of Atonement to be a specific day of property redistribution. In the 1870s and 1880s, black agricultural workers who were looking to move appropriated Exodus on a similarly literal level, as a mass migration. Others preferred more metaphorical readings. African American ministers and other well-established leaders often appropriated Exodus to describe the departure from white churches or the movement from slavery to citizenship, but rarely did they use the story to advocate for a mass migration. For Jubilee, a metaphorical reading by leaders and others could mean righting economic wrongs, or black prosperity, not necessarily a sudden act of property redistribution. Both stories were capacious enough to allow for literal and metaphorical interpretations.

In both literal and metaphorical readings, black leaders and migrants referred to the Exodus and Jubilee stories by shorthand: "Day of Atonement,"
"Jubilee," "Promised Land," "Moses," "silver trumpets," "land flowing with
milk and honey," etc. They rarely retold the entire stories, but their shorthand successfully evoked these biblical stories because their audiences were
already acquainted with each narrative and its implications for black life in
the postemancipation South. Even when black Southerners made no reference to Exodus and Jubilee, the stories' effect could be seen in the tension
between migration/colonization and economic justice/land ownership in
black thought. Even though black leaders and agricultural workers at times
staked opposite sides of the emigration debate, they all kept a keen eye on
the land, the agricultural labor market, and black economic interests in the
South. Interpreting religious narratives did not distract black Americans
from such practical considerations, which in fact helped them to discern
God's will. Rising political and economic fortunes supported arguments
that God wanted his people to stay settled, while political persecution, poor
crops, and economic injustice signaled God's will that they seek out the
Promised Land. Religious motivations were not separate from political and
economic ones.

In the immediate postemancipation period, former slaves placed their
hope in Jubilee, in the acquisition of land in the South. The freedpeople
who shared their "extravagant ideas" of property redistribution with Sinclair
certainly had Jubilee in mind. As the century progressed, however, more
and more black Southerners wearied in waiting for Jubilee, and placed their
hope in Exodus instead. From the end of Reconstruction through the Great
Migration of the 1910s, 1920s, and 1930s, African Americans entertained
ideas of relocation, including renewed interest in West Africa and large migrations from the Atlantic South to the Southwest and Deep South. In
North Carolina in the late 1870s, two small groups of landless black farmers
left the state in Exodus-inspired migrations: the one to Indiana and another
to Liberia. Black Protestant leaders opposed the migrations, intensified
their calls for economic justice and land reform in North Carolina, and appealed to black farmers to stay home. In 1889–90, in a mass migration out of
North Carolina, tens of thousands headed to states farther west and south
in search of a Promised Land. Such a large migration spoke to black North
Carolinians' unrest in waiting for Jubilee. Black leaders opposed this later
migration as well but had much less success in stemming the tide of emigrants.
Black Protestant leaders remained committed to Jubilee; they believed that

black land ownership and economic justice were possible in North Carolina. But increasingly, many of their followers placed their hope in Exodus.

In North Carolina, the tension in black eschatological thought between Jubilee and Exodus could be seen clearly in all three moments: the expectations of land during the Christmas season of 1865, the small migrations of the late 1870s, and the large migrations in 1889–90. For each of these moments, religious narratives shaped and inspired black action and debate. As African Americans drew on those narratives, they made strong, explicit connections between land and freedom, and, more specifically, between emigration (Exodus) and arguments for black land ownership (Jubilee). The search for land, be it here or there, remained central to the eschatological beliefs black Southerners forged during emancipation.

Jubilee Now: Postwar Expectations of Land

Across the South, newly freed slaves expected land to accompany their freedom. As one observer of Union contraband camps wrote, "The freedmen had got the impression that the abandoned lands of their old owners were to be divided amongst them." Rumors of General Sherman's promise of land, of slaves taking ownership of the Georgia Sea Islands, and of bills before Congress to confiscate and redistribute Confederate land fueled their expectations. In hindsight, it seems clear that large-scale land distribution would never have garnered enough support to be feasible, but in the moment, it seemed entirely plausible. The hopeful looked to government precedent in the Homestead Act of 1862, which took confiscated Indian lands out west and made them available and affordable to settlers. Could not the federal government take confiscated Confederate land and make it available and affordable to the freedpeople?[9]

In 1865, the answer appeared to be yes. The rumors of property redistribution had their basis in fact. Freedmen did take possession of confiscated Confederate land in isolated places—on the Georgia Sea Islands, for example, and in James City, North Carolina. In March 1865, Congress created the Bureau of Refugees, Freedmen, and Abandoned Lands and authorized it to lease almost 900,000 acres of abandoned Confederate land to former slaves and loyal white refugees. The law made provision for every male freedman to be assigned no more than forty acres; if the freedman rented the property for three years, he would be eligible to purchase the land and assume its title. Freedmen thus began to apply for land. When Andrew

TRENT RIVER SETTLEMENT, OPPOSITE NEWBERN, NORTH CAROLINA.—[SKETCHED BY THEODORE R. DAVIS.]

SCHOOL-HOUSE AND CHAPEL AT TRENT RIVER SETTLEMENT.—[SKETCHED BY THEO. R. DAVIS.]

NEGRO HUTS AT TRENT RIVER SETTLEMENT.

Trent River Settlement, 1866. The Trent River Settlement became James City, North
Carolina, one of a few places in the South where black farmers were able temporarily to
achieve the kind of property redistribution described in the practice of Jubilee. Image:
"Trent River Settlement," *Harper's Weekly*, June 9, 1866. Courtesy of Hargrett Rare Book
and Manuscript Library, University of Georgia Libraries.

Johnson's administration later decided that property redistribution was politically unviable, the federal government made it clear that the abandoned
and confiscated lands would be returned to their former owners. Nevertheless, black Southerners latched onto the free soil ideology that underpinned
the new Freedmen's Bureau. Radical Republicans in Congress envisioned a
nation where those who worked the land owned the land. It was akin to
Thomas Jefferson's vision of a free agrarian republic. So, in addition to biblical precedents for equating land with freedom, former slaves could turn to
American political ideologies to support their expectations of large-scale
property redistribution.[10]

In North Carolina, as elsewhere, expectations of property redistribution
were most intense in the fall and winter of 1865. As Agent Sinclair reported,

the freedpeople in North Carolina waited for something dramatic to happen on Christmas Day, 1865. In Duplin County, one group of freedmen stated their intention to own tracts of land "even if they had to shed blood to obtain them."[11] Most, however, prepared peacefully. Rumors circulated that the government would redistribute land to heads of households only. So, in the two days before a visit by a Freedmen's Bureau agent in August 1865, 150 black couples in Warrenton, North Carolina, tied the knot in order to be eligible for a land allotment. When the Bureau agent arrived, Warrenton blacks thronged to hear his announcement about the "new laws" regarding land ownership. The agent attempted to dispel the rumors but met resistance.[12] One month later, when African Americans gathered in Warrenton to elect a delegate to the State Freedmen's Convention in Raleigh, they reaffirmed their belief in an imminent plan for property redistribution, passing over one candidate who was dubious about land handouts, and electing the other who expected a "grand division" of land.[13]

Black expectations for property redistribution sparked fears of a violent revolt in the minds of white Southerners. The fear of insurrection and revolution began in eastern North Carolina in June 1865 and spread throughout the former Confederacy. In a diary entry, planter Samuel Agnew predicted "a negroe Jubilee insurrection." Others feared that the federal government would confiscate plantations and give the land to former slaves, or that blacks would turn violent when the government failed to do so, killing their former masters to take their land.[14] Donald MacRae, a white North Carolina merchant, wrote to his wife, warning her of the coming revolution, and confiding his fears that blacks would start a race war to take possession of the land; he encouraged her to learn to shoot a pistol. Some concerned white North Carolinians wrote to Governor Holden about the need to protect landholders from the coming Jubilee revolt.[15] One white North Carolina planter feared the worst: "a rehearsal for the South's Armageddon."[16] Rev. Burkhead recalled his fears of Jubilee-inspired violence in Wilmington in 1865: "[Freed slaves] began to threaten us with mobs, and even their preachers advised the colored people that the houses and lands were theirs and that they should get possession of them by violence if they could not be obtained by other means!"[17] Black expectations and white fears reinforced one another.

Even before rumors of insurrection spread throughout the South, black hopes for property redistribution took on an explicit millennialism. During the war, passersby heard communities of freed slaves singing:

Old master's gone and the darkies stayed at home;
Must be now that the kingdom's come and the year of jubilee.[18]

Even earlier, a black Union soldier camped in Virginia linked the coming Jubilee with the millennium: "so soon as the general jubilee is proclaimed throughout the Southern regions—so soon as this rebellion, originating from the power of slavery, is subdued, then we will have a glorious millennium of peace in this once slave-cursed country."[19] One group of African Americans in Mississippi put a precise date on the coming Jubilee and millennium. They heard a story that the Freedmen's Bureau had a "Great Document" sealed with four seals, which would be broken on New Year's Day 1866, when the federal government would deliver its "final orders" for land confiscation and redistribution. This was a dramatic retelling of St. John's vision in the Book of Revelation of a great document with seven seals, each broken seal releasing new terrors such as the four horsemen of the apocalypse. In the freedpeople's vision, the opening of the document paralleled the apocalypse, even if the contents of the document sounded more like Jubilee.[20]

Black Southerners continued to expect property to be redistributed, even when news came that the federal government would do no such thing. In mid-1865, when President Andrew Johnson announced that all confiscated lands would be restored to their former owners, General O. O. Howard, the commissioner of the Bureau of Refugees, Freedmen, and Abandoned Lands, delivered the bad news to former slaves across the South. An audience in Fayetteville, North Carolina, accused Howard of being a "Reb" dressed up as a Union general in order to deceive them. On one South Carolina plantation, when a black Freedmen's Bureau official informed the former slaves that the land would be restored to their former master, they lamented: "Christ has been betrayed by one of his own color." Why did black Southerners resist this news? They had believed in emancipation as part of God's plan, even when few had thought it possible. So when it came to land ownership, they were more likely to trust their eschatology than the word of Bureau agents. The criticism of the black agent in South Carolina is telling; former slaves accused him not of opposing black interests but of betraying Christ.[21]

Black Protestant leaders shared their followers' expectation of land and property, but many shied away from the dramatic Christmas Day predictions. Rev. J. C. Gibbs, a black Presbyterian minister, wrote the *Christian Recorder* from Wilmington urging other church leaders to take advantage of "confiscated rebel property." The U.S. military had already granted black churchgoers temporary rights over church properties abandoned by pro-Confederate clergy, and Gibbs believed there was "much property to be had for churches and schools."[22] He cited the recent "act of Congress" providing for the "withdrawing from confiscated rebel property, on the day of sale, such portions as may be needed for public purposes." Gibbs expected to very soon possess "a rebel's property, worth $15,000" on which he could build a church and a school. "Now is the golden moment," he told other leaders. Gibbs had every reason to expect property redistribution on a large scale, and he told others to "seize upon all these chances as quickly as possible."[23]

Other black Protestant leaders articulated visions for land ownership that looked less like a dramatic revolution and more like a steady rise in economic prosperity. Black leaders argued for the freedpeople's right to land, even if they distanced themselves from the rumors and fears surrounding Christmas 1865. They seemed hopeful that black Southerners could achieve economic independence from whites and create prosperous free black communities in the state.

Leaders at the Freedmen's Convention in Raleigh in September 1865 discouraged emigration, because they believed that land would be available in North Carolina. In an open letter to the convention, abolitionist Horace Greeley advised the delegates: "Stay where you belong. It may by-and-by be well to emigrate, but not now." Greeley extolled North Carolina for "her resources" and "sources of unsuspected wealth." He predicted that black North Carolinians could achieve financial independence from whites. As long as the state held promise for black land ownership and prosperity, Greeley reasoned, emigration made little sense.[24]

The delegates agreed. James Walker Hood told the convention in his presidential address, "Let us keep constantly in our mind that this State is our home." This was curious advice from a man born in Pennsylvania. He continued, "Some people talk of emigration for the black race, some of expatriation and some of colonization. I regard this all as nonsense."[25] Native North Carolinians concurred. After the convention, one delegate wrote, "It's not our purpose to emigrate or colonize, and we do not want to be driven away." African Americans, the delegate continued, wanted to live and die in "the Old North State" as landed and enfranchised men, "not as rogues, not as convicts, not as vagabonds."[26] The delegate's opposition to emigration remained wedded to a vision for land ownership and prosperity in North Carolina.

Black Protestant leaders consistently discussed emigration and land ownership in tandem. In an October 1865 editorial in the *Journal of Freedom*,

Edward P. Brooks chastised former North Carolina senator Kenneth Rayner for his "lugubrious sore-headed" plan to remove African Americans from the South. Brooks dismissed the plan on practical and ideological grounds, as black leaders had done for decades when they opposed white schemes for colonization. He cited "difficulties too numerous to mention" and accused Rayner of "hot-headed haste." But Brooks also used the editorial to argue for black land rights: "The blacks will remain here in the land to which their unquestionable loyalty gives them a better title than Rayner." Brooks's editorial placed him near the beginning of a long procession of black leaders who discussed and dismissed emigration as a segue to arguing for black rights to the land and other forms of economic justice.[27]

In 1865, very few black North Carolinians held title to land. The Christmas season did nothing to change that. The 1865 holiday season passed without incident—no Jubilee riot, no "Great Document," no property redistribution. Still, African Americans held out hope for land. Rumors of a coming Jubilee-like land scheme circulated again in 1867, 1868, and 1873.[28] Black laborers faced mounting debt, and the few who accumulated capital met resistance when they tried to purchase land. A few, remarkably, did become freeholders. Throughout Reconstruction, black leaders advised against emigration in hopes that land would become available at home. The African American editors of the *Fayetteville Educator* in 1874 still expressed enough faith in black opportunities in the state that they encouraged others to immigrate to North Carolina. The editors told readers that in North Carolina black men could become "freeholders." They enticed "all who wish land" to move to "a most beautiful and quite country," the Old North State.[29] African American beliefs in a dramatic reversal of fortunes—to go from slaves to landowners—were grounded in something more than rumors of redistribution schemes by the Freedmen's Bureau. They were grounded in black eschatology.

Still Waiting for Jubilee: Migrations in the Late 1870s

The promise of Jubilee during Reconstruction was strong enough to capture even the most ardent proponents of emigration. Even Martin Delany, the leading black advocate of colonization in Africa, quit urging migration after the war and instead worked for the Freedmen's Bureau and state government in South Carolina. Delany reconsidered his decades-old plan when he saw the work of God in emancipation. Even though he was not an advocate of property confiscation, Delany was fixated on land ownership as essential to black freedom.[30] In late 1865, in a series of essays on the "Prospects of the Freedmen of Hilton Head," Delany asked, "Will the negroes be able to obtain land by which to earn a livelihood?" As a Freedmen's Bureau official, in a plan he called the Triple Alliance, Delany wanted to sell small tracts of land to former slaves, with the aid of Northern capital investment.[31] Delany's conversion was energetic. Only years before, he despaired of a future for black Americans in the United States. During Reconstruction, he was creative and hardworking in making that future materialize. He even chastised others for not seeing the same glorious future that he did. In an 1866 letter to the Colored Convention that met in Washington, Delany explained why he had changed his mind about a future in America and why he was so willing to wait: "Do not forget God. Think, O think how wonderfully he made himself manifest during the war. Only think how he confounded ... the wisdom of the mighty of this land. ... He still lives. ... Bide your time."[32] Like other black Americans, Delany, who had been the loudest black voice in favor of emigration, interpreted the Civil War as an extraordinary intervention of God in human history, one that compelled African Americans to patiently observe what would come next. Bold predictions of the future accompanied emancipation. Delany remained interested in land for his landless people, but during Reconstruction he was willing to wait for the opportunity to own land in the South.

All across the South in the late 1870s, disgruntled African Americans grew tired of waiting. In North Carolina, one group enlisted help from the American Colonization Society to emigrate to Liberia; another turned to the National Emigrant Aid Society for their move to Indiana. Both groups cited their landlessness and economic troubles as cause for leaving, and both appropriated the Exodus narrative as their own story. Although both migrations were relatively small, they nevertheless made waves in North Carolina politics. Most black Protestant leaders opposed the migrations but used them as opportunities to push for land reform in North Carolina. More important than the migrations themselves were the debates they generated. In those debates, two things were clear. First, religious narratives shaped black expectations of land. Second, African Americans linked migration and land ownership; to oppose one was to argue for the other.

In 1877, Delany returned his attention to Africa. The same year, the American Colonization Society (ACS) in Washington, D.C., began receiving new petitions from North Carolina for transport to Liberia. "The people here are in a great uproar about going to Liberia," a white teacher from

Cabarrus County wrote to ACS secretary William Coppinger in August 1877. "The Colored people here are wide awake and are in earnest about going to Liberia," she informed him. "They say they expect to be ready by fall."[33] In the same year, Albert Williams described a similar readiness among Raleigh's African Americans, himself included. They held colonization meetings weekly and wanted to leave "at the earliest opportunity." The ACS responded positively to these requests, giving instructions on transport preparations.[34]

Across the South, groups prepared to leave for Liberia. Frustrated with the slow response of the ACS, would-be migrants in South Carolina formed the Liberia Exodus Joint Stock Steamship Company. By 1878, they had raised enough money to purchase the *Azor*, which harbored in Charleston before taking 206 passengers to Liberia on its first and only voyage. The steamship was auctioned to pay off the company's debts. The other would-be migrants had to search out other ways to get to Africa. Some continued to look to the ACS for help. Even before the *Azor* reached Liberia, black organizers were scouting the land for a colony of migrants from eastern Arkansas. In 1880, 100 refugees from Arkansas found themselves stranded and penniless in New York, having sold their possessions to get there in hopes of boarding ACS vessels for Liberia. By the following year, several groups of Arkansans had settled in Liberia. In Louisiana, as in North Carolina, local colonization groups sprang up with hopes of getting passage to Liberia, but few made the journey.[35]

Kansas then seemed a more practical destination. On one Saturday in July 1879, in Kinston, North Carolina, African Americans from across Lenoir County came together to discuss an exodus to Kansas. "The feeling was much more intense than anyone imagined," an observer noted. The large crowd greeted the prospect of emigration with the enthusiasm of "campaign times." The Kinston crowd listened to Sam Perry, a relatively unknown black leader, as he explained the reasons to move. Economic injustice, black poverty, and landlessness topped his list. Perry accused white landholders of "cheating them out of their earnings." Slave labor was valued at $150 a year, Perry reasoned, and if black farmworkers had received the true value of their labor since emancipation, each should have $2,250 in savings or real property. Perry's speech resonated with the crowd, and they responded with "repeated applause." Perry attracted followers because conditions at home failed to meet black expectations for property.[36]

Perry, a long-time advocate for colonization, had not served as a delegate to the Colored or Freedmen's Conventions, and he openly opposed their antiemigration consensus. "I had not much to do with the big professional negroes, the rich men. I did not associate with them much, but I got among the workingmen," he later recalled. Perry's populist message highlighted class divisions among the state's black population. Black business owners, schoolteachers, and church leaders were much more likely to oppose migration than were farm laborers. Despite organizing among farmers in Lenoir County throughout the 1870s, Perry met little success until 1879.[37] What changed the minds of those in attendance at the July 1879 meeting? Why did Lenoir County blacks suddenly favor a Kansas exodus?

The answer, at least in part, was the Landlord and Tenant Act of 1877. The North Carolina General Assembly revised previous laws on farm tenancy to privilege landlords over tenants. The new law declared that all crops and possessions held on leased land remained the property of the landlord until he decided all conditions of the lease agreement had been met. Perry later claimed that the infamous law gave "the landlord the right to be the court, sheriff, and jury." One section of the law made it a misdemeanor for sharecroppers or tenant farmers to move off rented land without the consent of the landlord, thus further empowering landlords, and limiting black tenants' freedom and financial growth. Nearly all the black North Carolinians who eventually followed Perry out of state cited the Landlord and Tenant Act as the reason.[38] In such a climate, "false emigration agents" preyed on black farmers' fears. In Kinston, two men sold worthless "little scripts of paper" for one dollar each, saying they were railway tickets to Kansas.[39] People were desperate to move. It was in this environment that sincere emigration advocates like Sam Perry found followers.

In September, Perry arrived in Washington, D.C., at the offices of the National Emigrant Aid Society, bearing petitions from would-be emigrants in Lenoir County. The Society discouraged Perry from organizing a mass migration to Kansas, for two reasons. Black migrants from Mississippi, Louisiana, and Tennessee were already pouring into Kansas, and there were not enough jobs or land for additional migrants. Second, the Society could subsidize transportation to the former northwestern states of Ohio, Indiana, and Illinois, but not the more expensive passage to the Great Plains. Perry heeded the Society's advice to organize a movement of black workers from North Carolina to Indiana.[40]

In November 1879, Perry returned to ready his followers for a journey to Indiana. A flyer posted around Lenoir County read:

EMIGRATION MEETING

A meeting of the colored citizens of Lenoir County will be held at the
Freedman's School House at La Grange, N. C.
on Saturday the 8th Day of Nov. 1879,
for the purpose of expressing our grievance to the Country and of
perfecting our plans of escape from the House of Bondage.[41]

Perry's group consciously appropriated the language of the Hebrew Exodus
to make comparison between peonage or sharecropping in North Carolina
and slavery in ancient Egypt, "the House of Bondage." They relived the Exodus story, as did their Deep South counterparts. The large numbers of exodusters fleeing Mississippi, Louisiana, and Tennessee for Kansas christened
the southern Great Plains "a new Canaan." Historian Nell Painter has argued that their exodus to Kansas not only appropriated the language of the
Hebrew exodus but also invested it with clear millenarian overtones.[42]

If Kansas was a dubious candidate for the land flowing with milk and
honey, Indiana was even less promising. But, as the flyer indicated, conditions in North Carolina, not in their destination, drove Lenoir County blacks
to flee.[43] One Baptist farmer seemed ambivalent about where he wanted to
go. "Some of my friends has gone to Indiana," Cary Bellamy wrote, "but a
great many are yet still getting ready for Liberia." Bellamy, like those at the
Lenoir County emigration meeting, was concerned with the lack of economic justice at home. "It has been so dreadful hard for a colored man to get
any money here in the south that . . . I shall do every thing that I can to leave
here." It mattered less to Bellamy where he was going.[44]

But to the success of the exodus, the place of destination mattered a great
deal, and Indiana came far short of the Promised Land. Train cars delivered
the migrants to Indianapolis, beginning in mid-November 1879, but they were
not warmly welcomed. As early as January 1880, some tried to return home.
Maria Bryant, who had emigrated to Indiana from Lenoir County, stopped
in Washington, D.C., on her way back home. According to a Washington
newspaper account reprinted in North Carolina papers, "she was stationed
[in Indianapolis] in a church, packed with emigrants of her own color, from
her own section, where she was compelled to remain two or three weeks,
receiving only one meal a day, and that a very poor one."[45] An AME Church
in Indianapolis had stepped up to care for the displaced Southerners, but
the church quickly depleted its resources. The disaster prompted Indiana's
Democratic senator Daniel Voorhees to call a Congressional hearing. At

that hearing, Perry, who had been called as a witness, confessed that "if [he] owned a lot in Indiana and one in hell, [he] would rent out the one in Indiana and live in hell."[46] Perry's followers would probably have made the same choice. Reports from Indiana agreed: "The emigrants cannot procure work, and are suffering and dying from cold and starvation."[47]

Those who followed Perry to Indiana numbered fewer than 1,500, and only 318 black North Carolinians left for Liberia. Even though the migrations were small, they received considerable attention, especially from African American ministers and politicians. In the late 1870s, black Protestant leaders debated, and by and large refuted, arguments for emigration and colonization for several reasons. Black emigration ran counter to black leaders' own interests. In the nineteenth century, black leadership was intensely local; the loss of local constituencies or congregations eroded a leader's influence and power. Emigration threatened the survival of institutions in which black ministers and politicians were so heavily invested. But leaders also sincerely believed North Carolina had more to offer than did other places. Migrants faced harsh conditions in Indiana and Liberia, and black leaders felt a duty to critique the rosy portrayals painted by those who did not have their congregants' best interests at heart. The central themes of their opposition to emigration were a belief in better prospects for black land ownership in North Carolina and a commitment to advocating for economic justice in the state. They wanted Jubilee, not Exodus.

When procolonization ideas began circulating in North Carolina in February 1877, Hood, by this time a bishop in the AME Zion Church, gave public speeches around the state denouncing the colonization schemes. Hood listed the disadvantages of Liberia: its bad climate, poor produce, and dangerous diseases. But Hood's central argument focused not on conditions abroad but on conditions at home. He turned his attention to the land. Hood "felt sure a brighter and better day was breaking upon the colored man," and he did not want black North Carolinians to miss it by relocating.[48]

Edward Hill, an African American legislator, made similar arguments in 1877 when the North Carolina House of Representatives debated a plan for black colonization in the American West.[49] Hill questioned "what was to be gained by it, especially when it was proposed to carry them among uncivilized Indians and grizzly bears ... and where for ten months in the year there is ice eight to ten inches in thickness." Hill critiqued the plan from all sides. Colonization, he argued, meant "giving up their church organizations and school houses," and, he worried, "beneath it slept the extermination of their race." He said to the House that there was "no better field than North Carolina for the colored man to develop himself." Hill had not yet given up on economic prosperity in North Carolina.[50] Hill's arguments even convinced the bill's author, who later joined other black leaders in their anti-emigration consensus.

That consensus became clear when leaders met in two State Colored Conventions in Raleigh, one in September 1877 and the other in January 1880, to issue statements against organized emigrations. Their opposition to the Exodus movements to Liberia and Indiana hinged upon an eschatological belief in a better day coming for African Americans in North Carolina. And they used the attention gained from emigration to argue for land reform and economic justice at home.

Ordinary African Americans were deeply interested in these State Colored Conventions. On September 15, 1877, African Americans in Edgecombe County filed into the Tarboro courthouse to elect delegates to the upcoming Convention. "Crowds from every direction poured in town," a Republican newspaper reported. "By 10 o'clock the streets were crowded to such an extent that persons could scarcely make their passage through the dense throngs." The meeting organizers abandoned their plans to hold the proceedings indoors, "the Court House being literally packed." When they moved outdoors, "the yard was completely covered." The reporter estimated that more than 2,000 were in attendance, roughly the size of the entire Tarboro black population from the previous census. At eleven o'clock the courthouse bell rang, and "everybody as if drawn by a magnet," made their way to hear the speakers, the first being the well-known and well-respected politician James H. Harris.[51]

Harris opened his speech by arguing that political defeat did not mean a surrender of claims to the land: "I said then [in the face of Democratic victory] what I repeat today, that we were born here, we were raised here, [and] our forefathers . . . by their sweat and toil [developed] the great resources of the South." The land the audience gathered upon, Harris argued, belonged to them. He cited cotton and tobacco production figures, claiming that black labor provided the wealth of white institutions. "I declare here today," Harris said, "that the black man is entitled to a home in this country, and so help him God here he's going to remain." The audience replied with applause and "cries of yes! yes!"[52] To Harris, colonization, beyond being "foolish," conceded that the political actions of Southern whites could interfere with black destiny. Some said that "there will be no chance for the colored people" now that Democrats have control, but Harris countered that Democrats could do nothing to prevent the elevation of his race "in the great drama of life." By not emigrating, black farmers could still stake claim to the land they worked.[53]

James E. O'Hara, an attorney who had served with Harris in the state legislature, spoke later at the same meeting. "At no distant future the negro will be the balance of power in North Carolina," he predicted, based in part on the progress made since emancipation. "A brighter day is dawning upon us," O'Hara proclaimed, "North Carolina regenerated and redeemed." In his speech, he applied language of individual born-again conversion to the whole state. In the familiar nineteenth-century narrative of conversion, the sinner reached his or her darkest hours before experiencing the joy of rebirth. O'Hara followed this narrative when he connected the language of rebirth ("regenerated and redeemed") to the dawn, as nineteenth-century evangelicals often did to explain individual conversion: "it is always darkest just before dawn." O'Hara, however, went beyond the individual, applying the metaphor to African Americans' economic and political circumstances in North Carolina. The dire straits in which many rural blacks found themselves did not argue for the need for Exodus, O'Hara hinted, but foreshadowed North Carolina's coming conversion.[54]

In the 1877 and 1880 conventions, the delegates passed resolutions opposing all emigration schemes. Despite their political losses and the landlessness of their people, black leaders affirmed that African Americans were, as convention leaders wrote in their public statement, "moulding their own destiny."[55] The 1880 public statement went one step further.[56] The authors walked a fine line, trying to convince whites of the legitimacy of black migrants' complaints while simultaneously convincing rural blacks to stay in North Carolina. Even though black leaders unequivocally disapproved of the movement to Indiana, not once did they castigate the emigrants. Instead, they placed responsibility for the migration on the shoulders of leading whites, identifying repressive Democratic policies as the "prime causes of the unrest." Their list of grievances focused on abusive land practices and black disfranchisement. Topping the list was the charge that "land owners exact exorbitant rents for their lands and necessary supplies, thereby sucking the life's blood from the colored sons of soil." This was strong language from men who valued tact and restraint. The document also cited the Landlord and Tenant Act, which they claimed "open[ed] a broad channel for unscrupulous landlords to defraud their colored tenants out of their hard earnings." The migration to Indiana captured white attention, and those at the January 1880 conference used that attention to attack unfair land policies in the state.[57]

The self-styled "representative colored men" of the convention intended to install themselves as liaisons between disgruntled African Americans and leading whites. Harris and his colleagues saw themselves as mediators, conveying black workers' grievances to leading whites and leading whites' anti-emigration advice to black workers. But even though they agreed with black workers as to the facts of oppression and economic injustice, the conference participants foresaw a better day ahead. The spirit of oppression among whites, they believed, was "now happily disappearing." Unlike the migrants, the convention delegates still believed that black economic prosperity was possible in North Carolina. They advocated specific land reform, such as the repeal of the Landlord and Tenant Act and limits on the fees and interest landlords and merchants could charge farmers. These reforms, they hoped, would provide black workers with decent wages, and, eventually, a degree of economic independence from whites. And in the preamble to the document, the conference delegates resurrected the moral claim that black North Carolinians had to the land. They reminded whites that black "labor, toil, suffering and affliction have changed North Carolina from a wilderness into a prosperous state." Black workers had endured a "long dark dismal night of bondage and oppression" and deserved a share of the prosperity their labor had produced.[58] It was a far cry from the radical call for property confiscation in 1865, but black leaders maintained a vision of black land ownership.

One black Presbyterian minister sharply contrasted emigration and economic uplift. He wrote in the *New York Evangelist* of two "Southern sensations" coming out of North Carolina. The first, the North Carolina Colored Exhibition, was the first full-scale black-run fair in the South, designed to exhibit the freedpeople's industry and arts. The exhibition told a narrative of advancement, of "material and mental improvement," and foretold brighter days for black Southerners. The second sensation, the exodus to Indiana, told a narrative contrary to black triumph or advancement. "The North Carolina exodus is a most miserable mystery," the minister wrote. "Running from place to place . . . would be more likely to hinder and hurt the peace and progress of the colored people," he argued. He interpreted the exodus as a concession, a defeat. The Presbyterian minister concluded that he had "no faith in any exodus but that led by Moses."[59]

Despite their opposition to exodus, black Protestant leaders benefited from the attention that mass migrations attracted. Migrations could publicize black concerns in ways that black institutions could not. Additionally, the threat of emigration gave black leaders negotiating power with leading whites. With black political voices increasingly marginalized, African Americans' ability to vote with their feet lent power to black leaders' demands, even if those leaders had very little control over migrants' decisions to move. The January 1880 document proved that leading black North Carolinians were willing to use this power. The document warned whites "to remove the cause of dissatisfaction" among black North Carolinians or face "the depopulation of the laboring element of our State." Emigration, though vehemently opposed by black politicians and ministers, became one of their favorite topics of discussion. It installed them as liaisons between powerful whites and would-be emigrants. It also reminded whites and blacks that African Americans were living out a certain religious destiny in the wake of emancipation: the pursuit of land. White Southerners needed to remove obstacles in the way of black economic prosperity, black leaders argued, in order to prevent their labor force from seeking out a distant Promised Land.

Mass Exodus: The 1889–1890 Migration

One decade later, black leaders were less successful in preventing an exodus. In Kinston, on November 15, 1889, crowds gathered around the train depot to bid farewell to 1,500 "negroes anxious to shake the North Carolina dust off their shoes and try their fortunes in some other State." The exodusters were heading west for Arkansas and nearby states. They piled the railway platform ten feet high with their luggage: "old meat boxes, various other boxes, barrels, trunks of all shapes and sizes."[60] The migrants from Kinston were not alone; tens of thousands of black farmworkers left the state in less than two years' time. In a *Christian Recorder* article, one AME minister tried to explain the frustrations of black sharecroppers in the state: "They have been striving for [over] twenty years to get ahead and to secure homes of their own, and the result is highly unsatisfactory." It was not surprising, he argued, that they were tempted to move elsewhere. "The marvel is that they have been content to pursue so long an experiment that has been without real encouragement."[61] They had waited for their own land long enough. Another AME minister, Rev. M. B. Sheppard of Burlington, North Carolina,

reported that "many of our people are suffering . . . an 'emigration Grippe.'"
Sheppard used the metaphor of disease in part to show that emigration was
"injurious" and in part to describe his own passiveness in the movement. This
new migration was happening to his people; he had no hand in it.[62]

Other preachers, particularly rural ministers less connected to their denominational institutions, did have their hands in the migration of 1889–90.
"When the exodus first began [in January 1889]," a *New York Herald* journalist
reported, "it was given a religious color." The religious movement started in
Wayne and Wilson counties, where congregations began planning an exodus to Kansas, Texas, or Arkansas. "It was preached from the pulpit," the
reporter wrote. Rural preachers declared that "God's hand was in it, and that
He was leading His people as the children of Israel were led aforetime."[63]
We do not know much about these pro-emigration ministers; they were not
well connected or well known. But they certainly held some sway. The
movement grew rapidly.

Beginning in February 1889, the movement ballooned into a mass exodus. "Since our last issue several hundred more negroes have left Wayne and
the surrounding counties," the *Raleigh Signal* reported on February 28.
"There are three hundred now in Goldsboro awaiting transportation . . .
about three hundred have left Wake county, and several hundred more are
preparing to leave in a few days." By the fall, the exodus reached unprecedented proportions. "The fever rise[s] higher and higher," a white man
from Jones County reported in November 1889. "My impression is, two-thirds
of Jones County will leave this winter."[64] Similar reports made headlines
across the eastern part of the state: "200 more negroes scheduled to leave
Wilson Friday for Arkansas";[65] "1,500 enthusiastic exodusters in town";[66]
"8,000 exodusters passed through Raleigh."[67] Such a large emigration frightened white North Carolinians. "In some sections of Pitt [county], the reporter is informed, every colored person has left," a contributor to the
Tarboro Southerner wrote with astonishment. "Some people may not believe
it, but land without labor to cultivate it is of little value."[68] By January 1890,
journalists tried to compile actual emigration numbers. One reported that
"35,000 have left [North Carolina] since January 1st, 1889," and another
concurred that "some estimate the total exodus at 25–35,000 negroes."[69]
Another estimate topped out at 50,000.[70] These estimates were not too high.

Between 1870 and 1910, some 700,000 African Americans, mostly from
Georgia and the Carolinas, migrated to Louisiana, Mississippi, Arkansas,
Texas, or Oklahoma. One historian called it "the Other Great Migration,"

citing demographers' estimates that one in ten African Americans migrated from one part of the South to another during the period, compared to one in eight who would move North decades later in the Great Migration.[71] The movement out of North Carolina in 1889–90 was but one part of an even larger mass migration.

What prompted so many to leave the state in such a short amount of time? The answer, once again, lay with land policy. Sharecroppers continued to complain of abuse from landlords, who exploited them using the Landlord and Tenant Act. Crop yields in 1888 were particularly bad. Black farmers, many already trapped in a cycle of debt and peonage, hit rock bottom with a series of bad harvests. What finally spurred some migrants were the stock laws (or fence laws) that took effect in a number of counties throughout the 1880s. These laws required farmers to fence in their livestock and not their crops, a reversal of longstanding agricultural practices. Small farmers, accustomed to letting their animals roam in common areas—the "root, hog, or die" method—now had to shoulder the expense of feeding enclosed livestock. Subsistence farmers soon had to grow more cash crops to afford the purchase of meat and other foodstuffs. Poorer white farmers, unable to make ends meet, moved off the land and worked instead for the state's growing industries. Their black counterparts, excluded from North Carolina's mills and factories, looked out of state to improve their lot.[72]

One black legislator blamed both black poverty and emigration on the stock laws. When he asked a crowd of black farmers at the Tarboro courthouse "Whose fault is it that people have to leave?" he answered his own question: "I claim that the white folks are the cause of it, when I look around and see the fences taken away and don't allow us to raise a pig." The listening farmers urged him on, shouting, "talk on." The legislator continued, "Ever since the fences have been taken away, we've been making short crops." Because of this, he had been fighting to repeal the stock law in the state legislature. In the meantime, he could sympathize with the black farmers who, faced with short crop yields, oppressive landlords, and no livestock, felt they had to leave the state.[73]

A few observers of the 1889–90 migration believed that black migrants' move made good economic sense. William Mitchell, a black businessman in Raleigh, told a reporter why black farmers left the state: because they were broke and could not break even as sharecroppers in eastern North Carolina. Norfleet Jeffries, whom a reporter described as "an old and well-informed Negro," sympathized with the exodusters, because wages were higher in the

Deep South and Southwest than they were in North Carolina.[74] When black Baptist missionary Rev. F. R. Howell traveled across the state in 1889, he found "poverty-stricken congregations" and observed how "the acts of the last Legislature . . . made it impossible for a farmer to live in some portions of the State." To those acquainted with the economic circumstances of black sharecroppers, the mass migration came as no surprise.[75] Arkansas, Louisiana, and Texas offered lower land prices and higher wages. As railroad companies completed new tracks in the western parts of the South, they sold off unused portions of land grants. Many African Americans were able to purchase land cheaply along the new railway lines.[76]

In April 1889, a group of pro-emigration leaders met in Raleigh to form the State Colored Emigration Association. The association included only a few leading black North Carolinians; most stayed away from the meeting. As a report at the meeting noted, "there was but one sentiment expressed and that was in favor of organizing and going to the southwest." Members of the association justified their position by listing grievances against North Carolina, almost all of which involved land policies: low wages offered by landholders, "the stock law which interfered with the right of common," and restrictions which prevented African Americans from hunting on whites' land. The situation in North Carolina, the association decided, "was more precarious now than ever before." The president of the Association, George W. Price, admitted he "did not know how much better they could do" in the Southwest, but concluded that "it could not be worse than here unless they went to hell." As Price's statement demonstrated, black workers left primarily because of their dissatisfaction in North Carolina and not necessarily because they found their destinations enticing.[77]

Observers, like the emigrants themselves, referenced the biblical Exodus story at every turn. The North Carolina Baptist Educational and Missionary Convention (NCBEMC) described the sudden loss of many of their members as "the great emigration fever . . . like the exodus of Egypt."[78] Whites, too, described the movement with biblical references. The *Raleigh News and Observer* criticized the movement: "We have shown them on the best authorities that these lands are not flowing with milk and honey."[79] Another white Democratic newspaper reported, in a mocking tone, that "Several colored families made a start for their promised land today."[80] Even as they critiqued the movement, white newspapers drew upon the same biblical language the exodusters themselves appropriated.

"Get a Home in Arkansas," 1904. This photograph comes from a brochure a decade or more after North Carolina's 1889–90 migration. As in earlier pamphlets, rail companies appealed to the desire for land ownership among would-be black migrants in the Carolinas and Georgia. Special Collections, University of Arkansas Libraries, Fayetteville.

Poverty and unfavorable land policies prompted the mass migration, but often labor agents made it happen. Southwestern and Gulf Coast cotton planters hired men to recruit labor from the Atlantic South, and these agents organized and orchestrated the movement. Railroad companies, too, sent agents to recruit black buyers for the excess land they acquired through generous land grants. Some migrants arranged for their travel independent of land and labor agents, but most did not. As one reporter observed, "The religious side of the movement was aided by agents, into whose hand it played."[81] By the fall of 1889, wherever would-be migrants gathered, labor agents followed, attracting the disdain of many black and white observers. Some whites blamed the entire movement on unscrupulous men like "Peg-Leg" Williams and W. P. Mabson.[82] "Doubtless many of the colored people who have been duped by Mabson and others and persuaded to emigrate West will regret it before they have been away long," the *Tarboro Southerner* editor opined. The editor accused Mabson (an African American) of hypocrisy:

"he does not seem to be anxious to leave himself, but remains here and reaps remuneration for persuading them to leave."[83] Men like Mabson were busy throughout the fall and the winter of 1889–90, organizing parties of migrants and arranging and funding their transportation.

The role of agents further intensified black debates over emigration. A number of black North Carolinians, like Mabson, worked as labor agents or on their behalf. Some of the pro-emigration leaders recognized that agents, by providing transportation, made possible the exodus on a scale previously unimaginable. Antiemigration leaders, still at the helm of black institutions, vilified the agents as modern-day slave traders. To take advantage of the fare-free travel that agents offered, some emigrants had to sign labor contracts, indenturing themselves to a particular plantation. Rev. I. F. Aldridge, pastor of the AME Church in Smithfield, compared the agents to cattle traders: "They talk about free transportation. Nonsense! It must all be paid for by work, hard labor in Arkansas. Those who go are locked up in the cars like cattle and carried by freight trains." Aldridge sympathized with the migrants' motivations, but he could hardly hide his disgust for the process: "It is a speculation in human beings, carried on by the cattle planters, railroads and agents of Arkansas."[84] Questions of freedom, land ownership, and the race's future turned into heated debates.

At one particular meeting, the disputes became physical. African Americans around Tarboro, North Carolina, called for a mass meeting at the courthouse in December 1889 to discuss the "emigration fever" sweeping through their part of the state, much as they had done ten years before. The local Republican Party chairman, George Lloyd, opened the meeting with nervousness and trepidation. He feared not only the hostility local whites might feel about the meeting but also the tensions within the black community that had resulted in the spread of slanderous rumors about him.[85]

Lloyd placed emigration in the context of emancipation and providentialism: "Many of you under the sound of my voice, whose heads are getting gray, prayed twenty-five years ago that the burden would be taken from you." Emigration, Lloyd explained, marked the opening of another act in the drama that began with emancipation. Like emancipation, this moment called for divine action and guidance: "Get all the preachers to pray for us all, we'll get all we want." Lloyd told the audience that he favored emigration, but only on black people's own terms. He opposed the work of labor agents. "We don't want to be taken off and sold like we were in slavery time," Lloyd told them, and the audience replied, "That's right." Lloyd advocated selecting a homegrown leader to organize the emigration, not someone paid to represent planters' interests. He and the audience seemed to be of one mind: "If you are going to have a leader, have one (cries, that's right,) you have agents to come here and pick you out like mules; we don't want to go that way (that's right)." Lloyd worried about black North Carolinians headed to the Deep South. He argued they were jumping from the pot to the frying pan. "The Mississippi bottoms are next to hell itself," he told the audience. The audience seemed to agree. When he asked, "Where should we go?" the crowd yelled back: "Kansas." Like most black leaders, Lloyd placed contemporary setbacks in the context of emancipation and argued that critical contemporary situations were momentous turning points in the race's God-ordained history. Unlike most leaders, however, Lloyd entertained emigration as a way for black Southerners to assert their autonomy.[86]

Not everyone shared Lloyd's outlook. The opponents he mentioned at the beginning of his speech stormed the stage. These men seemed to support the work of labor agents, and Lloyd's attack angered them. One of the men, Nathan Boyd, attempted to strong-arm Lloyd away from the podium. When Boyd tried to introduce a new speaker, presumably a labor agent, the struggle became violent. The audience laughed as the leaders brawled on stage, but the violence revealed the intensity of the debates over emigration.[87]

Black leaders rarely resorted to fist fighting, as they did at the Tarboro courthouse, but they took the 1889–90 migration very seriously. When black Baptists gathered at their state convention (NCBEMC) that year at Roanoke-Salem Baptist Church, they broached the topic with sobriety and gravity. Baptists predominated in poor, rural areas of the state. Poverty and emigration hit those churches hard. F. R. Howell explained, "And brethren, as every pastor knows, the spiritual condition of a church is soon impeded by its financial depression." They had not foreseen the downturn in the agricultural market or the migration of 1889.[88]

The Baptist ministers denounced Governor Daniel Fowle for his support of black emigration, because, they said, "we feel that we should share the privileges and benefits of this our native land." Their resolution reasserted black claims to the land. Later at the convention, delegate Henry P. Cheatham also opposed emigration by staking claim to North Carolina land. Cheatham, the U.S. congressman from North Carolina's Second Congressional District, was easily the most prominent man at the convention. He addressed his fellow Baptists, saying "The emigration of our people to the far South is a serious mistake, and ought to be discouraged." North Carolina boasted more and better black institutions. "Look at our schools and colleges. Look at our educated ministers and learned men," he continued. Cheatham himself, as the only African American in the U.S. Congress, served as proof of greater political opportunities in North Carolina. In Cheatham's opinion, staying in North Carolina made good sense, and it also allowed African Americans to continue fighting for specific rights. North Carolina, he said, "is our birthplace; our home; our native land, and we have a right to the undisturbed enjoyment of its rich blessings."[89]

Cheatham's message went beyond the four walls of Roanoke-Salem Baptist Church. The next day, the NCBEMC produced an antiemigration pamphlet and printed 10,000 copies. None of those pamphlets survive in full, but we can come close to replicating the message from the minutes of the committee meeting. The pamphlet laid out the relative advantages of black life in North Carolina and warned would-be migrants of the racial climate they would face in Texas, Mississippi, Louisiana, Arkansas, etc. The pamphlet asserted black farmers' right to land in North Carolina, or, at the very least, to a just share of the state's prosperity.[90]

Perhaps most important, the convention's pamphlet placed the troubles of 1889 in a broader theological context. As gathered from the convention proceedings, the tone of the pamphlet was decidedly optimistic: "we can see the hand of God at work for us." Black Baptists in North Carolina could mark significant progress since the days of emancipation, the committee argued. "We started out with nothing; we had no education as a race, nor any experience as a people; we had never felt any responsibility, nor never knew anything about leadership. But to-day we represent 120,000 communicants." By tracking progress since emancipation, Baptist ministers reassured their people that God was on their side, and that their future in North Carolina remained hopeful. Cheatham hoped in a better day coming—"I never felt happier over the condition than now"—and wanted other Baptists to feel the same way.[91]

A number of Methodist clergy agreed with Cheatham's assessment. The AME Zion pastor in Asheville, North Carolina, wrote a letter to his denominational newspaper to discourage any emigration. He denounced the "Negro Exodus" as "misleading, false and destructive to the race." He, too, worried most about the labor and land agents' motives. The pastor had harsh words for the agents who enticed his congregants to leave their homes without a penny in their pockets: "Their blood will be required at your hands."[92] The ministers present at the New Berne District Conference of the AME Zion

Church in January 1890 complained that unscrupulous men were organizing some of their parishioners into fraudulent emigration societies. These "bogus organizers" either planned exoduses contrary to the migrants' best interests or never planned trips, pocketing the societies' monetary collections "for their own personal benefit." So, the district conference "resolved that the ministers and influential brethren of the New Berne District use every effort to repel the present unwise, unprofitable, and speculative emigration fever."[93] Methodist clergy, no less than Baptists, wanted the exodus to stop.

John C. Dancy, the influential editor of the *Star of Zion*, however, found some good news in the exodus. Like most black institutional leaders, Dancy advised against the exodus of 1889–90.[94] But unlike his colleagues, Dancy appreciated the message that the exodus sent to whites: it broadcasted black autonomy and pride. The trainloads of emigrants leaving the state demonstrated that black workers were unwilling to tolerate "the deep humiliation and oppression to which they have been subjected by their masters." When landowners or the state militia stood in the way of black migration, Dancy became incensed. Mobility, Dancy believed, was a fundamental right of citizenship.[95]

Dancy hoped that the large-scale migration would force the state legislature to reconsider their repressive policies toward black residents. As the numbers of exodusters swelled, Dancy celebrated. He valued the movement for the way it taught white planters and legislators a lesson. In August 1889, he wrote in the *Star of Zion*: "The farmers whose legislature is driving them away need to thank themselves for the going. They may learn something from experience yet."[96] Dancy warned his readers against taking "a leap in the dark" by moving to "murderous Mississippi" or "wicked" Louisiana. Yet he could hardly contain his enthusiasm when he recounted how racist landlords were shooting themselves in the foot.[97]

In January 1890, after tens of thousands had left the state, Dancy made specific demands of lawmakers. In a lengthy editorial, he reminded them of his earlier statements: "We predicted that with the passage of such laws the State would soon become depopulated of some of its best colored citizens, and that quite fifty thousand would leave the state." His estimates were not far off. "The results," Dancy boasted, "have more than justified our prophecy . . . ten thousand leaving last week alone." He argued that the exodus mostly affected the class of planters who "sought hardest to humiliate and crush the remaining sparks of manhood out of the Negro." By disfranchising and cheating black laborers, wealthy whites found themselves without a workforce. Dancy reminded his imaginary audience of planters—they were not among his subscribers—that their land was "almost worthless without Negro labor." The only way out of the ensuing bankruptcy landowners would soon encounter was substantial legal reform. Darcy called for a number of specific changes. "Let the Landlord and Tenant Act be so changed as to encourage and protect the tenant as well as the landlord, and guarantee to the tenant some rights which the landlord is bound to respect," he demanded. Better yet, he offered, "Sell the Negro some land at a fair, reasonable price," so that African Americans will be invested in the state's prosperity. "Make him feel and realize his complete manhood, his full citizenship," Dancy pleaded. Without such reforms, he argued, nothing would stop the hemorrhaging of black labor from the state.[98]

Dancy stood out among black institutional leaders because he never unequivocally opposed the exodus. The 1889–90 migration played well into the political argument he was trying to make. But just like other black leaders, Dancy regularly associated emigration with land reform. His vision for the future involved the remaking of North Carolina's land and economy. If several thousand black workers had to leave for these changes to take place, Dancy was not going to stand in their way.

Dancy's rhetoric may have contributed to the notion that black leaders in North Carolina did little to stop the exodus to the Deep South. J. W. Rankin, an AME pastor in Louisiana, wrote a frantic word of warning to his colleagues in the North Carolina Conference: "Stay Away from Louisiana!" The Bayou State had little to recommend it to black North Carolinians, Rev. Rankin explained, and he was alarmed that so many were heading his way. Late in 1889, Rankin wrote other preachers, begging them to "instruct them from your pulpits not to come to Louisiana for their own good." He warned of brutal overseers, lynch mobs, and malnutrition. "Please sound the alarm as watchman on the walls." The warning implicated North Carolina clergy for falling asleep on the watch. As for those ministers who were in league with labor agents, Rankin expressed his pity and shame.[99]

The mass migration posed a serious challenge to prominent black Protestant leaders and betrayed the limits of their power. Despite their continued appeals against it, the migration went unabated. One scathing editorial in the *Christian Recorder* chalked the exodus up to North Carolina ministers' lack of manhood. Rev. J. H. Iford, AME pastor in Shreveport, Louisiana, described the exodus from North Carolina to Louisiana with despair. "For the last six or seven months our people have been under the control, advice and influence of what I pronounce Negro traders, huddled up like cattle and brought from North Carolina to North Louisiana, the hades of the South, where they have no more liberty than any other swamp hog." The situation, he argued, could hardly be bleaker. Iford expressed his disbelief that black leaders in North Carolina could have allowed the exodus to occur.[100]

Iford gave a gendered dimension to his critique. Black women, in particular, he reported, suffered from abuse in Louisiana: "They are whipped, the women are driven to work right along with the men . . . . These poor women are getting up at the ringing of the bell at 4 o'clock in the morning, getting ready for the new ground, to contend with the briers and thorns all day; half clothed, bare headed, bare handed, bare footed." By highlighting the women's suffering, Iford accused black leaders in North Carolina of failing to protect black womanhood. It was a serious charge. The critique assumed that black leaders, "the preachers and the teachers," had more control over black populations than they actually did. Black Protestant leaders worked hard to demonstrate their manhood by exhibiting the qualities of good citizens—respectability, sobriety, intelligence, and honesty—and by performing masculine duties such as providing for and protecting women and children. Iford's harangue, therefore, struck below the belt.[101]

The Louisiana pastor told his colleagues what to do: "Let the leaders of North Carolina rise up in the power of Israel's God and say out in the voice of manhood: 'We will protect and defend the virtues and sanctity of our women and put down this exodus and Negro trading which are doing more to damn the Negro than all other evils.' "[102] The solution was not that easy. Black Protestant leaders in North Carolina, with a few exceptions, had opposed the exodus from the beginning. They had used conventions, pamphlets, sermons, editorials, and in one case, their knuckles, to stop the labor agents. It was not until white landowners pushed through the legislature a prohibitive tax on labor agents that the exodus came to a halt.[103]

Beulah and Economic Opportunity

The migration of 1889–90 and emigration in general presented a crisis for black Protestant leadership in North Carolina. The railway cars full of black North Carolinians heading out of state carried the message that not everyone shared black Protestant leaders' visions for the future. In the 1879 exodus, pro-emigration leader Sam Perry exploited the class differences between the working populations of eastern North Carolina and the prominent ministers and politicians. But the charge that black Protestant leaders did not have sharecroppers' best interests at heart rang hollow; they had lobbied for land reform and had correctly assessed the migrants' destinations as unfavorable. Moreover, the majority of black North Carolinians stayed put. So, perhaps, "crisis" is too strong of a word. But leaders were alarmed nonetheless.

Emigration did, however, offer black Protestant leaders an opportunity to rearticulate their religious visions for the future. They seized that opportunity. In 1892, Baptist pastor C. C. Somerville preached that antiemigration people like himself were also on a journey, a "journey to Beulah." In Isaiah's prophecy, Jehovah renamed the Promised Land, christening it Beulah, meaning "the married one." It was a commitment by God to claim Israel as his bride and to heal or remake the land after it had been ransacked by enemies. When God renamed the land Beulah, he posted watchmen on the city walls to protect her from invaders.[104] Rankin, the Louisiana pastor who warned North Carolinians to stay away, alluded to this prophecy when he commanded his colleagues to be "watchmen on the walls." As the watchmen, or as those journeying to Beulah, black Protestant leaders offered a biblical interpretation to counter that of migrants.[105]

In this counter-interpretation, black Southerners had been metaphorically en route to the Promised Land since emancipation. To leave now in search of another Promised Land, to ministers like Rankin and Somerville, would be to reenact the Israelites' grumbling in the wilderness when the lack of food made them want to give up on the Promised Land and return to Egypt. Black migrants' desire to change course, in this counterinterpretation, demonstrated not a prophetic vision but a loss of hope. That was the message of one opponent to emigration in South Carolina. He told would-be migrants to Arkansas, "instead of fleeing to Little Rock, Arkansas, fly to the large Rock, Lord Jesus Christ." He argued that abandoning the struggle in South Carolina would betray a failure to trust God, like those who were afraid to conquer Canaan once they had already arrived in the Promised Land. Instead, black South Carolinians should stay put, trusting that they would conquer the land as Joshua did, "by his strong and faithful prayers, upon Gibson he stopped the sun, and in the valley of Ajelon the moon stayed." In Somerville's sermon, he, too, claimed the Exodus story: "If God delight in us, then will He bring us into this land and give it to us; a land which floweth with milk and honey." But he also claimed to already be en route to the land, right there in Fayetteville, North Carolina. By invoking Isaiah's prophecy of

Beulah in conjunction with the Exodus narrative, Somerville made the Exodus look more like Jubilee. He spoke of remaking the land and of God's commitment to a special people—a claim to land ownership, albeit less dramatic than that of the Christmas Scare of 1865.[106]

Antiemigration ministers expected God to change their people's status and condition in the South, to remake the South into a land for his special people. Bishop C. R. Harris, when he traveled to the Agricultural and Industrial Fair in Alexandria, Virginia, said, "We dismiss as contrary to the teachings of Providence, the idea that the Negro is to remain in a state of serfdom which seems to be the condition in which many of the Southern whites desire to keep our people." He then sang a couple lines from the often-quoted English hymn that expressed his eschatological confidence:

For Right is Right
Since God is God,
And Right the day must win.
To doubt would be disloyalty,
To falter would be sin.

Harris then gave a concrete example of what it meant to doubt and falter: emigration and colonization. "Deportation schemes," he argued, had symbolic power. They represented Plan B for African Americans, should the fight for full civil and political rights be abandoned. Whites, he reasoned, knew the symbolic power of the idea, which explained why "certain southern political leaders" hailed the merits of colonization or emigration even though they tried to prevent actual migrations. He clearly remembered the exodus from his own state a few years back: "If the South is so anxious to get rid of the Negro, why hinder agents from carrying them away, free of expense to the state or the nation?" The answer: talk of emigration distracted black Southerners from the journey they were already on, the journey to full citizenship and economic justice.[107]

In the 1890s, Harris surely found it difficult to assure fellow black Southerners that they were indeed on the road to full citizenship. But their fate, he argued, compared favorably to that of American Indians. "Where would the Negro be to-day had he not clung to the God of the oppressed? Let the fate of the American Indian answer." Harris did not argue that God had caused American Indians' suffering but rather that the Christian God, if followed, could have defended them against whites: "Unable to cope with his cruel, crafty, and powerful foe, he [the Indian] yet refused to bow to that

God who would vindicate his cause. To-day that people is a mere fragment, driven from their homes, though guaranteed them by the most solemn treaty obligation! If he be not completely blotted off the face of the earth, it will be because a purer Christianity shall effectually intercede for him and win him her protecting embrace!" Harris's comparison of Indians and African Americans illustrated two of his key tenets: first, that black progress since emancipation was attributable to God's protection of the race; second, that American Indians represented exactly what black Protestant leaders feared about emigration and colonization. Moving away in response to white supremacy would result in less land and fewer rights.[108]

The debate among African Americans over emigration, land, and religious destiny caught national attention. Booker T. Washington, in his famous Atlanta Compromise speech at the Cotton States and International Exposition in 1895, joined the debate. Scholars often situate his speech among various black responses to the onset of Jim Crow segregation; but Washington was just as concerned about emigration and land ownership. The line he repeated, "Cast down your bucket where you are," placed Washington firmly against "those of my race who depend on bettering their condition in a foreign land." As he urged white Southerners to employ African Americans in the region's young industry, he told black Southerners to focus their efforts on buying businesses and real estate in the South. Nowhere did Washington argue for radical property redistribution as many had decades earlier, but he firmly believed in black land ownership in the South. A few months later in a smaller venue at the same Cotton States Exposition, Henry McNeal Turner drew upon themes of Exodus and gave the opposite message: "There is no manhood future in the United States for the Negro." In his argument for migration to Africa, Turner explained that African Americans' sojourn as slaves in America was part of God's larger plan to create a new black Christian nation in Africa. Washington and Turner were both interested in the future of the race; both spoke of God's plan and the race's fate; both referred to the moment or purpose of emancipation; both outlined black Southerners' situation as a choice between financial prospects at home and migration abroad. Neither speaker in Atlanta stopped to hold a conversation about African American eschatology; neither explained the tension between land ownership and migration, or between Jubilee and Exodus. They did not have to; similar conversations had already set the terms of debate. Washington and Turner had but to pick a side.[109]

As evident in Washington's speech, land remained central to black Protestant leaders' objections to colonization and emigration. Most still waited, albeit in less dramatic ways than those who anticipated the Christmas Scare of 1865, for God to give them the land they worked. Joseph C. Price, an AME Zion minister and the president of Livingstone College in Salisbury, North Carolina, told an audience in Chester, South Carolina, "This sunny Southland, where lie the bleaching bones of my fathers, is dear to me, and I, too, feel to the manor born. This soil is consecrated by the labor, the tears and the prayers of my ancestors." Price not only claimed the land as his by birth but also expected God to give him the proceeds of the land. "I believe that God intends the negro race to work here in the South the highest stature he has ever attained," he preached. The South "will one day produce the richest harvest of prosperity the world ever saw, and I want to help reap it and enjoy it," Price told a cheering audience.[110]

Surely Price's prediction of black prosperity to be reaped from the land of the South seemed discordant with the realities of life as a sharecropper. Price spoke in January 1890, as the large-scale migration from the Carolinas to the West and Deep South continued. We can imagine someone in Price's audience responding with incredulity, "We have never seen the rich harvest that the South offers." To the would-be migrants in his audience, Price not only catalogued the practical reasons why black farmers were worse off in the American West and in West Africa, but also asked them to view the world with an impractical hope, seeing the divine forces operating around them. "He who would try to crush us deserves the pity—not the crushed!" Price concluded. "Though a hundred men fall around me, I will stand on the rock of my faith with an unshaken hope."[111] He bid his audience to resist the desire to leave, and to maintain the fight for land and economic prosperity. Black Protestant leaders argued, even when the evidence suggested otherwise, that in God's plan for the race, land would come just as surely as did freedom.

CHAPTER FOUR

A Jeremiad

Even before J. C. Price told South Carolinians that they had yet to see God's harvest in the South, he sounded a similar note in a speech for the National Temperance Society. As he assured the crowd, "I am sanguine. I believe there is a future, and a great future, ahead of the colored men." That great future, Price explained, had to do with the gifts, abilities, and intelligence that African Americans could use to further their progress. But the future Price described was one greater than that of black Americans' own making: it was a divine mission.[1] Two years later, in another temperance speech, Price sounded less sanguine. He told the African American audience that though "God set the Negro free," their immoral appetites still threatened to enslave them.[2] Taken together, the two different speeches, one of happy predictions and the other of doomsday warnings, represented well Price's temperance message. According to him, African Americans held an important place within God's plan for human history, and, to that end, God had decreed the progress of the race. Precisely because they had a "great mission to perform," African Americans needed to hold themselves to a high moral standard and guard against whatever stood in the way of racial progress.

Between Reconstruction and the Jim Crow Era, African Americans again had cause to reconsider their eschatological destiny. Were better days really coming, as Price argued? Not only had land ownership proved elusive for many, but racial violence and political persecution did not give way to an era of racial harmony and black progress. In these trying times, black Southerners often looked to the biblical prophets, who had harsh words for the Israelites. Their prophecies, much like Price's temperance message, worked to confirm Israel's favored relationship with God while warning of coming judgment if the people did not repent of immoral conduct. Late nineteenth-century black ministers concluded, almost unanimously, that intemperance was a serious obstacle for black communities. For them, the manufacture, sale, and consumption of alcohol threatened to arrest the God-ordained progress of the race. Black Protestants across the state enlisted in what they saw as a fight between good and evil, a fight upon which depended, as one minister said, "the hope of our race."[3] So, it was with particular zeal that

Rev. Joseph C. Price, 1895. One colleague called Price the "greatest orator" he had ever heard. Price was a tireless advocate for temperance and prohibition in North Carolina and across the nation. Image: J. W. Hood, *One Hundred Years of the African Methodist Episcopal Zion Church* (New York: A.M.E. Zion Book Concern, 1895). North Carolina Collection, Wilson Special Collections Library, UNC–Chapel Hill.

black temperance activists—ministers and their many male and female lay allies—campaigned for individual abstinence from alcohol and statewide prohibition, from Reconstruction well into the twentieth century.

Historians have paid little attention to black temperance activism, but when they have, they have placed it within the context of the black pursuit of respectability. By living a temperate lifestyle, black reformers believed they could rise above negative racial stereotypes and gain the respect of their white neighbors. A number of scholars have explained the importance, complexities, and problems of this bid for respectability. In contrast, this chapter shifts focus away from the white gaze and places black temperance activism within the religious narratives that African Americans told about themselves and for themselves. To be sure, African American reformers coveted the respect of leading whites, and temperance served those ends. But focusing on their bid for respectability mistakes a small part of the temperance movement for the whole.

Black temperance activists were motivated more by a desire to assume the special role God had assigned African Americans than by their desire to secure the respect of whites. When advocating temperance, they spoke principally of the moral and material development of the race, usually as an issue internal to black communities. Their message functioned as a jeremiad, a sermon in the style of the prophet Jeremiah, intended to warn, chastise, and rebuke a people even as it affirms them as God's chosen people. Price and other moral reformers warned African American communities of impending judgment—that intemperance could derail the race from its God-ordained progress. At the same time, by calling attention to the threat that alcohol made on race advancement, they reaffirmed beliefs that African Americans played a special role within God's design for human history.

To argue that black temperance was a jeremiad is to subordinate, not supplant, arguments about black respectability. Temperance activism was at the heart of late nineteenth-century bids for respectability and racial uplift. Black women's temperance activism played a large role in what historian Evelyn Brooks Higginbotham called "the politics of respectability." Higginbotham noted that black Baptist women's reform efforts showed both their "assimilationist leanings" and their opposition to racism. Black female reformers, Higginbotham continued, "reflected and reinforced the hegemonic values of white America," even as they "simultaneously subverted and transformed the logic of race and gender subordination." Even though Higginbotham acknowledged that black Baptist women pursued reform movements for their own ends, in her analysis, black reformers primarily operated for a white audience: to demonstrate black superiority in "manners and morals" and to "refute the logic behind their social subordination."[4]

Historian Kevin Gaines offered a decidedly less sympathetic reading of black reform movements, though he, too, placed black temperance activism in the context of respectability. Gaines argued that black ministers and other "bourgeois agents of civilization" called for temperance as a means to establish their moral authority and distinguish themselves from lower-class blacks. As they distanced themselves from poor blacks, black ministers and reformers sought respectability in the eyes of leading whites. To Gaines, these reformers suffered from "unconscious internalized racism"; that is, they blamed the black community for falling short of white middle class moral standards instead of pointing to the white oppression that prevented the black community from attaining those standards. Moreover, he argued, they sacrificed their common cause with lower-class blacks on the altar of white approval.[5] Higginbotham had a greater appreciation for the difficulties that black leaders faced. She could see the sincere, if sometimes non–self-critical, motives behind temperance activism, where Gaines could see only classist betrayal. But both scholars wrote as if black temperance activism existed principally for onlooking whites.

In contrast, we need to place black temperance within its eschatological context. My goal is to ask not what message black temperance activists wanted to broadcast to whites, but rather, what their message said about African Americans' role in divine plans for human history. When Price spoke before the National Temperance Society in 1887, it was more than two decades after the high point of emancipation but still before Southern states pursued widespread segregation and black disfranchisement. In the uncertainty that lay between Reconstruction and Jim Crow, Price returned to God's purpose in human history. What mattered most to Price and other activists was the race's place in the sacred historical design.

Initial Impulse

Black Protestants had a long history with the politics of moral reform. Early on, independent black churches embraced the temperance cause both because it resonated with their own theological beliefs and because it placed them in a movement peopled with their allies. Northern black churches adopted the cause nearly forty years before Southern emancipation. Beginning in the 1830s, AME and AME Zion conventions annually declared themselves opposed to the use of intoxicating liquors. In the antebellum North, temperance activism seemed wedded to abolitionism as part of a comprehensive national reform agenda. Leading black abolitionists also stumped for the temperance cause. As Frederick Douglass told an audience in 1846, "I am a temperance man because I am an anti-slavery man." The rhetoric of the two movements—temperance and abolition—bled into each other. Abolitionists accused slaveholders of being "drunk" with power. Temperance activists lobbied for a nation "freed from the chains" of intemperate drinking.[6] The early connection between these two reform movements helps explain why the white South, despite its evangelical population, was less fertile ground for nineteenth-century prohibition campaigns.

Black Protestants quickly gravitated toward the temperance movement, perhaps because it was part of a larger radical reform agenda. The temperance movement did not carry connotations of religious conservativism, as twentieth-century Americans would later attribute to it. Rather, temperance was allied with radical movements like abolitionism and feminism. Antebellum temperance activists, white and black, also joined any number of other Northern evangelical reform societies, the same societies that were so quick to send missionaries to the freedpeople in the South.[7]

When Northern white missionaries, like those from the American Missionary Association (AMA) and the American Baptist Home Missionary

Society (ABHMS), arrived to work among Southern black communities, they laid the temperance message on thick. Primers designed to teach freed-people how to read and write also taught abstinence from alcohol. The *Freedman's Spelling-Book* had students learn three-letter words by copying or reading aloud the following sentences:

> It is a sin to sip rum.
> A sot is a bad man.
> God is ho-ly; he can see if men sin.
> If a man sin, he is bad.
> A sot has rum or gin in his jug.[8]

Obviously, spelling was not the only lesson to be learned. As the students advanced, they moved on to four-letter and five-letter lessons about alcohol. In Atlanta, the Northern missionaries flooded black communities with temperance tracts from the American Tract Society. They organized African American youth into temperance clubs and encouraged them all to sign abstinence pledges. Similarly, African American missionaries from the AME and AME Zion denominations incorporated temperance activism into their postemancipation educational and church-building efforts. These tactics did not end in the immediate postwar period. Throughout the late nineteenth century, Northern missionary organizations sent free and unsolicited temperance newspaper subscriptions to black ministers and schoolteachers. The largest missionary organizations, the AMA and the ABHMS, maintained their focus upon freedpeople, American Indians, and immigrants, and central to their message was temperance.[9]

Black churchgoers' theology predisposed them to welcome the message of temperance. In the mid- to late nineteenth century, most attended Methodist and Baptist churches. Methodists espoused John Wesley's doctrine of perfectionism, a belief that Christians could attain a state of sinless perfection after experiencing a second moment of grace that followed sometime after their conversion. The grace of God, many Methodists argued, enabled believers to purge sin from their lives. Theologians and lay people developed different interpretations of this doctrine, but, however interpreted, Wesleyan perfectionism supported the belief that a life or a society without alcohol was possible and desirable. In antebellum North Carolina, one of the most important popularizers of this doctrine was Henry Evans, a free black Methodist minister in Fayetteville. Evans led a large, influential, and biracial congregation, and was considered by his bishop to be "the father of the Methodist Church, white and black," in the area. So, African American Methodists could claim perfectionism and temperance as authentically theirs by virtue of their race and denomination.[10]

African American Baptists, too, thought of temperance as consistent with their theology. Most black Baptists, like their Methodist counterparts, were heirs to the legacy of the Second Great Awakening and favored a free-will theology over the Calvinism of older Baptists. The added emphasis on free will brought more attention to law keeping; therefore, free-will Baptists spoke a great deal about the individual's responsibility to obey the dictates of God. At an early black Baptist State Convention in North Carolina, ministers stated for the record their belief "that temperance is a part of the Christian religion."[11] Temperance, then, for black Methodists and Baptists was of a piece with their religious life.

Black Protestants in North Carolina also organized nondenominational temperance societies soon after emancipation. When the Independent Order of Good Templars, one of the largest international temperance organizations, first arrived in the state in 1872, African Americans immediately petitioned for membership. The society admitted white and black members, but in the South, the Templars organized separate white and black lodges. White Templars in North Carolina balked at even restricted interracialism and withheld the necessary password from black Templars. Undaunted, black temperance advocates lodged a complaint with the national headquarters, the Right Worthy Grand Lodge, and soon black Good Templars lodges were established across the state.[12]

The Good Templars lodges quickly became interwoven with black religious life in the state. The lodges sometimes met concurrently with Sabbath schools or church meetings. The lodge meetings at times resembled revivals. An AME Zion bishop described one such lodge meeting. On a Monday night in early 1875, the Ark of Safety Lodge, Independent Order of Good Templars, met in Beaufort, North Carolina. Many from the community—members and nonmembers alike—turned out to witness the public installation of officers. The bishop was happy to observe that "this society is in a most flourishing condition" and that "the people here [seem settled] to drive the monster Intemperance from their midst." As the bishop's account shows, the meeting consisted of more than installing officers or planning temperance work. With preaching and singing, the gathering could have been a worship service: "During some part of the exercises, someone became so deeply impressed as to cry aloud, and before the Lodge closed, was happily converted."[13] The boundary between temperance organizations and black churches seemed blurry, to say the least.

Male-led temperance societies arrived first in North Carolina, but black women soon took the lead in temperance organizing. Until 1883, North Carolina was one of only two states without a chapter of the Women's Christian Temperance Union (WCTU). But after a visit from WCTU national president Frances Willard and strong backing from North Carolina's Quaker communities, the WCTU grew quickly. Black women across the state organized their own separate local chapters, often without the aid of local whites. In the late 1880s, black women attended the state WCTU conventions, but the poor treatment they received from white women led them in 1891 to establish North Carolina's WCTU No. 2. The separate state convention provided for both black autonomy and interracial cooperation, and, like the Good Templars, became enmeshed with black religious life. Mary Lynch, union president for its first twenty-five years, served on the faculty of the AME Zion Church's flagship school, Livingstone College. And, across the state, black women's temperance activism linked up well with the work of black women's home missions societies and Sunday School conventions.[14]

The temperance movement's abstinence message was one black Protestants had received from others, but one that they considered complementary and consistent with the rest of their religious beliefs and practices. Whatever else we say about black temperance activism, we must acknowledge that black Protestants embraced the cause not simply as a means to an end—respectability, for example—but rather as a natural extension of their deeply held convictions.

The Temperance Message: A Jeremiad

The temperance messages that black Protestants preached said a great deal more than the simple anti-alcohol lessons of the *Freedman's Spelling Book*. Temperance sermons, editorials, meetings, poems, and speeches spoke of the material and moral progress of the race, gendered expectations, supernatural battles, and black Christians' rocky but favored relationship with God. The messages functioned like a jeremiad. They rebuked black Christians even as they affirmed them as God's special people. As a literary and cultural genre, the American jeremiad has had a long and distinguished history, but it is best known as the favorite sermon topic of New England Puritan ministers. The Puritan jeremiads were political sermons delivered at almost every public event; they were "state-of-the-covenant" addresses. They were not happy speeches. Puritan jeremiads modeled themselves after their namesake, the rather grim Old Testament prophet Jeremiah whose task was to pronounce God's judgments on Israel for its wickedness. Jeremiah's prophecies included long lamentations over Israel's many sins and concluded with a rehearsal of the nation's military defeat and exile from its homeland, interpreted as a punishment from God. Likewise, the political sermons in New England recorded a litany of the community's sins and corruption and described or anticipated God's fierce judgment for its iniquity. For some observers and historians, the jeremiad signified the Puritans' predilection for self-castigation.[15]

But the Puritan jeremiad was not completely hopeless. Literary scholar Sacvan Bercovitch identified the affirming and optimistic side of these doomsday wailings: "For all their catalogues of iniquities, the jeremiads attest to an unswerving faith in their errand." Puritans believed they were a peculiar people, on a special mission from God. Precisely because they served such a special role in the "sacred historical design," their allegiance to God came under close scrutiny, and they suffered God's corrective discipline. Puritans used jeremiads, Bercovitch continued, "to direct an imperiled people of God toward the fulfillment of their destiny, to guide them individually toward salvation, and collectively toward the American city of God." The jeremiads reaffirmed the Puritans' status as a "chosen people" and spoke of God's watchful eye over them. Amid all the threats, hope remained.[16]

The American jeremiad outlived the Puritans, and, in Bercovitch's analysis, played a central role in the United States' national character through the twentieth century. As a Canadian, Bercovitch wondered how "a country . . . despite its arbitrary territorial limits, could read its destiny in its landscapes, and a population . . . despite its bewildering mixture of race and creed, could believe in something called an American mission." In all the contestations and rearticulations of the American mission—from the Puritan "city on a hill" to Jeffersonian agrarianism, from manifest destiny to the land of equal opportunity—American Jeremiahs chastised the nation for failing to live up to its grand purpose. As Bercovitch observed, "The question in these latter-day jeremiads, as in their seventeenth-century precursors was never 'Who are we?' but, almost in deliberate evasion of that question, the old prophetic refrain, 'When is our errand to be fulfilled? How long, O Lord, how long?'"[17]

If that particular refrain seems reminiscent of African American calls for the nation to live up to its democratic ideals, that is no coincidence. African

American critiques of the nation constituted the best examples of the enduring American jeremiad. Black abolitionists warned white Americans of God's impending wrath for the national sin of slavery. The black jeremiad drew upon common American commitments to Christianity and republicanism, as David Howard-Pitney has argued, to offer "sharp social criticism within normative cultural bounds." Like Puritan jeremiads, black abolitionist rhetoric rebuked the nation and simultaneously affirmed its favored status as a chosen people. Wilson Moses has described the ways that black abolitionists and the late nineteenth- and twentieth-century black leaders after them displayed "a clever ability to play on the belief that America as a whole was a chosen nation with a covenantal duty to deal justly with the blacks."[18]

In the African American jeremiad tradition, the nation was not the only or even the most important chosen people. As Howard-Pitney explained, black jeremiads conceived of "blacks as a chosen people within a chosen people." African American jeremiads were two different kinds of messages: one principally concerned with the failings of the American mission, chastising the nation for the sins of slavery, racism, or lynching, and the other concerned with black destiny, rebuking the race for failing to live up to its mission. When scholars speak of black jeremiads, they usually have in mind the former, but African American history teems with examples of the latter. Howard-Pitney identified Booker T. Washington as this second type of black Jeremiah. Washington affirmed his belief "in the promise of the black chosen people" with "stern remonstrations against their current failings" and by demanding "their socioeconomic repentance." Howard-Pitney argued that Washington's "critical reform rhetoric" toward African Americans closely conformed to the conventions of the jeremiad, perhaps more so than did black jeremiads against white Americans.[19] Traditionally, a jeremiad was delivered by an insider who fully identified with the people under rebuke and felt complicit in their wrongdoings.

By selecting Washington as his sole example of the black jeremiad for a black audience, however, Howard-Pitney belittled a large part of the black jeremiad tradition. He contrasted Washington's internal critiques and blind eye toward white racism with the outright denunciations of white supremacy by Ida B. Wells-Barnett and Frederick Douglass. For Howard-Pitney, Washington represented a deviation from the African American jeremiad tradition, one that stood in contrast to Wells's and Douglass's appeals for justice. In Howard-Pitney's analysis, internal critiques were incompatible with critiques of the nation. But most nineteenth-century black Protestants had no problem naming national sins and opposing white supremacy even as they leveled internal critiques against black communities. Black Protestant leaders embraced both kinds of jeremiads. They could warn the nation of God's impending judgment for its unjust treatment of African Americans in one speech, and in the next warn African Americans that alcohol threatened the race's freedom and progress.

For example, Rev. J. A. Tyler, a Methodist minister, remembered as "full of grit and grace," whose weighty sermons reportedly fell "like the blows of Cyclopes' hammer," delivered both types of jeremiads in one 1875 editorial. According to Tyler, black churches found themselves at the confluence of two dangerous eras: "an age of oppression" and "an age of intemperance." The first alluded to the voter fraud, corruption, and racial discrimination that characterized the end of Reconstruction. Tyler described the injustice meted out by the state legislature: "the wicked . . . rule and the people mourn, the needy are neglected and the poor cast out." The solution to the "age of oppression" was to be found in divine redemption and retribution. Here Tyler repeated the opinions of the authors of the Esther circular only five years earlier. Redemption, he argued, "the Lord does not love. He will defend [the poor and the needy] and break in pieces the oppressor." Tyler used the language of Old Testament prophets to assure his readers that their political persecution would be short-lived. Tyler argued that God would intervene in Southern politics on the side of the oppressed, an argument many black Protestants made. So, the "age of oppression"—the first of the eras Tyler identified—would not prove "detrimental" to black churches.[20] Up to this point, Tyler's was a familiar religious interpretation of Redemption. White supremacy movements were evil but futile because God would intervene on the side of the oppressed, as he had during the Civil War.

The "age of intemperance," however, posed a greater threat. Like oppression, intemperance created hardships for the poor and needy. Drinking, Tyler argued, led to the proliferation of crime, violence, and poverty, and wreaked havoc on struggling black communities. Intemperance could create as much misery for black Southerners as could hostile legislatures, but its effects were harder to remedy. Racial oppression would drive God to their defense, Tyler argued, whereas licentious living would only alienate them from God. It was a classic jeremiad; he chastised black communities for drinking even as he affirmed that God was on their side and would deliver them from the hands of white supremacists.

Some black Protestant leaders agreed with Tyler that the problems with alcohol were supernatural. The NCBEMC characterized the temperance movement as spiritual warfare. Temperance societies, Baptist ministers believed, would "help tear down the cause of Satan and in its stead establish the cause of Christ."[21] Baptists were not the only ones to equate the liquor trade or alcohol consumption with satanic or demonic forces. Bishop Hood wrote that God had plans for the race, and the liquor industry served as evidence that Satan had "summoned all the hosts of hell" to thwart those plans.[22] The rhetoric of Satan, hell, and demons not only dramatized the conflict between temperance activists and their opponents, but also viewed intemperance as an active external force that attacked black communities in order to thwart their progress. Presumably, black communities were vulnerable to these satanic attacks precisely because they were favored by God and because their progress brought about God's purposes on earth.

The forces of intemperance, many black ministers warned, held the power to delay or undercut the promises of God. Hood invoked the Exodus narrative: "If we are to wander forty years in this wilderness, I can see no cause for it but intemperance." Hood cautioned his congregation that drinking might push the entrance to the Promised Land further into the future.[23] God promised freedom for African Americans, as evidenced by emancipation, and intemperance threatened that plan. "This monster," Hood preached, "seems to have been waiting the results of the emancipation proclamation, that it might seize upon the freed people and enslave them again, before they were strong enough to resist its power." Indeed, Hood continued, "[Intemperance] has, in many cases, wholly nullified the intended effect of the freedom proclamation." Alcohol threatened to temporarily reverse or delay God's plan for black freedom. In fact, Hood drew a close parallel between the evils of slavery and intemperance, arguing that the latter was more dangerous than the former: "We, as a race, have lately escaped from a bondage most oppressive, degrading, and evil in its consequences—a system denounced by a great and good man as the 'sum of all villainies.' Whatever were the evils of that system, (and they were never half told), and whatever were the horrors to the enslaved class, or the curses upon the slaveholder, yet the victims of that system were in no such evil case as are the victims of intemperance!"[24] The *Star of Zion* published a speech from former Louisiana governor P. B. S. Pinchback in which he warned his fellow African Americans that licentious living would re-enslave them.[25] Speaking of temperance, one AME Zion minister argued that "the hope of our race is as much dependent upon this virtue, as any other, and possibly more."[26] The future of the race, according to black ministers, was contingent on the race's temperance.

In some jeremiads, black ministers spoke of God's favor upon the race as contingent upon their virtue and faithfulness to God. As AME Zion bishop C. R. Harris told an audience in 1892, "it is the duty of every lover of his race to exert his influence towards quickening the moral sense and enlightening the religious views of the people wherever such a condition exists. Only by so doing may we count upon continued favor of Almighty-God and fulfill the mission He has given us to perform."[27] Like Tyler's editorial in the *Fayetteville Educator* twenty years earlier, Harris's speech placed temperance in the context of African Americans' special relationship with God. That relationship, according to Harris, was covenantal or contractual. The people offered God loyalty, obedience, and moral rectitude; and God offered the people divine protection and a promising future.

In temperance jeremiads like Harris's, divine displeasure and satanic attack were not separate from the other ill effects of drinking, such as poverty, unemployment, and violence, which also threatened to derail the race from its eschatological destiny. As ministers recounted the damage drinking caused black communities, their rhetoric seemed hyperbolic, though certainly they thought it was no exaggeration. One Baptist resolution read: "Intemperance . . . is the most gigantic and terrible of all the evils of the present age; . . . it has ruined more souls; blighted greater hopes; crushed out noble ambitions; tarnished more characters; broken more hearts; shattered more homes; squandered more property, than all the evils combined."[28] Other leaders, too, placed the blame for any number of social ills on drinking. At the 1877 State Colored Convention, which was called to address black emigration, John H. Williamson, a leading black legislator, pushed hard for a strongly worded temperance resolution. As he told the other black leaders there, "Day by day, this prolific source of vice and crime, was contributing large numbers of our people to the penitentiary, already overflowing." Alcohol consumption in the state's African American communities, he concluded, "entail[ed] misery, want, degradation and death, upon thousands of innocent victims . . . . To this source might be traced four fifths, if not five sixths of all the crimes of our land."[29] Temperance advocates routinely issued dire warnings and grim assessments of alcohol's effect on crime, poverty, and violence.

Williamson leveled his jeremiad against black churches. At the convention, he accused "the church" of failing to meet the "requirements of this important issue." Black churches, he complained, had not said and done enough to address the crisis of intemperance. But the jeremiad cut deeper: "So far from throwing their powerful influence in the way of its onward and ruinous course, many professing Christians in the city of Raleigh, had favored and voted to continue the whiskey business." Several leaders present objected to his accusation. When one said that it was not the convention's job to critique the church, Williamson countered, "Many members of the church and ministers of the Gospel had not the backbone to meet this question." Some ministers defended Williamson. Rev. Ransom and Rev. Crosby told the convention "the delegate from Franklin had drawn the picture none too strong." Upon the ministers' recommendation, the convention passed a temperance resolution that included a critique of black churches.[30] Why would black Protestant leaders, many of them ministers, assemble together to pass resolutions condemning themselves and the institutions they led? To begin with, black communities and black churches never fully supported temperance. The regular communication by Methodist bishops telling clergy to stop drinking demonstrates the lack of full compliance. Other groups, such as fraternal organizations and business interests in the black community, often condoned drinking.

Black church leaders since emancipation had routinely complained that intemperance infested the ranks of the clergy. The 1872 State Baptist Convention was "sorry to learn that in some sections of our State the standard of morality among Baptist Ministers of our race is so low and unscriptural." "Tippling," or drinking, topped the list of ministerial transgressions.[31] Worse than the occasional bad apple was the willingness of congregations to tolerate them. The church convention seemed even more concerned that some Baptists failed to understand that drinking was a sin. The delegates regretted to admit "that so few of our brethren seem to appreciate the idea of an entire abstinence from the use of ardent spirits."[32] Baptist and Methodist church bodies routinely called upon ministers to forsake the use of alcohol; their repeated calls probably spoke to a lack of ministerial compliance. Churches passed regulations preventing drinkers or smokers from joining the ranks of the clergy. Nevertheless, as one AME Zion bishop reported, "the section of the general rules which forbids the use of intoxicating drinks is not strictly obeyed." As the bishop warned the annual convention, "Unless ministers in this conference cease to use intoxicating drinks as a beverage, you can not hope for success; drunken ministers cannot preach the gospel of Jesus."[33] The temperance jeremiad was a message not only internal to black communities but also internal to black clergy and churches.

The message of temperance advocates intertwined fears of moral degradation with those of financial decline. Black Protestant leaders marked progress since emancipation in terms of moral and material progress. They tracked statistics—the number of legal marriages, property accumulated, percentages of black landownership—and recounted anecdotes of moral and financial success. The statistics and stories described the moral and the material as twin developments, both key to the race's future. They reasoned that intemperance, as an enemy of God and the race, stood ready to inflict damage on black morality and property. Harris explained, "it involves a worse than useless waste of money, and the Negro cannot afford to be extravagant. The Negro is at the bottom of the ladder. Other forces of society are arrayed against him and he must deny himself of useless encumbrances, or he will be forever a hewer of wood and drawer of water." Harris envisioned a future when black communities were financially prosperous, and he argued that the way to "acquire wealth is by STRICT TEMPERANCE."[34]

Ministers and others often spoke of the spiritual and financial problems of alcohol as two sides of the same coin. At an NCBEMC convention, Dr. A. W. Peques made the connection between spiritual and financial welfare directly: "We need men in our Churches who will interest themselves in the moral and material welfare of our people. A people who are poor, ignorant, and oppressed on every side are in no condition to render acceptable service to God. Ignorance and Poverty are not religion."[35] Peques identified racial oppression and alcohol among the causes for black Baptists' ignorance and poverty. Fourteen years earlier, the same church body had committed itself to attacking "everything ... which tends to obstruct [black Americans'] intellectual, moral, and spiritual progress ... [and their] present condition of poverty and ignorance."[36] Baptist ministers saw their temperance message as complementary to their campaigns for racial justice. Both alcohol and injustice were roadblocks on the race's march of progress. Part of the church's job, they believed, was to oppose whatever stood in the way of God's plan for the moral and material progress of the race.

Black reformers also feared numerical or reproductive decline. Black birth rates fluctuated throughout the postemancipation period, and African Americans suffered from high infant mortality rates. The scientific racism of the day included predictions of race extinction, that African Americans as a race would die out because of poor health, degenerate moral behavior, and innate inferiorities. Often, white American ideas of progress treated people of color as relics of humanity's primitive past in a modern age.[37]

Black reformers, too, worried that the race was in danger of extinction—some said suicide—but they did not consider it inevitable as others did. Instead, they sounded warnings in order to raise support for improved sanitation, health care, and moral behavior.

To ensure the race's survival and progress, they often turned to gendered ideals. Temperance activists were concerned about alcohol's impact on women and on relationships between men and women, but they were particularly worried that drinking crippled black manhood. The *Fayetteville Educator*, North Carolina's second black-authored newspaper and the first to run for a year—a thirteen-month run in 1874–75—devoted more than a few columns to intemperance and gender.[38] The temperance message of the young editors often sounded like jeremiads. Even the masthead motto gave a sense of the paper's claim to moral authority: "Fearlessly the right defend— / Impartially the wrong condemn." In almost every issue, the editors included temperance lessons and news, yet they fostered the mystique that they and others said regrettably little. In one letter to the editor, the writer asked the paper to address temperance more: "It seems that there is one great mistake practiced among the masses which has not attracted the attention of our better thinking men . . . . It is the bad habit of drinking intoxicating liquors."[39] The letter writer worried that the issue had not attracted black leaders' attention, even though temperance remained one of the most-discussed topics in the state's only black newspaper, the annual state colored conventions, annual church conventions, countless public speeches, and dozens of temperance society meetings across the state. Perhaps one of the editors penned the letter; the notion that no one heard the watchman's alarm only confirmed the urgency of the jeremiad.

The editors of the *Educator* seemed particularly worried about boys in the black community. "Your boys are in great danger," they told the parents of the "colored boys of Fayetteville." Young black boys, they observed, were spending their time idly on the streets, and it was only a matter of time, they predicted, before they would become unemployed or incarcerated men. The triple sins of idleness, truancy, and drinking concerned the young editors. As the editors challenged black parents, "Will you make them men, such as will honor the race?" Idleness and alcohol, they told the boys, "does not only injure you, but our whole race as a people." The lament over black boys in Fayetteville was a jeremiad for the whole race.[40]

A Fayetteville schoolboy won a declamation contest by despairing over the loss of "many of our young men . . . who might have been noble men" to the bottle. Likewise, Tyler wrote in the *Educator* that he feared the "great, influential, and growing evil" of intemperance most acutely when it came to African American boys. Liquor and business interests, Tyler lamented, rivaled the church for rank in the community and were "leading our brightest sons astray from the cradle." Black boys became the focal point of the *Educator's* temperance jeremiads.

Temperance activists' concern with black manhood was widespread and long-lasting. They defined manhood as a specific set of gendered ideals, among them the exercise of upright character, self-restraint, independent self-reliance, and the ability to financially support and protect women and children. Beyond these particular attributes, black Protestant leaders exalted the terms *manhood* and *manliness* to mean everything laudable in a man. Historian Gail Bederman found a definition in the 1890 *Century Dictionary* helpful: "Manly . . . is the word into which has been gathered the highest conceptions of what is noble in man or worthy of his manhood."[41] Such an expansive definition could mean anything or nothing, and black writers continually redefined what it was to be manly or to have manhood. One editorialist equated manhood with religion: "Religion is as much as the total of manhood"; another equated it with "truth, honor, and bravery." Others described manhood as the self-respect that was denied black men under slavery.[42]

Whatever the attributes of manliness, black temperance activists emphasized that alcohol undermined them. As one black minister put it simply, "The real man is the sober man."[43] When AME Zion minister W. S. Meadows warned fellow preachers of the dangers of alcohol in an open letter to *Star of Zion*, he wrote, "intemperance cuts down manhood in its strength."[44] According to temperance advocates, by undermining black manhood (particularly qualities such as independent self-reliance and the provision for and protection of women and children), intemperance returned black men to the childlike dependence they experienced under slavery. As an anonymous poet explained in verse:

So the dread curse of slavery forever is gone,
But alcohol's curse doth remain,
And I would much rather be black and in bonds,
Than bound by this soul-cutting chain.
Arouse, men and women, and open your eyes,
O! Look on the misery around,

>Mark the works of this enemy so deadly and mean,
>Brilliant manhood he drags to the ground.[45]

The poet not only connected alcohol with slavery, a common rhetorical strategy in the black temperance movement, but also described the loss of freedom as the loss of black manhood.

Temperance activists also frequently wrote of the effect men's drinking had on women and children. At the 1884 North Carolina AME Zion Conference, Bishop T. H. Lomax called intemperance "the wife's dreadful woe" and the "children's tormentor." The victims of alcohol abuse, Lomax continued, were more often than not the innocent and helpless. Intemperance produced widows, orphans, and destitution.[46] At the same conference, Rev. C. H. Meade of the National Temperance Society portrayed "the scenes in a drunkard's family," of inebriated men and hungry children, of fathers bringing home whiskey instead of ham. His sermon "brought solemnity and tears in many eyes."[47] Meade's message echoed the one Meadows delivered to his fellow ministers. "Think," Meadows wrote, "of the poverty, of the destruction, of the little children tugging at the breast, of a weeping and despairing wife asking for bread, of the man struggling with imaginary serpents, produced by the devilish thing."[48] These speeches and articles were designed to appeal to a man's self-image as protector and provider. The temperance jeremiad was intended to alert black men to their failures to meet gender norms.

Black women were just as likely as men to issue temperance jeremiads about manhood. Cecilia B. Gwyn, president of the WCTU chapter that met at St. Augustine's College in Raleigh, considered it the job of black women to raise the alarm about drinking and black manhood. She described the ill effects of alcohol on husbands and fathers in familiar ways. Gwyn cited higher crime rates and financial downfall, but she focused her attention on the destruction of the home. She told her audience of well-educated women, "We, who are in our homes or other places of safety, can have but a vague idea of the dreary surroundings of a drunkard's children. They not only suffer physically; it is not [evidence from] their little bodies which are scantily provided for and, yes, we must say brutalized, that show the effects of intemperance." She told her WCTU chapter that the root of the problem was in "the character of man." But it was not solely a man's problem. "It is for us, who are receiving temperance instructions to exert our influence," she said, so that the race might boast of its progress.[49] Black women, as opposed to men, couched their temperance message in terms of home and family. They were more likely to work in tandem with white reformers, and white women's temperance rhetoric sounded similar.[50] Across racial groups, drinking was assumed to be a problematic male behavior but one with devastating consequences for women. For black women, however, the concern about manhood meant something more, because white supremacy already limited black men's ability to be protectors and providers.

The fears over black manhood that temperance advocates expressed remained consistent with their jeremiads over the race's progress as a whole. Black Protestant leaders frequently described the destiny of the race in terms of its achievement of gendered ideals. Price, five years after his speaking tour for the National Temperance Society, told a New York audience about the race's destiny "to gather up a Christian civilization that is unparalleled in [its] history." In the same speech, Price phrased his eschatological expectations differently: "The Negro is to build up a manhood and womanhood, [the likes of which] the world has never seen."[51] Other black ministers in North Carolina also marked the race's progress in terms of manhood (and womanhood). At a 1908 church convention, Baptist preacher J. A. Whitted boasted of progress since emancipation. He recounted the dire straits from which black churches emerged in the 1860s, and as proof that God was doing a mighty work among them, Whitted pointed to the black men in his audience "representing intelligence and Christian manhood, planting the old flag in every nook and corner of the Old North State."[52] If achieving manhood marked African American progress and destiny, then threats to manhood, temperance activists could claim, questioned whether the race would meet its mission. Temperance workers' discourse on manliness simply added temperance to the list of things that threatened black manhood, a list that already included slavery, white supremacy, and irreligion, things that conspired against the race's progress, and thus against the plans of God.

There was, of course, a positive side to all the wailings over poverty, crime, re-enslavement, and loss of manhood. Temperance activists reaffirmed the belief that a glorious day stood in the not-too-distant future for black Americans. And, in the case of alcohol, black communities had it fully within their power to remove the obstacle from their path, unlike other obstacles, such as oppressive landlords or voter fraud and intimidation. At the AME Zion District Conference in Fayetteville in 1884, Richard Williams reminded his fellow temperance activists what lay ahead of them if their reform efforts met success: "Nothing, I think, is nobler than reform. Fearfully it is needed among our own race, especially in the way of temperance." While his jeremiad began with a grim portrait, as did others, it ended on quite an optimistic note: "Should economy, uprightness, honestness, sobriety, each in their turn take the place of the many vices that we are addicted to or should the raging flood of intemperance which now sweeps through our land cease, this world of ours would be a happy one." What awaited black communities, Williams said hopefully, was "a Paradise on earth."[53]

Prohibition Politics

The reform that Williams promised would bring paradise on earth was one of moral suasion. The Good Templars and churches, and later the WCTU, recruited members who then signed pledges not to drink alcohol. Activists gave speeches, preachers delivered sermons, and Sunday School teachers taught lessons—all designed to stop individuals from drinking and to gain more activists for the temperance cause. But even though black temperance activism was largely focused on the demand side of the liquor trade, activists also touted supply-side solutions. In the 1870s, black temperance activists campaigned for local option laws to prohibit the sale of alcohol in townships throughout North Carolina. In the failed attempt to ban alcohol in an 1881 statewide referendum, black Protestant leaders made the jeremiad political. The African American community did not unite behind the referendum, and temperance advocates worried what the failure of the 1881 measure would mean for black North Carolinians' relationship with whites and with God.

The 1881 campaign began when a number of temperance organizations, leading citizens, and representatives from white and black churches converged on a State Prohibition Convention in Raleigh in January 1881. The Convention drafted a proposal to the state legislature arguing for a statewide ban on the sale of intoxicating liquors, and North Carolina's most prominent ministers and laymen signed it, including prominent community member Charles Hunter and black Baptist minister Augustus Shepard, founder of the Oxford Colored Orphan's Asylum.[54] "In the early part of the campaign," one white minister remembered, "all the ministers, white and colored, with but few exceptions, in the State, were for prohibition."[55] It was a biracial movement.

In the proposal sent to the state legislature, the Convention organizers boasted of unqualified black support for a new prohibition law. Not only were some of the leading prohibitionists African American, but black churches and organizations also passed resolutions favoring prohibition. In Raleigh, while the Prohibition Convention met, the North Carolina Prince Hall Masons, a black fraternal lodge, went into session and passed a unanimous resolution in favor of the proposed prohibition law. The Lodge's support—Masons were not reliably dry—was, white prohibitionists argued, "an incident highly creditable to our colored citizens." In fact, leading white activists saw the Masonic resolution as the first fruits of full black support for prohibition.[56] Rev. R. H. Whitaker, a leading white temperance activist and editor of a temperance newspaper, recalled, "The colored people, if anything, were more favorable to it than were the whites."[57] Black temperance organizers presented a unified front.

State legislators refused to pass a statewide ban on the sale of alcohol. Instead, they put the issue before the voters in a popular referendum set for August 1881. Prohibitionists quickly mobilized a campaign targeted at the state's electorate. This, too, was a biracial effort. Price—"the greatest orator I have ever heard utter a sentence," according to one colleague—stumped the state.[58] His speeches attracted interracial audiences. One speech in High Point, North Carolina, attracted "the largest audience ever assembled in this part of the State (supposed to be ten thousand)." Observers marveled at Price, "a Negro as big and black as he was eloquent and learned," and delighted in his "grace and eloquence" and his "logical reasoning and solid arguments."[59] Black women, too, worked tirelessly in favor of the prohibition referendum. About the movement in Raleigh, Rev. Morgan Latta said, "Of course [the women] were in favor of prohibition," as if women's involvement was so widely known as to need no comment.[60] And in Charlotte, black churchwomen organized the Ladies' Prohibition Association, which caught the attention of the white press.[61] Male and female prohibitionists' interracial campaign appeared to be working well, and by the early summer of 1881, nearly everyone expected the prohibition measure to pass.[62]

But anti-prohibitionists were ready for a fight. On June 1, North Carolina liquor dealers organized a convention to oppose the referendum. Nearly three hundred delegates arrived in Raleigh to chart their course. According to local newspapers, about one-fourth of the delegates were African American. Prominent black leader James E. O'Hara, who had spoken out earlier against emigration and who would later represent North Carolina's Second Congressional District in the U.S. House, joined the anti-prohibitionists. Many of his friends and colleagues felt betrayed. O'Hara came onboard the

State Anti-Prohibition Association's executive committee and helped craft the strategy to defeat the 1881 referendum.[63]

The liquor dealers and anti-prohibitionists demonstrated political savvy by creating a new political party, the Liberal Anti-Prohibition Party. This party poised itself to challenge the Democratic Party leadership, many of whom had come out in favor of the 1881 referendum. The state's Republican Party leadership, including O'Hara, welcomed the arrival of a third party. The Republican Party State Executive Committee, in a controversial 3-to-2 vote, issued a statement opposing the prohibition referendum. Republicans hoped to absorb the Liberal Anti-Prohibition Party (which they would do three years later) and to challenge the decade-long dominance of the Democratic Party. Two institutions that normally made good bedfellows, black churches and the Republican Party, turned against each other.[64]

When Baptist minister Morgan Latta gave speeches in Raleigh in favor of the referendum, he met resistance from black audiences who dismissed the measure as "nothing but a Democratic ticket." Frustrated, Latta told those assembled that "there were no politics involved in this measure." The people responded by accusing Latta of "selling their interests to the Democratic Party."[65] According to Whitaker, a leading white prohibitionist, the Republican Party leadership tried to convince black voters that prohibition was just one of the many ways Democrats planned to restrict their rights or "to put them all back into slavery."[66] Given small-scale disfranchisement measures and unfair landlord-tenant laws unleashed by the Democratic-controlled legislature, the association between the Democratic Party and curtailment of rights had to be strong in black voters' minds. A number of black North Carolinians found the description of prohibition as a curtailment of liberties a convincing one. Latta encountered black voters who believed that "to take whiskey out of the State was infringing upon their material rights that were granted to them in the Fourteenth and Fifteenth Amendments of the Constitution of the United States."[67] Whitaker and Latta were unsympathetic, even mocking, of this perspective on prohibition, but some black voters were reluctant to give the state more power to limit their personal choices.

In August, voters defeated the prohibition referendum by a margin of three to one. Almost immediately white and black temperance advocates began interpreting the defeat, both practically and theologically. Some white North Carolinians blamed the defeat on black voters. The *Charlotte Observer* and the *Carolina Watchman* concluded, with little evidence, that the black vote went almost entirely against the referendum and that the white vote was split. But because black voters made up less than one-third of the state's electorate, it was not entirely believable to blame the election results on them. Whitaker, however, found a way: "as soon as it was seen the negro vote would be cast almost solidly against prohibition, hundreds of white men who had intended to vote for it, began to ease off." As dubious as Whitaker's reasoning was—that white voters took their cue from black voters—the idea caught on. A consensus among white temperance leaders emerged that, despite initial black support for prohibition, the 1881 referendum failed in large part because of African American voters.[68]

Black temperance leaders, in contrast, argued that both the white and the black vote split on the issue, but they were equally disappointed with the outcome. Bishop Hood told the North Carolina Annual Conference of the AME Zion Church in Beaufort in December of that year, "the members of our church contributed a full proportionate share of [the prohibition] vote, yet it is painful to know that some were active opponents of the measure."[69] Black leaders' contention that the African American electorate cast a split vote seemed easier to substantiate than did white leaders' accusation of a solidly wet vote. Black churches and temperance organizations maintained an active campaign throughout the summer of 1881, and, in subsequent local-option prohibition campaigns, newspapers reported a mixture of black support and opposition. After several 1886 elections, the *North Carolina Presbyterian* reported, "Some of our successes in the late elections were due to freedmen. They refused to be hood-winked by the clap-trap about liberty and freedom."[70] Whatever the racial makeup of the 1881 vote, the anti-prohibitionists won by a landslide. It was a deafening defeat for both black and white temperance activists.

The prohibitionist camp searched for answers, trying to make sense of defeat. Hood put the defeat in the context of emancipation and supernatural warfare. "Nothing since emancipation has reflected so badly upon our people as their action in this matter."[71] Hood was tracking the race's progress since emancipation, as almost every other black leader did, and to him this was a momentous, if depressing, point in human history. It was also part of supernatural history. Hood told his church that "Satan must have looked upon the anti-prohibition movement as his last great effort ... in defense of his tottering kingdom." Hood often described earthly events as the work of both human and supernatural agents. So, even though he blamed the defeat on "the hosts of hell," which he meant literally, he also pointed fingers at certain groups of people. Hood attributed the election results to the "slanders of politicians or rum-sellers" and to white leaders who claimed to be "friends of the temperance cause" yet "found fault with the bill's [wording]." He challenged those leaders, who "are most likely to control the next Legislature," to produce a better prohibition measure, and if they did so, black churches would stand ready to help. Hood also considered the 1881 prohibition referendum a test that his church and his race had failed, and so he issued a stern warning to his colleagues. Anyone who rejected "total abstinence from all intoxicants as a beverage," Hood warned, "has denied the faith . . . and forfeits his right to a place among us." The faithful would continue to "make war" on intemperance, to "follow the path of duty" that God had laid out before them, Hood preached. It was a jeremiad of the first order. The jeremiad tapped into black communities' existing beliefs about emancipation and race destiny.[72]

The success of the anti-prohibition message in black communities—and how successful it was was not entirely clear—depended upon its ability to produce a jeremiad of comparable credibility to that of the prohibitionists. We know very little about why black Protestant leaders like James O'Hara opposed the 1881 measure. But we know from others' accounts that O'Hara was hardly alone. Part of their opposition came from their vested interests in the Republican Party and their willingness to try maneuvers aimed at regaining a Republican majority in the state. Some of the bill's black opponents may simply have wanted a place to drink. But it also seems probable that leaders like O'Hara might not have considered their support for temperance and their opposition to prohibition to be inconsistent. The concept of manliness, which, again, black temperance activists often invoked, emphasized a man's ability to control himself. Seen in this way, imposed state control took away a black man's ability to exercise the key virtue of manhood: self-control. Moreover, when black leaders used the concept of manhood, it was almost always in contrast to white paternalism. As manly men, black men wanted to regulate themselves and to prove they could do so without white supervision. Opposition to prohibition, then, for leaders like O'Hara, may have stemmed from longstanding black Protestant support for the virtues of manhood and for black political liberty.

Whitaker's memoir, which intended to demonstrate the "nonsense" of anti-prohibitionists, unintentionally revealed their rationality. Anti-prohibitionists marshaled numerous biblical stories to argue that prohibition ran counter to God's will. Passing such an antibiblical measure, they insisted, would im-

Anti-Prohibition Speech, 1905. Rev. R. H. Whitaker blamed the failure of the 1881 prohibition referendum on black voters, as seen in this cartoonish illustration of revival-style anti-prohibitionist meetings. Image: *Whitaker's Reminiscences, Incidents, and Anecdotes* (Raleigh, N.C.: Edwards and Broughton, 1905), 199. North Carolina Collection, Wilson Special Collections Library, UNC–Chapel Hill.

peril the race's freedom. This counter-jeremiad, as it were, seemed to resonate well with black audiences who held biblical stories in high regard and who worried that their newly won liberties were in danger. Black anti-prohibitionists issued the same kind of warnings about freedom and race destiny that black prohibitionists did. A shared eschatological framework inspired opposing political opinions and set the terms for debate.[73]

Whitaker reported seeing a number of open-air camp meetings, akin to revivals, in the summer of 1881, where anti-prohibitionists convinced black worshippers that prohibition ran contrary to their own interests and to the word of God. In his memoirs, Whitaker offered a composite sample of the speeches he heard, and he provided a sketch. In the sketch, a white man preaches from a makeshift pulpit of two whiskey barrels and a plank of wood. He stands on a soap box, with a liquor bottle in his back pocket and his fist in the air. An audience of black men and women, some barefoot and wearing farmers' hats and headscarves, gathers in an outdoor meeting place. At first glance, the scene could be one of a camp meeting revival: indeed, the text in Whitaker's account of the anti-prohibition speech sounded very much like a sermon. According to Whitaker, the "whiskey power" preacher preyed on African Americans' fear by calling attention to the "danger of losing our most sacred right—the right to eat and drink as we please." The language of rights and freedom, Whitaker worried, was an underhanded way to gain the support of a people "who were ignorant and very much afraid they might be put back into slavery again." The anti-prohibition preacher raised additional fears when he claimed, rather vaguely, that "there's something behind" the bill, something "concocted by the enemies of a free and independent people." The fact that many Democrats supported prohibition and that the Republican Party State Executive Committee opposed it, no doubt, lent weight to the whiskey preacher's arguments.[74]

The preacher in Whitaker's account went further, claiming that prohibition contradicted the teachings of the Bible. He drew upon the familiar passages of Jesus's miracle at Cana, where he turned water into wine, and Paul's advice to Timothy to take a little wine for his stomach infirmities; and he quoted the proverb, "Give strong drink to him that is ready to perish." The speech reached its climax when the preacher asked the congregation, "And didn't the blessed Savior say, 'Not that which goeth into the mouth defileth a man, but which proceedeth out of the mouth?'" People in the crowd cried out, "Bless de Lawd, de Bible's on our side!" These biblical arguments combined with political arguments made an effective case for anti-prohibition, and Whitaker lamented that it was "no wonder" that black North Carolinians believed it.[75]

There is reason to question the accuracy of Whitaker's account. First, it was an imagined composite; his story named no specific people or places. Second, the tone of his memoir was so openly derisive of African Americans as to lose any semblance of objectivity. And lastly, the failure of the 1881 prohibition campaign left Whitaker bitter, and he, like many white North Carolinians, scapegoated black neighbors for his own frustrations. Other sources, however, including white and black religious newspapers, corroborated some aspects of Whitaker's story. African Americans in North Carolina were apprehensive about any further curtailment of their rights; and they found biblical stories that seemed to condone drinking more persuasive than general moral arguments against the practice. There were striking parallels between the anti-prohibitionist sermon in Whitaker's memoir and the typical jeremiad of black temperance activists. Both argued that black North Carolinians were on a path to full citizenship and that certain barriers threatened to stop or reverse their progress. Both gave warnings and both appealed to the authority of the Bible. For folks on both sides of the issue, prohibition raised questions about the freedom and progress of the race and the directives of God.

After the 1881 campaign, prohibition politics in North Carolina remained racially charged. The national Prohibition Party held its first convention in North Carolina in December 1885. The convention frightened Democratic Party officials, who feared defection from their ranks. Democrats held too precarious a majority to back a statewide prohibition measure, an unpopular move if the 1881 election proved anything. But by not backing prohibition, the Democratic Party risked losing one wing of the party to the new Prohibition Party. Party officials, therefore, sent a clear message to their own members: any third party risked splitting white votes and electing black officers. Instead, prohibitionist Democrats threw their weight behind local-option prohibition campaigns, hoping to defuse the issue at the state level.[76]

But even local prohibition elections became racially charged, although wet and dry never fell neatly along racial lines. The *Winston Sentinel* claimed that Winston's black residents voted "almost solidly for the dry ticket" while newspapers in Charlotte reported that only "two Negroes voted for prohibition, notwithstanding nine tenths of them are members of the church."[77] The traveling editor of the AME Church's *Christian Recorder*, Benjamin F. Lee, observed a strong prohibition sentiment among Raleigh's black population. In 1886, that city voted dry in a local-option prohibition referendum, and, one year later, the issue again came before the voters. As a result, Lee noticed, "the prohibition question was in hot discussion in the town." Lee described prohibition meetings convened "under a large canvas tent" where "colored and white assembled together night after night, speaking, singing, yelling and rolling on the prohibition subject." The meetings were interracial, but, as Lee recounted, the African American community was the "most pronounced in favor of reform." Black women showed the most commitment, as they "declared themselves ready to die martyrs to the glorious cause." African American prohibition activism in Raleigh fed into the city's race-baiting politics. According to Lee, white anti-prohibitionists warned white voters that to vote for prohibition was to ally with "the nigger side." It is hard to say how effective that intimidation was, but at the next election, Raleigh voters opted for a wet city.[78]

Prohibition politics in North Carolina became increasingly racialized. Black temperance leaders, who spearheaded parts of the earlier campaigns, found the movement snowballing out of their control. When black churches gave their full support to the 1881 referendum, the movement failed, and white prohibitionists blamed the black community. When black churches renewed their commitment to prohibition, as they did in the 1886–87 Raleigh local-option campaigns, some whites used black prohibitionist sentiment to drum up white support for the opposing side. After the 1881 campaign, Bishop Hood declared, "We care not who leads in the suppression of intemperance; what we desire is that the evil be banished from the land, and we will follow any man's lead to that end."[79] Black ministers and women organizers had championed the interracialism of the temperance movement, not principally to gain respectability or white approval. Rather, working with whites served as a means to another end: to stop threats to African Americans' progress. But interracial cooperation became trickier and more volatile as the century came to a close. The movement for prohibition in North Carolina became a story largely about whites, not because black temperance activists retreated or lost interest, but because they found themselves unwelcome among their former allies.

In fact, a number of leading white temperance advocates reasoned that black suffrage stood in the way of statewide prohibition. They cited allegations that African Americans would always vote wet. Frances Willard, the national president of the WCTU, said in an 1890 interview in Atlanta, "The problem on their [white Southerners'] hands is immeasurable. The colored race multiplies like the locusts of Egypt. The grog-shop is its center of power."[80] At the 1896 North Carolina state WCTU convention, Belle Kearney, the keynote speaker, listed black suffrage among the primary hindrances to temperance legislation.[81] But the other part of their reasoning had little to do with speculation as to whether black men would vote dry or wet. White prohibitionists argued that Democrats were reluctant to split white votes over a controversial measure like prohibition as long as black politicians stood ready to capitalize on their discord. Race baiting sounded the death knell for prohibition legislation in North Carolina. Southern white prohibitionists argued that by disfranchising black voters they could take the race card from their opponents' deck.[82]

Later, when North Carolina would disfranchise black voters, the *Biblical Recorder*, the weekly journal of the white State Baptist Convention of North

Carolina, hailed it as a boon to prohibition: "As was long hoped, the first fruits of disfranchisement of the negroes bids fair to be progress in legislations prohibiting saloons."[83] Other white prohibitionists anticipated more success now that state elections were nearly all white. As historian Daniel Whitener explained, "Since the Negro was eliminated, they said, prohibitionists were now at liberty to leave any party that persisted in licensing and upholding 'a business that demoralizes and debauches society.'"[84] In 1905, in a popular referendum, North Carolina became the first Southern state to ban completely the manufacture and sale of all alcoholic beverages.[85]

Chastisement and Destiny

It is tempting to see the long, troubled history of black involvement in the temperance movement as a failed bid for respectability in the eyes of whites. The movement's leaders before and after 1881 were keenly concerned with how whites viewed them. But that is certainly not how black Protestants interpreted it. In fact, black temperance advocates looked back upon their foray into prohibition politics as a crucial moment in the race's peculiar relationship with God. They interpreted their failures in the 1881 campaign as the sin for which black North Carolinians would later suffer God's chastisement with the arrival of Jim Crow segregation in the late 1890s.[86]

Bishop C. R. Harris wrote in an editorial for the *Star of Zion* that, to understand the violent white supremacy campaign that came at the end of the century, black North Carolinians needed to reflect on their relationship with God since the days of emancipation. "Thirty years ago or more," he wrote, "God was for the Negro and the Republican Party." Harris argued that black Republicans had been so hungry for power, with such blind loyalty to the Party, that they made alliances with unscrupulous and immoral men. Harris explained God's reaction:

> But, as with Israel in the days of old, God did not suffer us to desert Him without a Prophet to warn and persuade us. He saw the Negro had just emerged from the black night of slavery; he can not easily discriminate between right and wrong in party politics. "I will try him with a moral issue." So in 1881 He sends upon the political arena a prophet like Isaiah and Jeremiah . . . God even here "tempered the wind to the shorn lamb." He separated it from the word "Party" and named it "Bill"—Prohibition

Bill. In the contest that ensued, God, with His preachers, white and black, were found upon one side, allied with the best people of the State, Republicans as well as Democrats.

According to Harris, black North Carolinians did not pass the test that God sent. When they failed to ride the tide of the prohibition campaign to victory, "its ebb drug back the Negro into well nigh irretrievable defeat." What was its result? Harris answered, "Righteousness was defeated without regard to color or party, and corruption has ruled politics since."[87]

Harris's account of the 1881 prohibition referendum election laid out some practical consequences. Because black voters listened more to the Republican Party than to their own consciences, white prohibitionists abandoned the idea of biracial politics and instead threw their weight behind white supremacist politics. But Harris's story was also supernatural. "God has deserted the party," Harris explained. The subtitle of his editorial explained even more: "The Negro Leaves God—God Leaves the Negro." Harris drew the parallel with ancient Israel very closely. African Americans, being God's chosen people, entered into a special reciprocal relationship or covenant with God. Their faithfulness ensured God's protection and blessing, but their unfaithfulness—amid the warnings of prophets—led God to withdraw blessing and to issue divine chastisement. In light of the recent chastisement, Harris said, "So may the Negro now cry 'O preacher, preacher! Had I but served my God as I have served my party, He would not now have left me prostrate and bleeding.'"[88]

Harris's good friend and colleague Bishop Hood agreed with Harris's interpretation. He, too, at the turn of the century, mourned the lost opportunity of the 1881 prohibition referendum. Before the Central North Carolina Conference of the AME Zion Church, Hood recounted the story of the 1881 election. He reminded his audience of the Republican Party's decision to support "the rum interest," and the "sorts of lies" opponents spread about a loss of freedom, or a return to slavery, that would result from the prohibition measure. "We were read out of the party and our preachers generally who favored Prohibition were denounced as enemies of the race." Hood spoke just three weeks after racial violence in Wilmington, and he related the recent events to the 1881 election: "In 1881 we had the opportunity to divide the white vote so widely that it could never have been consolidated again—not on a political issue, however, but on a great moral issue . . . If the mass of our people could have been induced to vote for Prohibition and thus secured its adoption, the white people would have seen that we could be depended upon to support such measures . . . and what we have now passed through could never have occurred." Like Harris, Hood lamented the results of the 1881 prohibition campaign, and blamed on it the failure to forge long-lasting biracial alliances.[89] Hood recast the history as a supernatural story. Because of the Republican Party's stance on the prohibition measure, he argued, "the curse of God has rested upon the party in this State from that date to the present." Hood's and Harris's pronouncements of God's judgment sounded as grim as the original jeremiads. But, for all their talk of God's chastisement, their messages were not self-loathing but rather self-affirming. By rebuking black voters, Hood in no way meant to exonerate the race's political enemies. White supremacists, Hood felt certain, would suffer God's wrath for their "lawlessness."[90] That is, black reformers like Hood were not suffering from "unconscious, internalized racism."[91] We know this because the story that Hood and Harris and other temperance activists wanted to tell was not about whites, though obviously they desired biracial alliances and the friendship of white men "worth standing with" to accomplish their purposes. Instead, the story they told was of black Americans' relationship with God and the special mission God had granted them in human history.

The story black temperance activists told, despite the setbacks of 1881 and the onset of the Jim Crow era, was a triumphant one. Their chest-beating, like that in Puritan jeremiads, gave way to predictions of a glorious day and affirmations of their role as God's special people. Hood ended his editorial on an upbeat: "Not withstanding the bitterness of the recent campaign and its results, I cannot allow myself to believe that the future of my people in this State can be as dark and discouraging as some are now prophesying." In the column next to Harris's editorial in the *Star of Zion*, Bishop Alexander Walters explained why ministers like Hood might still hold out hope: "Truly the outlook is gloomy. But we have seen gloomier times than the present (a short while before the war, when the fugitive slave law was passed) and were brought triumphantly through the God of battles."[92] Even in the 1890s, the memory of emancipation as an act of God remained strong. Walters expected divine intervention on behalf of his people. In all the doomsday warnings and admonitions to stop drinking, black temperance activists were sending another message: that African Americans occupied a high place in the sacred historical design, and that as God's special people, their eschatological destiny was progress and triumph.

CHAPTER FIVE

A Table Prepared by Our Enemies

Even before North Carolina's white supremacy campaign of 1898, African Americans across the South knew the times were troubling. Beginning in 1890, state legislatures and popular referenda imposed racial segregation on rail travel and considered ways to disfranchise black men. Lynching peaked in 1892, with mob victims topping two hundred per year. Rev. S. F. Hamilton, a black Methodist minister in Monroe, North Carolina, was troubled about his race's future and with good reason. He viewed recent political events as portentous signs. Hamilton conveyed his fears to fellow church members in a *Star of Zion* column. "The times are stringent, it cannot be denied. . . . We have reached the danger line," he reported. In the history of the race since emancipation, Hamilton wrote, the 1890s were a critical turning point. "What God has done for us in these twenty-nine years is a wonder of wonders!" He described racial progress as a reenactment of the biblical story of the conquest of Canaan. In that story, Joshua sent out spies to scope out the dangers ahead before the people crossed the Jordan to enter the land. "We as a nation are in arms' reach of the goal," Hamilton narrated. But, he continued, "There seems to be a great Jordan between us and the 'Promised Land.' Many difficulties to remove before we eat of the corn of the land." As the race worked to reach the Promised Land, Hamilton predicted the 1890s would be a decade full of difficulties. He wrote, "We must achieve victory in the next decade, or to some extent a great defeat will send a shock of cowardice on the Negro race . . . which will be felt for succeeding generations." Hamilton foresaw the new assaults on black rights, the beginnings of the Jim Crow era, and warned his colleagues to fight hard against it.[1]

Though Hamilton saw omens of defeat for black Americans—lynching, low wages for black farmers, and disfranchisement measures in other states—he nevertheless spoke confidently about the race's coming triumph. "I believe a brighter day is coming; that we are on the eve of a millennial age, in which the pure gleam of heaven will be inhaled by the nations," he wrote. With such an eschatology of hope, Hamilton explained, black Americans could weather and defeat the forces of Jim Crow. "If we are God's people, 'no weapon that is formed against us shall prosper,'" he wrote, softening his alarmism. He used apocalyptic language: "Let God but unstable His fiery horses and they will paw the mountain into cinders and beat the world into ashes in a moment; but even then hitched to the car of our redemption, shaking their fiery manes among the stars, and flashing through the constellations will roll us up to God—the fires of hell tossing below with the damned."[2] He invoked the image of the four horsemen of the apocalypse, in a more detailed way than black freedmen in Mississippi had done three decades earlier.[3] It was a frightening image, but one that black Protestant leaders had used before. In this case, the apocalypse was scary only for those who stood in the way of God's people, and Hamilton seemed little in doubt that black Americans were in fact God's people. Despite the very real warnings that Hamilton gave in the beginning of his column, he concluded with a much more upbeat message. The column ended, "The 'living wheels' of the Almighty cannot be hindered by man. Be courageous for the trembling gates of hell shall not prevail against her [the church, or God's people]. No never." Hamilton seemed at ease mixing and matching biblical prophecies—the living wheels of the prophet Ezekiel's vision and the gates of hell from Jesus's prophecy to Peter—in order to forecast the triumph of right over wrong.

Hamilton had two seemingly contradictory aims. First, he wanted to alert "every leader" to the political dangers facing the race and to motivate them to seek practical and human ways to avert those dangers. Second, he insisted that the future of black Americans lay in God's hands, and thus, despite the machinations of white supremacists, the race would enter the twentieth century triumphantly.[4] Those aims were precisely the same taken by James Harris and other black leaders when the Klan stood ready to control the state some twenty-five years earlier.

Hamilton's predictions of a contentious and difficult decade proved true. Just months after his column appeared in the *Star of Zion*, the People's Party (composed of reform-minded white farmers) and the Republican Party (composed largely of African Americans) formed a coalition in North Carolina that produced a Fusion slate of candidates in the 1894 election. The success of the Fusion ticket in 1894 and 1896 ignited fierce race-baiting campaigns by white Democrats in an attempt to regain control of the legislature and the Governor's Palace. In 1898, black North Carolinians fielded a company of volunteers for the Spanish-American War, which they hoped would erase the color line but which instead bolstered white supremacy at home and abroad. The white supremacy campaigns in North Carolina peaked in the corrupt and bloody November 1898 election, an election that delivered the state to the Democratic Party. Two days after the election, a violent coup d'état in Wilmington deposed and exiled the city's elected biracial leadership and left at least a dozen African Americans dead. Within three years' time, the state instituted de jure segregation and passed a constitutional amendment designed to disfranchise African Americans. The rise and fall of black fortunes in North Carolina were more dramatic than they were in other states, but the outcome followed similar events in the rest of the South. African Americans in Louisiana, too, experienced the rise and fall of power in their own Fusion. North Carolina was but the seventh ex-Confederate state to pass disfranchisement measures, and the remaining four did so by 1908. And although the coup in Wilmington seemed unparalleled when it occurred, similarly devastating race riots soon followed in New Orleans (1900), Atlanta (1906), and elsewhere. The turn of the century, as Hamilton worried, proved disastrous for black interests in the region.

Contemporary white Southerners who engineered this shift in racial politics thought of it as a permanent solution to the race problem. Among historians, the turn of the twentieth century has earned the reputation as the nadir of American race relations.[5] The rather dramatic and drastic political changes—disfranchisement and segregation—along with a peak in lynching marked the descent into the long night of the Jim Crow era.

Given the devastating events of the late 1890s, one might have expected black Protestants to abandon the thoroughly hopeful eschatology that they had preached since emancipation. Instead their theology endured the onset of the Jim Crow era intact, albeit with some important revisions. Black Protestant leaders' descriptions of the time period seem incongruent with those of historians and contemporary whites. First, black political victories in 1894 and 1896 only strengthened their faith in a better day coming. Until 1898, black leaders in North Carolina could describe the years following emancipation as ones of steady progress. What, though, could sustain their hope given the events of the turn of the century? Previously, black Protestant leaders had celebrated nonpolitical markers of progress, things like church membership, church property, schools, and black land ownership. After 1898, they turned to these markers almost exclusively. Also, black leaders in the state increasingly turned to the narrative of Jesus's crucifixion, more so than at any time since slavery. In Jesus's suffering on the cross, they saw their own suffering at the hands of mobs. The crucifixion provided a powerful way to admit the severity of black Southerners' pain at the close of the century while still expecting a glorious resurrection.

Col. James H. Young, 1899. Young served in North Carolina's Third Volunteer Regiment, the only all-black regiment with an all-black officer corps in the Spanish-American War. Image: "The Military and Historical Portrait Group of the Officers of the Third North Carolina U.S.V. Infantry in the War with Spain" (Asheville, N.C.: Thomas L. Leatherwood, 1899). North Carolina Collection, Wilson Special Collections Library, UNC–Chapel Hill.

Not all black leaders could imagine that resurrection within the United States, and some exiled from North Carolina during white supremacy campaigns chose never to return. Yet, as in earlier setbacks, both those who remained hopeful about the South and those who did not situated their circumstances within a larger story about God's plan for the race. Because black eschatology took the shape of biblical narratives, ministers and other leaders had at their disposal many stories that helped to contextualize their current defeat within a larger story of triumph. Jesus's crucifixion and resurrection was the most vivid story, but not the only one. Some leaders regarded the setbacks as God's chastisement of his beloved people—further proof that God favored African Americans and reserved for them a special role in history. Others couched the political conflict as supernatural warfare between the forces of hell and heaven. Many black ministers and laypeople were deeply troubled by the 1898 election, disfranchisement, and Jim Crow legislation. Those events, as they understood them, constituted an undeniable setback but not an insurmountable one. For most black Protestant leaders in North Carolina, the turn of the twentieth century was no nadir, only a bump—albeit a sizable one—on the road to a great preordained destiny. African American religious responses to the politics of white supremacy clearly show that, in the millennial worldview of black Protestant leaders, the reality of emancipation always overshadowed and outweighed the reality of Jim Crow. At the dawn of the twentieth century, black Southerners remained in the age of emancipation.

Fusion

Peculiar political developments in North Carolina bolstered black Protestants' belief in a better day coming. Populism and strengthened biracialism promised to redistribute political power; the promise of a new political landscape fed millennial hopes and raised prospects for the state's African American population. When neighbors to the south experienced a wave of defeats—beginning with black disfranchisement in Mississippi in 1890 and the separate railcar law in Louisiana the same year—black leaders in North Carolina boasted that their state followed a different path. In 1892, J. C. Price told an audience in New York, "While North Carolina does not profess perfection in this matter [race relations], it is far in advance of many of her sister states in the South."[6] In 1896, the state's Second Congressional District elected George White as the only black member of the U.S. Congress. Throughout most of the 1890s, Price and his colleagues celebrated the absence of Jim Crow laws in North Carolina. At the 1893 annual meeting of the NCBEMC, Dr. J. O. Crosby, the president of Greensboro's A&M College, decried the introduction of Jim Crow cars on railroads in states farther South, and he urged those assembled to make use of the opportunities that their brothers in "the southland" did not have.[7]

Later in the decade, black Protestant leaders in North Carolina continued to compare their state favorably to others. In the summer of 1898, Bishop C. R. Harris of Charlotte, put forth "the absences of jim-crow cars" and the prosperity of black businesses as evidence of the "good feeling which exists between the races in this State." The economic and political climate, Harris argued, "justifies the North Carolina Negro in deeming this the best of all the Southern States, and he sings with gusto, 'Hurrah, Hurrah, for the good old North State forever, / Hurrah, hurrah, for the old North State.'"[8] A year later, Rev. S. N. Nass, the District Secretary for the American Baptist Publication Society, burst with state pride, too: "Our people are a superior people to those you meet in other states—both white and colored."[9] Even as black ministers routinely criticized state leaders for the curtailment of black rights, they continued to extol North Carolina as the most racially progressive state in the South.

The elections of 1894 and 1896 underscored North Carolina's exceptionalism. Across the South and Midwest, the People's Party formed temporary coalitions with the Republican Party to pursue a number of economic and electoral reforms. Nowhere was this two-party coalition more successful than in North Carolina. If the Populists and Republicans ran a joint slate of candidates, the party leaders reasoned, they would have the numerical strength to defeat the incumbent Democrats and to pass legislation favorable to both. It was a strategy, as the *New York Times* labeled it, of "Anything to Get Votes," but it also revealed the similar class interests of white and black farmers and laborers. Fusion, as the two-party coalition became known, was an assault by the working classes and the marginalized upon the Democratic oligarchy.[10]

Some black clergymen, like Walter Pattillo, embraced the strategy wholeheartedly. Pattillo, a prominent Baptist who helped organize the Colored Orphanage in Oxford, celebrated Fusion not only because it offered black North Carolinians a return to political power but also because Populist reforms would benefit black farmers and sharecroppers. In 1890, Pattillo served as the elected state organizer and lecturer for the Colored Farmers' Alliance, and, by the early 1890s, the organization claimed over 55,000 members in North Carolina. In 1891, Pattillo represented the organization at a Confederation of Industrial Organizations convention in Washington, D.C., and, a year later, he attended the St. Louis meeting that organized the People's Party.[11] Pattillo exemplified the close connections between Populists and rural Baptists in the state. The People's Party and Baptist churches drew support from the same populations: rural farmers, black and white.

As recent scholars have noted, they also shared a similar eschatological outlook. One flyer for the People's Party in North Carolina bore the title "Look to Jesus!" Populists in North Carolina, like black Baptists, drew upon a millennial outlook. Speakers decried the nation's decline from the liberty enjoyed in the early Republic to the despotism and oligarchy they observed in the late nineteenth century. Populist organizers foretold God's judgment on the nation for its betrayal of freedom and democracy and saw themselves as prophets like those in the "Good Book," as one leader said, who "warn nations, cities, and individuals of danger to come." They also told of better times to come. An agrarian reformer from Edgecombe County, North Carolina, told his fellow members of the Farmers' Alliance: "Rejoice, ye multitude! . . . . Millennium is coming! Who shall say the Alliance is not a factor to hasten it?" To be sure, Populists' brand of millennialism differed from most black Protestants'. The American Revolution, not emancipation, served as the chronological fulcrum, and the population of the United States, not African Americans, were God's favored people.[12] Still, Populism's apocalyptic warnings and triumphant millennialism sounded quite similar to what black Protestants in the state preached.

At the same time, religious biracialism gave black North Carolinians more cause for optimism. Both Populists and rural Baptists engaged in rather extraordinary biracial cooperation in the 1890s. Baptists linked arms in a biracial Christian education project known as the Plan of Cooperation. In 1894, local black Baptists, Northern whites in the American Baptist Home Missionary Society, and Southern whites in the Southern Baptist Convention drew up a plan for short-term ministerial training institutes all across rural North Carolina.[13] And at the same time, the state's white and black farmers considered a political alliance to address their common economic concerns. There is not enough evidence to argue that one of these rural biracial alliances led to the other. Did the biracial relationships forged in the Plan of Cooperation pave the way for black and white farmers' political cooperation? Figures like Pattillo, who advocated for both black involvement in the Populist Party and black Baptist involvement in the Plan of Cooperation, suggest a strong correlation. In any case, the similarity and concurrence of the two biracial alliances are noteworthy. Certainly, for leaders like Pattillo, they went hand in hand.

Responses from other black clergy, however, were mixed, and many black ministers at first eyed Fusion with suspicion. Rev. George Clinton, editor of the *Star of Zion*, raised a number of concerns. In April 1894 when party officials began discussing the possible coalition, Clinton wrote an editorial arguing against it. He believed that Populists were "as much if not more opposed to giving fair play to the Negro" than were Democrats. According to Clinton, the People's Party attracted "the element of white people which has always been opposed to the progress and best interests of the Negro." His words hinted at a class prejudice against working-class whites, whom he called "special classes and unfit leaders." But he also cited the attempts at Fusion in Alabama as evidence that white Populists seemed unready to extend a friendly hand to black voters. There was nothing in Fusion, Clinton wrote, "that will prove of benefit to the Negro." He also had concerns about the viability of a third party. Only the Republican and Democratic parties had any chance at a working majority, Clinton argued. Third parties in American politics were short-lived, he maintained, and therefore he discouraged African Americans from building a long-term political strategy dependent upon the survival of the Populists. Black Americans, he argued, should not hitch their train to an engine that would soon run out of steam.[14]

Clinton's opposition to Populism also stemmed from his loyalty to the Republican Party. Had God chosen the Republican Party in emancipation only for African Americans to abandon it for new third parties? He was forever devoted to the party of "Lincoln, Sumner, and Grant." Ultimately, he believed that true principles—not coalitions of convenience—would ensure the long-term success of the Republican Party; so he called for a return to the party's "pristine principles." His belief in the effectiveness of "pristine" politics rested upon his belief in an active God that worked in human affairs: "We believe God raised up the men who founded and manned the Republican party for a purpose. If that purpose is carried out, He will see that the party succeeds." For decades, many black leaders had considered the success of emancipation and Reconstruction as proof that God would finish the job of securing black rights. In this viewpoint, there was not a need to change political strategies; Fusion might even be seen as a failure of faith. With God ready to defend the Republican Party, Clinton felt free to let Fusion pass on by.[15]

Ignoring Clinton's advice, North Carolina Republicans embraced Fusion as a promising venture. Republicans and Populists held concurrent conventions in Raleigh during the summer of 1894. Party leaders found a number of shared interests: unseating Democrats, democratizing local and county governments, and enacting electoral reforms, such as color-coded balloting to assist illiterate voters. The parties put forward a single slate of candidates for state offices, mostly white Populists and white Republicans but a number of black Republicans as well. In September, when the parties published the slate, the Fusion ticket met with widespread black support. The editors of the *Star of Zion*, who had opposed the coalition just a few months before, now endorsed the Fusion ticket.[16] Republicans and Populists won a landslide two-thirds majority in the state legislature, with ten black lawmakers earning seats.

The victory emboldened black North Carolinians in ways that resembled emancipation. Among the spoils of the 1894 victory was the power to replace North Carolina's Democratic senators in Washington. "Every Negro in North Carolina," editor Clinton wrote, "ought to rejoice that fouled-mouth, Negro-hating, and foxy Senator Ransom will be among the slain after March." In the 1896 election, the Fusionists increased their majority in the legislature to three-fourths and elected a white Republican as governor. Black North Carolinians struck a triumphant chord. Their union with Populists had succeeded, in numbers greater than anyone expected, in "wrest[ing] the State from the hands of hidebound and one-sided Democracy."[17] It was reminiscent of the biracial politics of Reconstruction, and black North Carolinians seemed as hopeful as they had been a generation earlier. Their political victories and the Fusionist reforms fueled and confirmed black Protestants' expectations of a better day coming. As the *Star of Zion* editor beamed, "The long oppressed and discouraged Negro will now take courage again."[18] Things were looking up.

War with Spain

Even as the nation prepared for war in the spring of 1898, black Protestant leaders foresaw a grand future. With sympathy for the Cubans' bid for independence, African Americans, like most other Americans, greeted President William McKinley's declaration of war against Spain as a cause for celebration. John C. Dancy, a leading state Republican and the editor of the *AME Zion Quarterly Review*, seemed particularly sanguine. "There is a growing opinion that the war with Spain is wiping out race, sectional, and class prejudice all at one time," he wrote in the summer of 1898. Black soldiers' participation in the fight against Spain inspired Dancy: "What wonderful changes. Who would have thought thirty years ago that Negro troops with colored officers would be commanded in a war with a foreign power?" Former Confederate generals served alongside free black regiments, Dancy boasted. "God, indeed, makes the wrath of men to praise Him." The positions of honor that black men held in the war fit well into the narrative of progress and destiny that black Protestants told and retold. Dancy added it to a long list of proofs that a better day indeed lay ahead, that progress was sure: "Publication Houses, successful beneficial associations, cotton factories, building and loan associations, great Church organizations, and regiments of soldiers commanded by our own people—these are some of the beginnings of the future of a recently emancipated race." Dancy and others invested the Spanish-American War with manifold meaning. "Everything is beginning to come our way after thirty years of freedom—even the isles of the sea with their large contingent of colored population."[19] Dancy hoped that good race relations forged in wartime would snuff out the race hatred igniting the Deep South and elsewhere.

If black military service—and the accolades, respect, and citizenship that came with it—tasted sweet, black autonomy in North Carolina's Third Regiment of Volunteers was sweeter. "North Carolina again leads," Dancy declared.[20] The Third Regiment, unlike all other black volunteer regiments in 1898, marched with a full slate of black officers. North Carolina black volunteers, perhaps emboldened by recent political events, refused to field a regiment with white officers. Their mantra—"No officers, no fight!"—along with the newly elected Republican governor's support ensured "a full quota of officers—all Negroes."[21] N. N. Bruce, a Baptist leader, soldier, and instructor at Shaw University, wrote a letter to the Raleigh *News and Observer* shortly before the Third Regiment had been formed, explaining the significance of the regiment, and expressing hope that black military service would translate into equal citizenship rights. "Nobody seriously suggests any want of patriotism, courage, intelligence or boldness on the part of the black soldier boys," he wrote. "It seems to be a settled truth that these can fight and fight well and long and hard."[22] For black Protestant leaders like Dancy, the regiment communicated a message: that black men took a complete and equal share in the body politic. Dancy wrote, "The State has three regiments and our race has one of these. This gives us our precise quota according to our population. No other State in the Union can say as much. North Carolina really leads—the other States simply follow." A precise quota meant full representation in the state, further evidence that in North Carolina black men had the power their numbers afforded them.[23] Democrats, in contrast, pointed to the regiment as proof that Republicans, despite substantial evidence to the contrary, were hell-bent on "Negro domination," an allegation they would wield in upcoming elections. Ultimately, the regiment, which never saw conflict, held more importance for state politics than for the war effort.

For Bruce, the war was an instrument to usher in a new era of peace, justice, and egalitarianism. Bruce wrote, "The war was begun for Justice to Humanity—Justice at home as well as abroad, and if this is true, it will not end until any and every color of American man will be gladly welcomed into the trenches alongside of the other boys to fight for Christ's peace and justice on earth."[24] The war with Spain fit into a larger narrative about the coming of "Christ's peace and justice" and racial harmony.

AME Zion minister Rev. L. S. Slaughter discerned spiritual parallels between the war with Spain and the Civil War. His retelling of the Civil War followed literary conventions of Old Testament histories. It read like a page from Genesis or the First Book of Kings: "The South said, 'We will secede and set up a kingdom of our own and have for our king Jeff. Davis.'" The point of his retelling was to show how God used human actors, like Lincoln and Davis, who unwittingly accomplished God's purpose in emancipation. Slaughter allegorized, "Here we have in those two men a Moses and a Pharaoh—one to lead and the other to drive, and God the great General to command." He hoped that the Spanish American War would likewise accomplish divine purposes even as the nations involved pursued their own interests. If good were to come from the war of 1898, he believed it would have to come from "the Lord who will see that justice is done."[25]

But Slaughter worried that the current war would parallel the Civil War in less desirable ways. "After the [Civil] war," he recalled, "the Negro," despite his exemplary military service, "was treated by the Government as a poor man treats his horse after a hard day's work—turned out to graze on a dry pasture." He worried that the same mistreatment might follow the present war and noted that "nearly as many Negroes ... have died by lynching since the close of the war as died in the war." He remained mystified why the United States would go to war to protect and liberate Cubans while refusing to offer the same protections to its own citizens. "Our patriotism is being chilled because our willingness to help to defend the flag is not appreciated." The war, according to Slaughter, had not accomplished what Dancy and Bruce had hoped. In fact, the war heightened racial tensions and intensified calls for white supremacy.[26]

As the war came to an end, many black Americans agreed with Slaughter's assessment. As historian Willard Gatewood has argued, African Americans reevaluated their enthusiasm for the war when the expected blessings failed to materialize. The accolades black soldiers received for their service in Cuba and elsewhere "proved both brief and illusory." As Gatewood explained, the sectional unity that black leaders like Dancy expected "actually meant northern acquiescence in the 'southern solution' to the Negro Problem." The black volunteer regiments frightened whites, and, as Gatewood argued, "the reward for the Negro's demonstration of patriotism and valor was a tightening of racial lines." Perhaps the most frightening development of all to the black leaders who heralded the war was the nation's new imperialist ideology—the white man's burden—that taught white men to exercise control and care over dependent and inferior people of color. The employment of white supremacy abroad only strengthened campaigns for white supremacy at home.[27] This foreign and domestic nexus of white supremacy

certainly played out in North Carolina. While members of the North Carolina Third Regiment of Volunteers wrote letters to the Army lamenting their
poor treatment in the garrison, their family members wrote them complain-
ing of racial violence at home.[28] It would test their theology more than any
event since emancipation.

The 1898 Campaign and the Wilmington Massacre

Frustrated by their defeats in 1894 and 1896, leading Democrats launched a
fierce race-baiting campaign in the summer and fall of 1898. With the major
newspapers and printing presses in their control, Democratic leaders like
Josephus Daniels, editor and owner of the Raleigh *News & Observer*, were
well positioned to spread their message. The message was three-pronged.
First, Democrats tried to convince Populists that Republicans were exploit-
ing them for their votes without showing due concern for their interests. At
times they argued the opposite, that Populists exploited white Republicans.
Second, Democratic leaders trumpeted evidence of corruption and ineptitude
within the Fusionist government. The third prong, the threat of "Negro
domination," was their sharpest. By focusing on race, Democrats aimed for
Fusion's Achilles' heel. In rallies, stump speeches, editorials, and vivid political cartoons, Democrats alleged that a vote for Fusion was a vote for "Negro
domination." The cartoons portrayed the relatively small number of black
officeholders as ubiquitous and powerful. Often, Democratic newspapers
argued, black men served as supervisors for white men, thus inverting the
racial order. And, most alarmingly, the papers warned shrilly, "Negro domination" put white women under the power of black men. The leaders of the
race-baiting campaign consciously exaggerated the prevalence and power of
black officeholders to stir up fear among white voters. Their alarmist messages about "Negro domination" were carefully coded to raise the fear of
black male sexual access to white women.[29]

The campaign put black church leaders on edge. The NCBEMC met in
Rocky Mount, North Carolina, in October 1898. At the meeting, ministers
expressed concern that the intense race-baiting campaign would lead to violence against blacks. "The people of North Carolina are going through a
heated and most bitter political campaign, and the prejudice between the
races is being greatly excited," one committee explained. The ministers blamed
the "politicians and partisan newspapers" for "daily aggravating the passions

of the people by inflammatory remarks and utterances, menacing the peace and welfare of our commonwealth." The Baptist leaders' acute concern was the prospect of violence, and they asked God to "control the passions of the people for the general good of our citizenship." Considering the racial tensions in the state, they believed that any perceived transgression by African Americans would provoke a disproportionate backlash from whites. They therefore urged members of their own denomination to "restrain themselves from excessive anger, and avoid provoking race conflict."[30] In a short period of time, the political climate had turned hostile.

According to the editor of the *Star of Zion*, the level of racial tension in the state was unprecedented. "There have been many hot and bitter campaigns in old North Carolina, but the one now raging is the bitterest known in the history of the State," J. W. Smith wrote in October. The whole affair—race-baiting and intimidation used to fracture a biracial alliance—unsurprisingly, reminded Smith of Reconstruction: "The blaze of hatred and persecution of reconstruction days has been re-lighted and is now burning with deeply intense fury against the Negro." The Democrats' strategy to equate Fusion with "Negro rule" was a "scare-crow, a false alarm," shouted only for political gain. Black political hegemony was no threat, Smith explained, "while there are three white men in North Carolina to one black man."[31]

Smith feared that a cheap political trick—the "cry of 'nigger domination,' the last and only trump card"—would continue to haunt the state's black communities for some time. Democratic leaders, Smith believed, were short-sighted, focused only on winning the elections in November, but their tactics threatened to permanently increase racial hostilities in the state. Like his Baptist colleagues, Smith feared violence. He tried to impress upon his out-of-state readers the danger that black North Carolinians faced. The state's Democratic leaders, Smith reported, were listening to Benjamin Tillman, South Carolina's strident white supremacist senator, who advised them to "carry the State . . . with shot guns." Black South Carolinians had suffered their own disfranchisement three years earlier, also in a conflict between white farmers and elites. Smith urged caution: "Let the white and black voters keep cool now and say and do nothing rash. Let the Negro go quietly to the polls and vote against every man that coughs up the race issue." Even beyond the risk of immediate violence, Smith saw disastrous consequences: "The day is coming when the Democrats in all the Southern States will attempt to disfranchise the Negro." It had already happened in six states.[32]

Smith still believed that God had good things in store for African Americans. Nevertheless, because black North Carolinians were contending with a "diabolical campaign" led by "fallen angels [trying] to regain the Paradise which their folly excluded them," they needed to prepare for a supernatural conflict.[33] It was the same theological move made by James Harris when Democrats violently overthrew Reconstruction nearly thirty years earlier. To call Democrats demons was to affirm their evil and the danger but also to highlight their futility. In the end, God always wins.[34]

Aided by voter intimidation and ballot box stuffing, the Democrats won at the polls on November 8. In the run-up to the election, black and white Republicans experienced violence designed to keep them from voting. The night before the election, Alfred Waddell, a leading white supremacist in Wilmington, instructed his supporters, "If you find the Negro out voting, tell him to leave the polls, and if he refuses, kill him, shoot him down in his tracks. We shall win tomorrow if we have to do it with guns."[35] The violence and intimidation worked to keep many black voters at home. An organization of African American women in Wilmington encouraged black men to brave the streets in order to cast ballots. The Organization of Colored Ladies wanted to remind black men that the fight was supernatural, between God and "the demons who are now seeking to take away the most sacred rights vouchsafed to any people." For them, "trusting in God to restore order" involved marching down to the precinct poll and casting a vote for the Republican Party.[36] Despite the women's impassioned plea, many black voters stayed home on Election Day. The Democratic Party regained a majority in the state legislature and recaptured most local and county governments.[37]

Two days after the election, the threats of violence erupted in Wilmington, the state's most populous city, and black churches found themselves in the center of the state's worst race riot. The most divisive issue involved Alexander Manly's editorial in the Wilmington *Daily Record*, the only black daily in the South. In the article, Manly criticized Rebecca Latimer Felton, a white Georgia woman who advocated the lynching of black men—"a thousand times a week if necessary"—to protect white women from rape. Manly argued that if the accusations of rape were accurate, "her plea would be worthy of consideration," but he countered that liaisons between white women and black men were often consensual. When white newspapers reprinted the editorial, white residents of Wilmington clamored for the destruction of the *Record*'s printing press and for Manly's exile.[38]

Rev. J. Allen Kirk, the pastor of Wilmington's Central Baptist Church, first entered the Manly editorial fray when businesses pulled advertisements from the *Daily Record*. He and the other black ministers in town, afraid that the *Record* might fold, called upon their congregants to subscribe. They wanted to back the only black daily newspaper in the South without endorsing Manly's inflammatory editorial.[39] The distinction was lost on Wilmington's white residents, who soon identified black churches with Manly's "Infamous Attack on White Women."[40] Some local whites threatened to exile the members of the Interdenominational Ministerial Union. In fact, rumors spread through the city that black churches were organizing the black community for a violent backlash. Some white newspapers reported that black leaders were using churches "to deliver incendiary speeches and impassioned appeals to blacks to use the bullet" and to encourage church members to torch whites' crops and property.[41] Black ministers, despite attempts to distance themselves from Manly, found themselves in the middle of a tense and dangerous situation.[42]

On Thursday, November 10, an armed white mob burned the *Record* office and then descended upon black neighborhoods, searching out specific men. Believing churches to be the black community's ammunition warehouses, the mobs ransacked the buildings in a fruitless search for weapons. Rev. Kirk and his family, along with many others, fled into the swamps outside of town. Armed men forced the white Republican mayor and the city aldermen onboard trains out of town. At the end of the day, at least a dozen African Americans lay dead, hundreds more were in exile, and martial law replaced the elected government. It was the first and only coup d'état in the United States.[43]

Events in Wilmington produced grief and horror in black religious communities across the country. Editors at the *Christian Recorder* called the bloody massacre a "hell-born conspiracy," and mourned the death of "a score or so of sable-hued human victims."[44] The paper displayed a picture of white mobs in front of Manly's burnt office and asked readers to "let your hearts go out in sympathy to the people affected."[45] Many in the black community hoped that President McKinley would condemn the lawlessness when he addressed Congress in December of 1898. His failure to mention the massacre dismayed black religious leaders. AME bishop Wesley Gaines told *Atlanta Constitution* readers that, because of the Wilmington massacre and the subsequent inaction by the federal government, he was "beginning to despair of race harmony in this country."[46] AME Zion bishop Alexander

Walters considered "the outlook... gloomy" because no governmental body stood ready to protect African Americans from the strong-arming of white supremacists. "The city officials of Wilmington, N.C., were the leaders of the mob that ruthlessly murdered more than a dozen Afro-Americans on the 10th of last November," he explained, and the state officials and federal government answered black appeals for justice and protection with silence. All levels of government, Walter lamented, "abandoned us to our fate."[47] It was a time for mourning.

Indeed, a spirit of mourning prevailed at the North Carolina Conference of the AME Zion Church when it met in Washington, North Carolina, one month after the 1898 election and the Wilmington massacre. The ministers and lay delegates sang the hymn "And Are We Yet Alive?" with gusto, because it captured their mixture of pain and hope. An observer noted that "the members of the Wilmington District seemed to lay especial emphasis upon it in their singing":

> And are we yet alive,
> And see each other's face?
> Glory and thanks to Jesus give
> For His almighty grace!
> What troubles have we seen,
> What mighty conflicts past,
> Fightings without, and fears within,
> Since we assembled last!

Dancy, a mainstay at the conference, was in temporary exile, as were other delegates who had escaped Wilmington. One church reported the loss of two hundred members. The delegates dispensed with a committee on the State of the Country, presumably because no one had enough distance to objectively evaluate their circumstances. When they adjourned, the conference delegates scheduled the next annual meeting for Kinston and prayed that "no occasion will call forth the singing of the song, 'And are we yet alive?'"[48] The same month, Bishop Hood opened the denomination's Central North Carolina Conference in Carthage, North Carolina, with similar solemnity. Recent events, he said, "have brought sadness, sorrow, and gloom to many hearts."[49] The church sustained substantial personal and financial losses.

At the 1899 NCBEMC in Newbern, black Baptist leaders, too, tallied their losses. There present was Dr. Charles Meserve, a Massachusetts-born

John C. Dancy, 1908. Dancy, the editor of the *AME Zion Quarterly* and the collector of customs for the port of Wilmington, was among those exiled by the 1898 coup d'etat. Image: J. W. Hood, *One Hundred Years of the African Methodist Episcopal Zion Church* (New York: A.M.E. Zion Book Concern, 1895). North Carolina Collection, Wilson Special Collections Library, UNC–Chapel Hill.

white missionary who closely identified with black Baptists when he moved to Raleigh to serve as Shaw University president. He made a sober assessment: "We live under different conditions than we did a year ago." J. A. Whitted said, "I need hardly call your attention to the fall elections of '98, and the bitterness resulting therefrom." He told those present at the meeting in New Bern, "You are yourselves aware that business enterprises and work of all kinds were obstructed and necessarily hindered." Those in gospel ministry, Whitted explained, had suffered just the same. Churches struggled to rebuild and reorganize in the wake of 1898. Whitted confessed, "At one time the obstructions were so great, and the discouragements so numerous we feared lest we would have to give up in hopeless despair." Somehow, the work of planting and building black churches continued, but the losses were great.

As Bishop Hood expected, the political changes brought by the white supremacy campaign did not end in 1898. Hood told the annual Central North Carolina Conference, "I do not know to what extent we shall enjoy the right of the elective franchise hereafter."[50] Democrats had promised that if they won the election in 1898, they would not seek the disfranchisement of black voters. Rev. George Clinton stood ready to "give them the credit of sincerity,"[51] but Hood and others put little faith in the Democrats' promise. As early as January 1899, black North Carolinians braced themselves for a wave of anti-black legislation. J. W. Smith expected the following: "Jim

Crow cars, disfranchis[ement], the withdrawal of taxes paid by the whites to help support the colored public schools, etc."[52] The legislature mandated racial segregation on railways in 1899; and as Hood and Smith predicted, the new legislature put before the people a constitutional amendment in August 1900 designed to take the ballot away from black men. Those who would have opposed such an amendment were so badly bruised by the 1898 election that they hardly made a showing in the 1900 election. The party of white supremacy easily won reelection, including the governorship, George White's Congressional seat, and the disfranchisement amendment needed to cement their hold on power.[53]

Black ministers received this news with horror but not shock. They had seen it coming. What did shock them, however, was the lack of support they received from the state's white Republicans. Dancy wrote that the entire "colored race in North Carolina" waited for white Republican leaders, for whom black voters had risked life and limb at the polls, to oppose the measure. When they failed to do so, Dancy complained: "our supposed friends have deserted us, wronged us and forsaken us."[54] The theme of abandonment recurred throughout black religious responses to the white supremacy campaigns. Bishop J. B. Small, an Afro-Caribbean minister in the AME Zion Church who spent much of his ministry in North Carolina, wrote, "God has left us in the hands of our enemies, and they maltreat us without mercy, while all seem to look on approvingly—none even advise to the contrary. A terrible plight!"[55] The theme of abandonment by God would have reminded black congregations of Psalm 22 or Isaiah 53, passages about the brutal treatment of God's faithful servant. Christians associated both passages with God's abandonment of Christ as he suffered on the cross. Within two years' time, black Protestants watched North Carolina transform from a relatively racially progressive state, without de jure segregation and with significant black political influence, to a white supremacist state willing to enforce segregation and black disfranchisement with violence. It was a terrible plight indeed.

Interpreting Jim Crow Politics

Black Protestants in North Carolina saw the events of 1898–1900 as significant and tragic. But it is possible to overstate the impact of these events on their outlook. Glenda Gilmore poetically described black North Carolinians after 1898 as "searching . . . for a place to stand after the earth and sky fell away."[56] In one way, Gilmore's picture captures the grief and bewilderment that many felt in the wake of the white supremacy campaigns. But in another way, the image conjures up something much more dismal and cataclysmic than appears in contemporary black religious writings. In response to the grim new political climate, black Protestant leaders searched out new political strategies. And although their theology looked different as well, much of their eschatology survived the events of 1898–1900 intact. They wrote their experiences of Jim Crow politics into biblical narratives, and reiterated their unwavering belief in their status as God's favored people and their hope in a better day coming. The persistence of this eschatological hope shaped the way black North Carolinians viewed the events of 1898–1900 and the way they responded to the new political climate. For them, the devastating events comprised a short episode in a God-ordained drama in which emancipation—not Jim Crow—remained at center stage.

African American church leaders interpreted the arrival of Jim Crow politics in several different ways. After initial expressions of lament and despair, many quickly looked for God's hand in the events. Bishops Hood, Clinton, and Small, among others, reckoned the events of 1898–1900 as God's chastisement of a beloved and favorite people. Hood told the Central North Carolina Conference in early December 1898 that African Americans had committed "two very great blunders" that incurred the "curse of God." The first, he explained, was the failure to support the statewide prohibition measure in 1881. The second occurred when black Republicans allied with white Republicans and Populists in Fusion. The alliance, Hood admitted, brought political advantages, but it also compromised black Republicans' integrity. "To my mind, there is not a plank in the Populist national platform to which an honest Republican can subscribe," he told the conference. Fusion cast further shadows upon the black community, Hood continued, because the sudden success enticed self-seeking, unscrupulous, and unqualified men into office. The follies of Fusion, which Hood named by category and not by incident, returned to haunt African Americans in the most recent election. According to Hood, God meant for black Southerners to learn a lesson from the election of 1898: "to have more religion in our politics." His phrase— "more religion in our politics"—meant higher moral standards for office-seekers and a return to the principles of the Republican Party during the days of emancipation and Reconstruction.[57]

When Hood's address hit the press, it provoked a chilly response from Christopher J. Perry, the editor of the *Philadelphia Tribune*, a fifteen-year-old African American weekly. Perry chided Hood for his failure to condemn the white supremacist attack. In the editor's opinion, Hood had mild words for the murderous mob but harsh words for the black victims. In his response, Hood assured the editor he strictly condemned the lawlessness that accompanied the 1898 election. If his words of condemnation were mild, well, Hood argued, it was because he was a mild man: "If any expect me to rant and rage and curse and rip, they are mistaken in the man." But Hood went further in his defense. The *Tribune* editor, comfortably situated in his office north of the Mason-Dixon Line, had little perspective from which to criticize Hood, who had "been down here for many years." In general, black leaders in the South, in contrast to their Northern counterparts, responded to the politics of white supremacy with more caution than outrage. Hood boasted of his success in and knowledge of the South. After thirty-five years in North Carolina, Hood felt confident in his own judgment. "I have faith in ultimate success on the line on which I believe I am directed by the Holy Spirit. For me to turn back while thus convinced would be a sin as great as that of Lot's wife." His experience and his religious convictions told him to stay the course.[58]

Ultimately, however, Hood gauged his differences with Perry to be more theological than regional. Hood considered Perry one of "many of our leaders" who "trust too much in the arm of the flesh." In Hood's assessment, Perry saw only the material and temporal realities of the situation. Hood, in contrast, paid attention to the supernatural realities behind worldly events. His commentary on the Wilmington massacre went deeper than condemning the bloodshed and lawlessness, censures he thought went without saying. In the address before the Central North Carolina Conference, Hood did what he thought ministers were supposed to do: explain the supernatural significance of earthly affairs.[59]

Likewise, Bishop C. R. Harris, Hood's colleague, saw divine lessons in the defeat of 1898. "The Negro has been departing from God," he wrote, "now God has departed from the Negro." Harris listed numerous biblical precedents—the lamenting, God-forsaken Psalmist; the wayward, idolatrous people of Israel; the prophet Jeremiah—to demonstrate that God chastises those who stray from the right path. Like Hood, Harris lamented that the Republican Party had lost its way and hoped that it would become a "Moral Reform Party." He, too, made reference to the failed prohibition referendum of 1881. Harris denounced the corruption that ruled politics, and took the fact that "the preacher as a potent factor in politics is unknown" as evidence that indeed the Republican Party was in moral decline. But by Harris's reckoning, God's lesson was not "more religion in our politics," as Hood believed, but rather that loyalty to the Republican Party had outstripped the race's loyalty to God. And God, in his jealousy, destroyed the race's idol.[60]

Bishop J. B. Small saw a consensus emerging in the pews and pulpits of churches across the country. For most black Protestants, Small maintained, it was not hard to see "the pointings of the finger of Providence." In the "severe suffering of the colored people of . . . North and South Carolina," he wrote in an 1899 editorial, there was a clear rebuke from God. He reminded readers of the reciprocal relationship between God and the Old Testament Israelites. As long as the Israelites remained in God's service, God prospered their work, but when they strayed from God's commands, they fell into the hands of their enemies. God sent suffering to the Israelites to chastise them, so they might return to faithfulness and righteousness. African Americans' defeat in 1898, Small reasoned, had the same divine purpose.[61]

God had abandoned black Americans, Small argued, precisely because he cared about their future. "The colored people of this country have a special mission to fulfill, and God will have them perform the intention of His Providence, if it must be done through suffering." According to Small, African Americans shared several similarities with Old Testament Israelites: a deep devotion and piety, a proclivity for sin, and a divine mission that conferred with it the moniker of "God's own people." To rein in their proclivity for sin and to prepare them for their mission, God rebuked black Americans just as he did ancient Israelites. In Small's view, God willed President McKinley to remain silent about the Wilmington massacre "to teach us . . . there is no true friend save God." He continued, "What we really need is to serve God with an honest heart and true intent, work to our own interest and let parties go to the bats." No doubt Perry would have accused Small of blaming the victims and retreating from politics. However, Small did not advocate an absence from politics. Rather, like Harris, Small interpreted the crushing defeat of 1898, along with betrayals from white Republicans, as God's way of directing African Americans away from partisanship.[62]

In 1900, John Dancy, too, interpreted North Carolina's disfranchisement measure as God's chastisement. In his view, evidence of chastisement was cause for rejoicing. Dancy passionately defended black voting rights, but if disfranchisement were chastisement from God, then it conferred God's favor. "Whom the Lord loveth He chasteneth," he quoted from the letter to the Hebrews. "How do we know that the very fact of our recent chastenings is not proof conclusive that the Lord loveth us far beyond our knowledge or even belief," Dancy asked.[63] To interpret disfranchisement as God's chastisement was not to condone the work of white supremacists, nor was it an expression of self-loathing. Rather, the interpretation reaffirmed African Americans' identity as God's beloved people. By seeing God as the principal actor, black Protestants could belittle the power of white supremacists, who could only do as much damage as God would permit. Perhaps most important, the interpretation placed black people at the center of the action, precisely when whites had been, at first glance, so successful at marginalizing them.

Even those who shied away from naming specific sins of the black community that occasioned God's rebuke nevertheless saw divine purpose in the community's suffering. Suffering, in their view, was redemptive. So, even among black Protestants' frank assessments of the new circumstances, there remained a chorus of optimistic voices. Meserve told his fellow Baptists in 1897, "The colored race is getting more out of adversity than any other race ever did."[64] Two years later, Meserve reiterated his message: "I am not in favor of persecution, but let us remember that God has some purpose even in persecution. I believe in the purposes of God. He can and will, sooner or later, make the wrath of man praise him." Meserve opposed disfranchisement, but said, "Some fear that they can never vote again; some good may come out of this."[65] Some black listeners may have struggled to speak as optimistically as Meserve, a sympathetic white, did. But the final 1900 issue of the *AME Zion Quarterly* opened with a string of similarly upbeat messages: "No blow struck the Negro race is of sufficient force to incapacitate him for further effort. Indeed the race that strikes us suffers more from the effect of the reaction than we do from the blow itself. Continue the upward stride."[66] The *Quarterly* offered the same insight four years later: "It is remarkable that every move against the Negro helps him. He is used to overcoming great obstacles."[67] Having weathered the events of 1898–1900, black Southerners in North Carolina and elsewhere stood stronger and tougher, waiting for God to work good out of their ill.

African Americans in North Carolina concentrated on other markers of progress as evidence that God indeed was doing good things among them. They remarked on advances in denominational publishing houses, missionary and youth activities, women's auxiliary membership, literacy rates, modern architecture of church buildings, and the number of clergy with seminary education. The month after the 1898 election, Warren C.

Coleman, a wealthy black Methodist layman, opened the Coleman Cotton Mill outside Concord, North Carolina. The black-owned and black-run mill made headlines. The editor of the *Christian Recorder* thought it difficult to overestimate the mill's significance: "Now that the factory has actually started, the race has more in its turning spindles, its flying shuttles, its marketable fabrics, to enlist its interest and furnish far-reaching object lesson than all the industrial education theories proposed by friends, or all the political troubles precipitated by foes." The textile factory stood as brick-and-mortar proof of "Negro possibilities and prospects in the Southland." Coming as it did on the heels of the Wilmington massacre, the Concord mill offered a reassuring contrast. The *Christian Recorder* cited the mill as evidence of the "folly of looking to politics." Entrepreneurial success was the real benchmark of black progress.[68]

So, too, was church growth. In the first decade of the twentieth century, revivals and church planting continued to grow black Baptist and Methodist churches. Even during the heat of the white supremacy campaign in North Carolina, Rev. W. M. Anderson was more concerned with the revival in his small mountain town. "The Lord has blessed us with a glorious revival throughout our work this year," he reported, "and many souls have been happily converted and Zion's borders enlarged."[69] J. A Whitted took time to reflect at the 1908 NCBEMC. He marveled at how quickly the conference had grown to represent 180,000 church members. And he noted, "It is a proud day when [the Baptist] women alone in a single Annual Convention can report eleven hundred and forty dollars in cold cash." The maturity and wealth of black church institutions—such as twenty-two schools, and the oldest, Shaw University, approaching forty-four years—gave Whitted cause to proclaim a steady progress since emancipation.[70]

In 1899, Baptist delegates to the annual convention in Newbern heard some unusual advice from Meserve: "Get homes; get farms; put one or two rooms to your house; get a bigger mule for your farm." Delegates may have chafed at a transplanted white man advising them to do what they had striven to do for decades, but Meserve turned to the subject of farms and mules to move his listeners beyond the political defeats of 1898.[71] African Americans in North Carolina, since emancipation, had focused their energy on land ownership; it remained the unfulfilled promise of Jubilee. But as black political fortunes plummeted, African Americans increasingly looked to black land ownership for a rosier picture of black life in North Carolina. In 1910, black-owned land in the United States topped fifteen million acres, a high-water mark from which black land ownership rates subsequently declined. North Carolina figures tell a similar story. The number of black-owned farms in the state steadily increased from emancipation to 1910.[72] So, in the first decade of the twentieth century, black Southerners had cause to be optimistic, if their eyes fixed upon economics instead of politics. George Clinton told as much to Northern audiences: "All over the South, wealth, education, and general progress can be noted. The South is the battleground where the Negro is destined to reach the highest plane of progress."[73]

Black Protestant leaders seemed rather deliberate in their search to find only evidence of progress in black life at the turn of the century. One minister wrote in 1904, "We must not be discouraged. To do that is [to] half surrender the fight. Let us see nothing but victory despite all the clouds and difficulties."[74] Black Protestant leaders evaluated their circumstances as part of both human history and divine history. For them, the greater reality was divine history. So, many were unashamed to seek out only evidence from human history that aligned with their understanding of divine history. If God had ordained victory for the race, then they need only look for affirmations of that fact. Accordingly, they saw victory in black land ownership, church growth, and the development of black institutions.

African American church leaders' most hopeful interpretations of Jim Crow politics, however, focused on the past, not the present or the future. Black eschatology had always been as much a reading of history as a prediction of days to come. Black ministers reminded their followers of a sacred history and urged them to place the events of 1898–1900 within that context. In order to cast segregation or disfranchisement as temporary setbacks, black ministers weighed them against the black experience before emancipation. After the Wilmington massacre, Bishop Alexander Walters had to overcome his melancholy: "we have seen gloomier times than the present." He recalled the fugitive slave law that passed Congress shortly before emancipation, a measure surely more devastating to African Americans than the disfranchisement measures before them at present. "And we were brought triumphantly through by the God of battles."[75] Devastating setbacks sometimes preceded monumental victories. If any found the news of the day depressing, they could turn to the lessons of history for reassurances that God was on their side.

Meserve made those lessons explicit. "Count your blessings," he said, "review your history." To encourage fellow Baptists, he offered an impromptu catechism: "What were your darkest days? The days of the African slave stealer."[76] Their darkest days had passed. Emancipation had inaugurated a new era. In light of the larger historical narrative of slavery to freedom, a narrative presided over by "the God of battles," surely the election of 1898 and the curtailment of black freedoms thereafter seemed a rather small setback. The bigger story was freedom—not white supremacy. It was still the age of emancipation.

To situate Jim Crow politics into that broader story of freedom, black Protestants turned to another biblical narrative, the crucifixion. African American leaders in North Carolina revisited the central Christian story— that of Jesus's death and resurrection—as evidence that God redeems suffering for a greater good and frustrates the plans of evildoers. According to R. A. Williams, a missionary from the Woman's Baptist State Convention, black North Carolinians were living through the sufferings of Christ. African American men and women lived "through the 22nd Psalm," she said. Christians understood the psalm, written several hundred years prior to Jesus's birth, as a foreshadowing of his crucifixion. In the gospel accounts, Jesus himself quoted the psalm from the cross: "My God, my God, why hast thou forsaken me?" Williams's use of the psalm would have prompted her audience to think of the crucifixion, to see themselves in that story, and to echo Jesus's sense of abandonment by God.[77]

Williams, like the psalmist, found hope amid the suffering. The psalmist, after initially accusing God of abandoning him in his suffering, turns near the end of the song to praising God, who "has listened to [his] cry for help." Williams told her audience that "we need to learn the lesson of Christian progress." Before redemption comes suffering. Before the resurrection comes the crucifixion. In their suffering, Williams argued, black believers saw glimpses of redemption. She explained, "We are moving into the 23rd Psalm," a psalm that describes God as a good shepherd taking care of his flock. "In fact," she concluded, "we are being invited to sit down at the table prepared by our enemies. God be praised." As Williams quoted the psalm, she rewrote it. Where the psalmist described a table "in the presence of mine enemies," she spoke of a table "prepared by our enemies." In doing so, Williams claimed that God's provision for the race would come not only in spite of white supremacist campaigns but through them. Her rewording of the psalm strengthened the connection she made between the psalms and Jesus's death. In the crucifixion narrative, Jesus's enemies were defeated at precisely the moment when they assumed they had won. By killing Jesus, the authorities had set the stage for his resurrection and triumph. The lesson of the crucifixion—and that of the psalms that prefigured it—was to wait for the resurrection.[78]

Around the turn of the century, a number of African American writers identified Jesus's crucifixion with black suffering. One newspaper editor wrote that if "[Christ] were living in Kentucky to-day, [he] would be cooped up in the 'Jim Crow' cars."[79] Theologians searched scriptures to find Jesus's African ancestry. Willard Hunter published *Jesus Christ Had Negro Blood in His Veins* (1901) and argued that "if He was living in the United States of America to-day He would be called a negro." Scholars often trace claims that Jesus was black to radical black theologians of the late 1960s and 1970s or to Countee Cullen's famous 1929 poem "Black Christ," but, as Paul Harvey has argued, the claims go much further back.[80] W. E. B. Du Bois explained where the black identification with a crucified Jesus came from: "Jesus Christ was a laborer and black men are laborers; He was poor and we are poor; He was despised of his fellow men and we are despised; He was persecuted and crucified, and we are mobbed and lynched." When in 1906 Atlanta experienced a race riot deadlier than Wilmington's, Du Bois connected black Americans' suffering with Christ on the cross in a published litany of prayers, asking why God had abandoned them. Why had God allowed "the innocent be crucified for the guilt of the untouched guilty?" He prayed, "Let the cup pass from us," as Jesus had done on the night of his betrayal. Even as Du Bois railed against God, he also discerned a better end to the story, when God would right the injustices of the world. Still, in the wake of the riot, Du Bois resisted a happy and hopeful Easter story. The tone of the litany remained one of pain, betrayal, and anger.[81]

Bishop George Clinton made a similar point but much more triumphantly at the 1904 Emancipation Day celebration in Charlotte. Before addressing black suffering under Jim Crow, Clinton placed emancipation in a broader context. He ranked emancipation among the four greatest milestones in human history and compared it to the Jewish Year of Jubilee. Clinton contrasted the historical significance of emancipation with the fleeting "anti-Negro spirit of the times." Even though Jim Crow deserved less attention than did emancipation, the current persecution of African Americans demanded some sort of interpretation. Clinton thought it fitting to parallel whites' attempt to "keep the Negro . . . in 'his place'" with the crucifixion of Christ. In Clinton's retelling, Jesus's enemies doubted his ability to rise from the dead, in much the same way that white supremacists spoke of "Negro inferiority and incapacity." The enemies not only doubted but also attacked, as if they did not trust their own rejection of Jesus's claim. Again, it paralleled black experience in Jim Crow. All the effort whites expended to keep African Americans "in their place" only showed that African Americans did not fit very well in that place. And white supremacists' attempt to suppress black Americans, Clinton argued, would work as well as Jesus's enemies' effort "to keep the Nazarene from rising."[82]

As Clinton told it, Jesus's triumph over the grave gave hope that African Americans too would experience a resurrection. The resurrection in Clinton's retelling frustrated God's enemies and all the plans they had concocted. Clinton told the crowd assembled before him at Grace AME Zion Church in Charlotte to wait for their own political resurrection. Those "who made all sorts of declarations against the Negro, especially against his success," like those who sought Jesus's death "may have a like disappointment." According to Clinton, the enemies of God and of the race may win the battle, but they would lose the war.[83]

The battle waged by white supremacists at the turn of the century, black ministers attested, had been devastating to African American communities. But by placing the battle in a larger historical context, one where emancipation loomed large, black Protestant leaders downplayed the long term significance of their political defeat. And by writing their suffering and defeat into biblical narratives such as the crucifixion—ones where, in the words of Dancy, "the density of this darkness only foreshadows the brightness of the approaching dawn"[84]—they found hope in their eschatological destiny.

Two scenes from the streets of Wilmington stand in stark contrast. The first, from February 1865, features black soldiers marching triumphantly through the city. As they took control of Wilmington, they set slaves free and sent remaining white Confederates fleeing. Thirty-three years later, in November 1898, armed white men marched Wilmington's streets. As they took control of the city, black residents fled for safety out of town. In the first scene, the marching troops symbolized for black residents the triumph of emancipation. In the latter scene, the troops represented the forces of white supremacy and the limits of black freedom. Taken together, these two scenes illustrate a narrative of decline for black interests in the state. But black Protestant leaders nearly uniformly resisted that kind of narrative. Their theology allowed them to fit these two scenes into a very different narrative, one of hope and purpose, orchestrated by a God active in human affairs. One *Star of Zion* editorialist confided in 1898, "I have unalterable and abiding faith in my race—the Negro race—and I am not yet prepared to denounce it or renounce it. In all human history it is families, nations, races, to whom Almighty God has given mission, and as a race we have a mission."[85] The triumph of white supremacy at the turn of the twentieth century did little to mitigate the sense of purpose and the eschatological hope that black Protestants had expressed since the Civil War. They narrated their own story with an arc that used emancipation as the anchor, or starting point, and ended with a world transformed by justice. Even those pro-emigration black Protestants who despaired of progress in the South and left the region in large numbers (as seen in chapter 3) did so because they remained hopeful that the race had a bright destiny, albeit somewhere else.

Contrast the staying power of black Southerners' theological hope with that of early twentieth-century white Protestants. Liberal Protestants held postmillennial views that God's kingdom on earth was steadily advancing. All around them they saw progress—in science and medicine, in government and diplomacy, in religion and good will. A good number of these postmillennialists predicted the end of war. When subsequently confronted with the carnage of World War I, many white liberal Protestants abandoned their belief in world peace and progress.[86] World War II raised even more questions about the inevitability of human progress. Postmillennialism faded from white Protestant circles, replaced with more sober assessments of human nature and the future of humanity. They looked around at the world, at the disasters of the twentieth century, and reasoned that the march of progress either had been abruptly arrested or had only been an illusion.[87]

During the nadir of race relations black Protestant leaders in North Carolina and across the South experienced no similar disillusionment. As a way to make sense of their social circumstances, their eschatology proved amazingly elastic and powerful. They were not naïve about the realities of segregation and disfranchisement. But they saw in the turn of the twentieth century what they expected to see: a God active in human affairs working on their behalf, a continuation of the advancements made since emancipation, and a better day coming.

Of late, historians have been chipping away at the Jim Crow era from both ends. Jim Crow, as a solid system of segregation and oppression, was slow in coming and took many years to construct. Historians have argued for earlier and earlier dates for the start of the civil rights movement, as they unearth evidence of black political activity, protest, and progress in the first half of the twentieth century. The move to consider much of the twentieth century as one long civil rights movement has come out of a recognition that black Americans never acquiesced to Jim Crow policies. This new periodization in American historiography—one that sees continuity in African American history since emancipation—approaches black Protestants' own view of history. Their eschatological expectations forced them to see their own struggle for freedom as uninterrupted by the politics of Jim Crow, a position that historians have now belatedly adopted.[88]

Epilogue
Some Great Plan

Courage! Look out, beyond, and see
The far horizon's beckoning span!
Faith in your God-known destiny!
We are a part of some great plan.
—James Weldon Johnson, 1917

Between 1913 and 1916, dozens of American cities held conventions and parades to celebrate the semicentennial anniversary of emancipation. Black leaders successfully lobbied the U.S. Senate for a quarter million dollars to hold a national celebration, but the House of Representatives voted the measure down. At the larger exhibitions in Richmond and Chicago, black organizers assembled exhibits to demonstrate fifty years of progress. At the New York semicentennial, W. E. B. Du Bois designed an African American history pageant, the "Star of Ethiopia," that showcased the glory of ancient African kingdoms. A similar pageant in St. Louis boasted a fifty-person orchestra, a caravan of camels, and a herd of elephants. African American playwrights and musicians timed performances to coincide with the anniversary. These performances, like so many before, retold the race's past as a way to lay claim to a different future. Yet the organizers struggled to attract the attention of most white Americans, whose Civil War semicentennial celebrations focused on unity between North and South. Often national memory of the war sidestepped emancipation altogether, and Northerners and Southerners could be reconciled because of their common commitment to white supremacy. Black Americans found it difficult to use the memory of emancipation in order to claim ground politically.[1]

Others questioned the reason for celebrating in an age of entrenched restrictions on black freedom. For example, preparations for the celebrations coincided with the release of the widely popular film *Birth of a Nation*, which glorified the Klan's role in Redemption. Were things really better for African Americans in 1915 than they had been in 1865? The editors of the *Chicago Defender* said the semicentennial would celebrate "semi-freedom," as black

Southerners would have to ride Jim Crow cars and avoid "lynching bees" to get to the event.[2] The promise of full citizenship rang so hollow in the 1910s that many found it difficult to celebrate.

In fact, by the 1910s, the local annual practice of celebrating emancipation was already waning. Many African American communities across the nation ceased to celebrate Emancipation Day. For nearly five decades, black Americans had used Emancipation Day to publically commemorate the end of slavery with speeches, parades, fairs, and worship; why would the celebrations gradually stop drawing crowds after 1910? As Mitch Kachun has argued, local white leaders were less willing to lend their support, and some black institutional leaders worried about the behavior of the lower classes at public events. This was particularly the case in North Carolina, where black ministers publically voiced opposition to what they saw as raucous demonstrations and excursions. And as public spaces became increasingly segregated, localities restricted where and when black Americans could gather to commemorate anything, not to mention problems with segregated lodging and transportation. Kachun also suggests a more profound obstacle to emancipation celebrations. By the turn of the century, Americans almost exclusively used commemorations of the past to bring stability to the present social order. African Americans' desire to see in the past hope for a drastically different future—or to issue jeremiads—now seemed completely out of step with the nation's relationship to its past.

Moreover, an entire generation of black Americans writing at the time of the semicentennial had not lived through the emancipation of Southern slaves. Older leaders wanted to remind the new generation of the progress since slavery. Others, like an editor in the *AME Church Review*, found it tiresome to keep "counting the milestones of our progress or enumerating our material wealth or intellectual gains." It seemed ill-fitting to celebrate nothing but progress to a generation that had witnessed the onset of Jim Crow but not the end of slavery. The editor called for "a new emancipation," not the memory of an old one.[3]

The older generation of African American Protestant leaders believed that they had witnessed a decisive, cataclysmic inbreak on their world. The divine act of emancipation called African Americans to a new era of freedom and justice, one where they lived in the center of history. As they turned to different biblical narratives to understand that inbreak, they found ways to imagine and claim their place in the new age of emancipation, even with the onset of the Jim Crow era. But that generation no longer led black institutions by the 1910s. In North Carolina, Augustus Shepherd, leading black Baptist minister and founder of the Colored Orphan Asylum, died in 1911. James Walker Hood died in Fayetteville in 1918 at the age of eighty-seven; his colleague Bishop C. R. Harris passed away the year before. Perhaps local Emancipation Day celebrations ended because a new generation no longer gave emancipation the eschatological importance that black Southerners once did.

These changes did not necessarily signal the end of a hopeful eschatology for black Protestants, only that the Civil War–era emancipation of Southern slaves no longer anchored it. Even in the nineteenth century, when emancipation remained the most important piece of black eschatology, other features of that eschatology had been diverse and dynamic. Let us remember that from the beginning, black Protestants' theology of emancipation had been changing. In the 1860s, they readily employed biblical stories of conquest and nationhood to understand African American destiny, but some turned more to exile or wilderness narratives when Reconstruction collapsed. Some who had believed North Carolina to be on the verge of a literal Jubilee property redistribution left the state for a different Promised Land only years later. The theological need to see progress meant that black Protestant leaders changed their markers of progress, and with the resurgence of violent white supremacy, they identified more closely with Jesus's crucifixion. The declining importance of emancipation, however, marked a more fundamental theological change, one that needed, as the *AME Church Review* editor called for, a new emancipation.

Several different movements in twentieth-century African American history promised just that. On the heels of the semi-centennial, those who left the rural South during the Great Migration understood their flight as a "second emancipation."[4] Migration was nothing new; black North Carolinians had a long history of seeking their fortunes elsewhere. Although the destinations differed and the numbers increased, the new migration sparked similar debates as earlier ones did. Could the new labor shortage in the state be leveraged to argue for greater political rights? Would black emigration hurt black institutions? Proponents argued that the movement was a fulfillment of scripture. And just as before, many more African Americans remained at home than left. Still, we can understand why migrants and subsequent scholars have considered the migration of over a million black Southerners a new emancipation. It was the defining moment of a new generation, and it wrought significant changes to African American religion and politics. The rather separate worlds of the rural South and the urban North came together. The African American freedom struggle became less regional and more national; and disparate black religious traditions collided. Many observers drew close parallels between the Great Migration and emancipation. One writer for the *Negro Year Book of 1918–1919* explained why: "No event since Emancipation of the Negroes from slavery so profoundly influenced the economic and social life of the Negro. It may be said that whereas the Thirteenth Amendment granted physical emancipation, the conditions brought about by World War I made for the economic emancipation of the Negro, in that he found for the first time, opportunity to go practically anywhere in the United States and find employment along a great many lines."[5] Like the Civil War–era emancipation, this new migration seemed a divine act, as Milton Sernett has argued, "because of its suddenness and size."[6]

Twentieth-century activists railed against Jim Crow segregation using the prophets Isaiah and Ezekiel's messages of redemption, of a return from exile.[7] Members of Marcus Garvey's Universal Negro Improvement Association in the 1910s and 1920s believed that the creation of strong pan-African state "would usher in a golden age of racial solidarity, self-rule, and economic power for all black people worldwide."[8] Garveyites preached an eschatology, but for them, pan-African politics and economic collectives—not emancipation—marked the climax of human history. Even non-Christian movements like the Nation of Islam depended on an eschatology that renarrated ancient history and forecast a special destiny for the African race, much as nineteenth-century Protestants had done. What became so striking about leaders of the civil rights era, one scholar has noted, was their conviction that change would come because God intervenes in human history on behalf of the oppressed, not because human institutions naturally progress toward reason.[9] Even though these movements retained a sense that history had a sacred design, none centered human history around the experience of emancipation. None narrated progress as uninterrupted since 1865.

Black Protestants' reliance on biblical narratives to explain their own experience meant that their theological understanding of history was always diverse and changing. This way to read the Bible represented a kind of narrative theology, a term used by some late twentieth-century theologians to describe seeking knowledge of God through a community's familiarity and identification with biblical stories, as opposed to constructing a systematic theology of carefully arranged, internally consistent propositional statements.[10] African American Christians' emphasis on narrative made their eschatology elastic and durable. Because many white Americans' view of progress was tied to an onward and upward understanding of history, not the ups and downs of biblical stories, they were ill-equipped to make sense of the scale of tragedy and mayhem of the twentieth century. Postmillenni-alist views of uninterrupted progress could not account for two world wars or the Holocaust. In contrast, black eschatology's reliance upon many bibli-cal narratives gave it the flexibility to account for suffering, disappointment, periods of waiting, triumph, and progress. That flexibility is what makes it difficult for us to make sweeping statements about how black religion worked and instead calls us to investigate the particular implications of different narratives.

Black Protestants' use of biblical narratives made their theology directly applicable to African American life and politics. Narrative theology could be quite concrete, because biblical stories involved real, tangible things: ty-rants and armies, harvests and famines, floods and flogging. Black Protes-tants found concrete parallels between their own experience and these biblical stories. For almost every moment from slavery to Jim Crow, there was a rel-evant narrative. African Americans' theology, and particularly their escha-tology, was hardly esoteric; it was, as *The End of Days* has labored to prove, integral to black Southerners' understanding of their political, economic, and social circumstances. Black Protestants' eschatology was not the only source for African American political thought, but it holds considerable ex-planatory power for understanding their politics in the period. Their em-phasis on emancipation as a divine, earth-altering act did eventually fade, but not in the immediate aftermath of Redemption or Jim Crow. The same theology also carried into the twentieth century a challenge to the story that the *Birth of a Nation*, early historians of Reconstruction, and many Americans continued to tell. Whereas Southern whites proclaimed disfranchisement and segregation as permanent solutions to the so-called race problem, African American Protestants balked at such pronouncements, confining the policies of Jim Crow to the footnotes of a story that, as they saw it, had always been about black freedom and destiny.

Notes

Introduction

1. Report of Speech by Edwin Jones, August 22, 1867, Letters Received, Oaths of Office, and Records Relating to Registration and Elections, 1865–69, ser. 1380, Post of Wilmington, Record Group 393 Pt. 4, National Archives, quoted in Foner, "Reconstruction and the Black Political Tradition," 62.

2. Let me offer some prominent examples. W. E. B. Du Bois's *Black Reconstruction* offers a Marxist reading of black political consciousness in the aftermath of freedom. The work concerns the interests and actions of the black worker but does not look deeply into black Southerners' religious or theological outlook. Eric Foner's *Reconstruction* in many ways follows Du Bois's work, by centering black experience and by critiquing the Dunning School of Reconstruction history. Foner, unlike Du Bois, shifts attention from blacks as the proletariat to black use of republican ideology. Foner also differs from Du Bois in his attention to religion. Foner recognizes that religious language was as common as republican ideology in the articulations of black leaders in Reconstruction. But though he attempts to give religion its fair share of attention, he fails to give it its fair share of analysis. Foner recognizes the prevalence of religious

language but does not delve deeper. Religion, in Foner's analysis, is a language with which African Americans convey political messages or inspire political action. But religion does not seem to have much content that deserves unpacking. Steven Hahn's *A Nation under Our Feet* takes its title from the forty-seventh Psalm and the title of its middle section, "To Build a New Jerusalem," from the last two chapters of Revelation, but you would not know it from reading Hahn. In the introduction, Hahn explains that the book began with his attempt to understand why and how African Americans were so politically motivated in the years immediately following emancipation. Where did such an active political culture come from? Hahn answers the question by reaching back to the political culture of slavery and tracing its development into the twentieth century. Along the way, he encounters and recounts numerous theological references, but leaves them unexplained. I argue that the frequent references to biblical stories and theological concepts give us insight to black political culture, and find it surprising, given his questions and the title of his book, that Hahn does not. Labor historian David Roediger has resurrected Du Bois's description of emancipation as a "general strike" among slaves. In his recent work *Seizing Freedom*, Roediger employs the term Jubilee in its specific biblical meaning and agrees with my assessment that the explanation of the biblical reference matters for interpreting what slaves wanted when they emancipated themselves. See 29, 44–45n32.

3. The *Oxford Companion to the Bible* defines eschatology as "the teaching concerning last things, such as the resurrection of the dead, the Last Judgment, the end of this world, and the creation of a new one." *Oxford Companion to the Bible*, s.v. "Eschatology," http://www.oxfordreference.com/views/ENTRY.html?entry=t120.e0229 (accessed July 28, 2008). The *Concise Oxford Dictionary of the Christian Church* defines it more broadly, similar to my own definition: "the doctrine of the last things, that is the ultimate destiny both of the individual soul and of the whole created order." *Concise Oxford Dictionary of the Christian Church*, s.v. "Eschatology," http://www.oxford reference.com/views/ENTRY.html?entry=t95.e1976 (accessed July 29, 2008).

4. Wilmore, *Last Things First*, 29.

5. I am indebted to Reginald Hildebrand for helping me formulate this observation. The phrase quoted here appeared in several of King's public speeches but has its origins in the nineteenth century. See Parker, *Ten Sermons of Religion*, 84–85.

6. Acts 17:26, KJV; Revelation 7:9 KJV; see, for example, Editorial, *SOZ*, January 26, 1899; "Dangerous Advice," *SOZ*, November 17, 1898; Butler Harrison Peterson, "Is the Negro Morally Depraved as he is Reputed to Be?" in D. W. Culp, ed., *Twentieth Century Negro Literature*, 240; Latta, *The History of My Life and Work*, 198–99; *Journal of Freedom*, September 30, 1865; Clinton, *Christianity under the Searchlight*, 54–56; Francis Grimke, "Christianization of America," in D. W. Culp, ed., *Twentieth Century Negro Literature*, 431–33.

7. Fulop, "Future Golden Day of the Race"; a particular reading of history accompanied these interpretations of Psalm 68. In numerous race histories, black Americans wrote of a mythic glorious past that placed their ancestors in the ancient civilizations

Egypt and Ethiopia, civilizations that predated and outstripped the West. And as Raboteau argues, it was "surely as legitimate a fictive pedigree as white American claims of
descent from Greco-Roman civilization." Raboteau, " 'Ethiopia Shall Soon Stretch
Forth Her Hands to God,' " 397–413. Laurie Maffly-Kipp explains, "African participation in ancient history was a useful counter to the white claim that the Negro had
always been, and would remain, a degraded race." Maffly-Kipp, "Mapping the World,
Mapping the Race," 618; and Maffly-Kipp, "Redeeming Southern Memory: The Negro Race History, 1874–1915," 170, 179, 184. According to Maffly-Kipp, these race histories exhibited the many tensions within the black community. Often writers were
well-educated middle-class Northern blacks who criticized Southern blacks for their
primitive spirituality. Moreover, these black elites rarely held approval for the actions
and beliefs of the black masses. Race historians also disagreed among themselves.
And in one sense, their histories removed Negro history from the realm of a personal
God favoring his people to a liberal understanding of inevitable progress. But Maffly-
Kipp concludes that race historians had more in common than not. Their common
message was that African Americans had a prominent place in history and the future,
and their common purpose was to foster the building of a successful free black community.

8. See Glaude, *Exodus!*, 12–15. For a discussion of how these two themes competed
in African American missions to Africa, see Wills, "Introduction," xix–xxii.

9. See Wright and Dresser, eds., *Apocalypse and the Millennium*. Sacvan Bercovitch
first used the phrase "sacred historical design" to describe how Puritans saw themselves in God's plan for human history. I borrow the phrase to refer to the similar
ideas among African Americans. Bercovitch, *American Jeremiad*, 7–8.

10. Numbers and Butler, eds., *The Disappointed*. Dispensationalism began in the
early nineteenth century, but did not gain significant popular following until after the
publication of the *Scofield Reference Bible* in 1909. Dispensational premillennialism is
today the most popularized and most visible eschatology of conservative American
Protestants.

11. Weber, *Living in the Shadow of the Second Coming*, 9; Roll, "Garveyism and the
Eschatology of African Redemption," 30.

12. Timothy Miller, *Revivalism and Social Reform*.

13. Their faith in human progress and in the essential goodness of human nature
inspired the Progressive reforms of the early twentieth century and faltered in the
face of the two world wars that followed. See Morehead, *World Without End*, and
Curtis, *Consuming Faith*.

14. AME minister Theophilus G. Steward's 1888 *The End of the World* displayed
classic tenets of premillennial thought, envisioning the return of Christ before the
coming millennium. Many racial "uplifters" held to postmillennialism, believing that
their work to educate, reform, and evangelize would usher in the millennium. James
Walker Hood, the only black author to pen a theological commentary on Revelation
during the period, sided with amillennialism. Fulop, "The Future Golden Day of the

Race"; Steward, *The End of the World*; Hood, *The Plan of the Apocalypse*. Rural Garveyites in the early twentieth century blended elements of premillennialism and
postmillennialism when they discussed their *cause Afric*. Roll, "Garveyism and the
Eschatology of African Redemption," 29–30.

15. NCBEMC *Proceedings*, October 1894: 17.

16. Raboteau, "African-Americans, Exodus, and the American Israel," 9.

17. Cone, *God of the Oppressed*, 102–3.

18. There is considerable debate about how closely grouped by ethnicity and language African slaves were in the Americas. There was significant clustering of groups,
but it is possible to exaggerate the possibilities for slaves to maintain linguistic and
kinship ties. See Hall, *Slavery and African Ethnicities in the Americas*.

19. Wimbush, "The Bible and African Americans," 82–83. Italics added.

20. See Glaude, *Exodus!*

21. Raboteau, *A Fire in the Bones*, 12. Rev. Morgan Latta, of Raleigh, North Carolina, for example, invited a direct comparison between ancient Hebrews and African
Americans: "people have said that God was not just, allowing other nationalities to
predominate over them [Hebrews] and hold them as slaves . . . God works things to
suit Himself, and if God, in His own mysterious ways, in managing things, has promoted the Hebrews to prosperity, then it is prima facie evidence that the same God
that promoted the Hebrews will promote the negro race." *The History of My Life and
Work*, 53–54.

22. Hobson, *The Mount of Vision*.

23. Callahan, *The Talking Book*, xii–xiv.

24. Modern theologians to work on Jesus-as-Israel include N. T. Wright, M. D.
Goulder, Robert Horton Gundar, G. B. Caird, and Peter Leithart. As a starting point,
see Caird, *Jesus and the Jewish Nation*, and "The One and the Many in Mark and
John," 43–46.

25. Cone, *God of the Oppressed*, 122–26.

26. Du Bois, "The Conservation of the Races," 2; Theophus Harold Smith, *Conjuring Culture*, 234.

27. Maffly-Kipp, *Setting down the Sacred Past*; Trulear, "Sociology of Afro-American
Religion," 52–53. Italics added.

28. Cone, *God of the Oppressed*, 103.

29. Wilmore, *Last Things First*, 83; Bryan R. Wilson, *Magic and the Millennium*, 6–7.

30. Moltmann, *Theology of Hope*, 15–16.

31. Cone, *God of the Oppressed*, 116.

32. Albert J. Raboteau's work serves as a starting point for almost all inquiries into
nineteenth-century black religion. Eschatology is no exception. His essay "African-
Americans, Exodus, and the American Israel" traces out the deep connections that
African Americans saw between themselves and Old Testament Israel, and Raboteau
suggests that their reading of the Old Testament, in particular the Exodus story, had
ramifications for nineteenth-century politics. See "African-Americans, Exodus, and

the American Israel," 9. Raboteau's essay on black Christians' use of Psalm 68:31 ("Princes shall come out of Egypt; Ethiopia shall soon stretch forth her hands unto God.") develops briefly the second part of black eschatology that I want to highlight— beliefs in the race's destiny. Raboteau, "'Ethiopia Shall Soon Stretch Forth Her Hands to God.'" Allen Dwight Callahan's *The Talking Book* details the centrality of biblical narratives to black experience and to black understandings of justice. Timothy Fulop delves deeper into this topic, examining the various millennial beliefs that black Christians espoused in the late nineteenth century. His approach is one of high intellectual history; he is concerned with millennialism, in the traditional and narrow definition and not the more expansive topic of eschatology as a whole, and he draws heavily on the most educated and published of black authors. Fulop argues, quite convincingly, that the traditional categories of millennial thought that pay attention to timing/dating do little to illuminate black thought, and offers instead a categorization based on the character of the millennium. Fulop, "The Future Golden Day." Wilson Moses and Eddie Glaude both pay attention to black identification with Old Testament Israel and black notions of race destiny in their attempts to understand the religious origins of black nationalism. Both draw from Eugene Genovese's thesis in *Roll, Jordan, Roll* that black Christianity gave African Americans the tools to conceive of themselves as a nation. Those tools were the stuff of eschatology. Black Americans found in their appropriation of biblical narratives a common history and a common destiny. This allowed them to undertake the project of nationalism. Glaude largely finds this project laudatory, and wants to rescue it as an alternate to the kind of black nationalist ideology that relies on biological race or that necessitates a rejection of all things white and American. *Exodus!*, 3–43. In contrast, Moses sees black appropriation of passages like the Exodus story and Psalm 68:31 as inherently "racially chauvinistic." The belief in a common history or common destiny, in Moses's estimation, necessitated a belief in consanguinity and shared the false assumptions of whites that blood or biological origins of a people endowed them with shared characteristics or a certain place in society. Moses, *Black Messiahs and Uncle Toms* and *Classic Black Nationalism.* For Glaude's critique of Moses, see *Exodus!*, 12–15. For African American prophetic traditions, see Hobson, *The Mount of Vision*. Studies of two African American literary and oratory genres shed further light on black eschatological thought. Most important are studies of an intriguing nineteenth-century black literary genre: race histories, or African American communal narratives. In these histories, black authors charted the development and trajectory of the race, often beginning in antiquity, climaxing with emancipation, and forecasting a better day coming. Studies of this genre, though few compared to those of slave narratives, reveal black Americans' differing ideas of the race's past and future. And many of these authors wrote with an emphasis on discerning God's purpose and plan for the race in human history, the same preoccupation that I have found in the writings of black North Carolinians. My entrance to this genre comes from Laurie Maffly-Kipp, *Setting down the Sacred Past*. See n. 7 above. Another genre, that of the African American jeremiad, has likewise garnered scholarly attention and speaks to black understandings of human and divine history. In the jeremiad, African Americans positioned themselves as prophets, declaring God's favor upon specific peoples while warning them of impending judgment if they failed to amend their ways. Howard-Pitney, *The African American Jeremiad*. For more on jeremiads, see chapter 4.

33. Mitchell, *Righteous Propagation*, 7–10.

34. There were so few black Catholics in nineteenth-century North Carolina and fewer still in the historical record that I cannot presume to speak to their experience when I analyze the actions of black Methodists, Presbyterians, and Baptists. So, I use the signifier *Protestant* more often than I use *Christian*, to be more precise. To be consistent with twenty-first-century usage, I use the terms *black* and *African American* interchangeably—even though both were rarely used in the nineteenth century—to signify all persons of African descent who identified with others of African descent, especially those living in the United States.

35. Gilmore, *Gender & Jim Crow*; Sims, *The Power of Femininity in the New South*.

36. Wills, "Introduction," xxiii.

37. Historians of the Atlantic world sometimes refer to the period beginning with British abolitionism in the 1780s and ending with the last abolition of slavery in Cuba and Brazil in the 1880s as the "age of emancipation." See, for example, Davis, *The Problem of Slavery in the Age of Emancipation*. Here I use the term differently to refer to the roughly fifty years in the United States after the start of the Civil War, when the meaning of emancipation featured prominently in African American discourse.

Chapter One

1. William McKee Evans, *Ballots and Fence Rails*, 22. *Ballots and Fence Rails* provides a detailed account of the capture of Wilmington and of Reconstruction in the Wilmington area, as well as a brief account of the prayer service at Front Street Methodist that this chapter recounts in greater detail.

2. Arnold, Wilmington, N.C., March 29, 1865, letter, in Edwin Redkey, ed., *A Grand Army of Black Men*, 165–67; Burkhead, "History of the Difficulties," 37.

3. Waddell, *Some Memories of My Life*, 57; William McKee Evans, *Ballots and Fence Rails*, 22–23.

4. Burkhead, "History of the Difficulties," 37–43; Psalm 9:6, KJV; Hildebrand, *The Times Were Strange and Stirring*, 36–40; Wright, ed., *Centennial Encyclopedia of the African Methodist Episcopal Church*, 122.

5. Raboteau, *A Fire in the Bones*, 17.

6. See Miller, Wilson, and Stout, eds., *Religion in the American Civil War*, and Noll, *The Civil War as a Theological Crisis* and *America's God*.

7. Latta, *The History of My Life and Work*, 169–70.

8. Williams, *Narrative of James Williams, an American Slave*, 74; Fountain, *Slavery, Civil War, and Salvation*, 95.

9. Walker, *Walker's Appeal*, 5, 18.

10. Ibid., 6–7.

11. Ibid., 45, 43 (italics added).

12. Ibid., 49.

13. "Second Inaugural Address of Abraham Lincoln, March 4, 1865."

14. Crow, *Black Experience in Revolutionary North Carolina*, 88–89.

15. Morgan, *Slave Counterpoint*, 648–49.

16. Ibid., 650.

17. Genovese, *From Rebellion to Revolution*, 7.

18. *CR*, November 15, 1862.

19. Ibid., October 11, 1862.

20. Colonel Heckman's Report to Governor Olden, March 15, 1862, in J. Madison Drake, *The History of the Ninth New Jersey Veterans Vols, A Record of Its Service from Sept. 13th, 1861, to July 12th, 1865* (Elizabeth, N.J.: Journal Printing House, 1889), 65–66, quoted in Browning, "Visions of Freedom and Civilization," 75.

21. Derby, *Bearing Arms in the Twenty-seventh Massachusetts Regiment of Volunteer Infantry during the Civil War, 1861–1865* (Boston: Wright and Potter Printing Company, 1883), 94–95, quoted in Mobley, *James City*, 2. Here I have taken the liberty to edit the derogatory dialect transcription that nineteenth- and early-twentieth century whites sometimes used when recording the words of African Americans. I have changed the spelling but none of the words.

22. William Wells Brown, *The Negro in the American Rebellion; His Heroism and His Fidelity* (New York: Lee and Shepard, 1867; reprint, New York: Citadel Press, 1971), 132, quoted in Hildebrand, " 'Brother, Religion Is a Good Thing in Time of War,' " 3.

23. *CR*, February 4, 1865, quoted in Hildebrand, " 'Brother, Religion Is a Good Thing in Time of War,' " 3–4.

24. Thomas Wentworth Higginson, *Army Life in a Black Regiment* (New York: W. W. Norton, 1984), 133, quoted in Hildebrand, " 'Brother, Religion Is a Good Thing in Time of War,' " 3.

25. Keith P. Wilson, *Campfires of Freedom*; Hildebrand, " 'Brother, Religion Is a Good Thing in Time of War.' "

26. Hildebrand, *Times Were Strange and Stirring*; Dickerson, "Liberation, Wesleyan Theology and Early African Methodism," 109–20.

27. See Glaude, *Exodus!*

28. Burkhead, "History of the Difficulties," 44.

29. Raboteau, *A Fire in the Bones*, 12. Latta, *History of My Life and Work*, 53–54.

30. See, for example, Report of Speech by Edwin Jones, August 22, 1867, Letters Received, Oaths of Office, and Records Relating to Registration and Elections, 1865–1869, ser. 1380, Post of Wilmington, Record Group 393 Pt. 4, National Archives, quoted in Foner, "Reconstruction and the Black Political Tradition," 62.

31. Burkhead, "History of the Difficulties," 44.

32. *Wilmington Herald*, September 8, 1865, quoted in William McKee Evans, *Ballots and Fence Rails*, 87.

33. Isaiah 66:6–9, KJV.

34. *Columbia Herald*, October 29, 1869, quoted in Ash, *Middle Tennessee Society Transformed*, 209; Isaiah 61:1.

35. Burkhead, "History of the Difficulties," 44–45.

36. Ibid., 43–44.

37. Ibid., 64–65.

38. For narratives and analyses of independent black church movements, see Melton, *A Will to Choose*; Gravely, "African Methodisms and the Rise of Black Denominationalism," 239–63; Montgomery, *Under Their Own Vine and Fig Tree*; Dvorak, *An African-American Exodus*; and Richardson, *Dark Salvation*.

39. The antebellum desire to separate from white Southern churches, coupled with slaves' long history of secret, independent worship (the "invisible institution") prepared black worshippers to assume and assert their independence during the Civil War and Reconstruction. See Dvorak, *An African-American Exodus*; and Raboteau, *Slave Religion*.

40. Whitted, *A History of Negro Baptists*, 14–15; Micah 4:1–4, KJV.

41. Hood, *One Hundred Years*, 185–88, 289–300.

42. Ibid., 55, passim.

43. *CR*, April 1, 1865.

44. Whitted, *A History of Negro Baptists*, 14–15.

45. "Letter from Rev. J. C. Gibbs," *CR*, May 6, 1865.

46. Hood, *One Hundred Years*, 289–93.

47. Ibid.

48. Ibid., 292–94.

49. "Letter from Rev. J. C. Gibb," *CR*, May 6, 1865.

50. Ibid.

51. Burkhead, "History of the Difficulties," 95.

52. Arnold, Wilmington, N.C., March 29, 1865, letter, in Redkey, ed., *A Grand Army of Black Men*, 166–67.

53. Burkhead, "History of the Difficulties," 95.

54. Ibid., 47–50, 56, 61, 73; Teed, "Loyalty and Liturgy," 54–56.

55. Nannie R. Alexander, "Personal Reminiscences of the Founding of Seventh Street Presbyterian Church and Biddle University by Mrs. Nannie R. Alexander who assisted her husband, the late Rev. S. C. Alexander, D. D., Founder of both Church and School," handwritten memoir, Willerstown, Pa., December 6, 1910, History of JCSU Collection, Box 1, Folder 1, Inez Moore Parker Archives and Research Center, James B. Duke Memorial Library, Johnston C. Smith University, 23–24.

56. *CR*, April 1, 1865.

57. Hood, *One Hundred Years*, 55–56; see Dvorak, *An African-American Exodus* and Harvey, *Freedom's Coming*, 8–19.

58. Fountain, *Slavery, Civil War, and Salvation*, 6–40, 93–114. Fountain's thesis is a formidable challenge to the consensus that the practice of Christianity was the center of slave culture. Fountain's survey results may be less significant than they first appear. In revivalistic evangelical Protestantism, converts almost always narrate the earlier parts of their lives as ones of irreligion, even if Christianity profoundly shaped their ideas and practices before conversion. Moreover, slave narratives, starting with Olaudah Equiano's, took as their genre model the spiritual autobiography, substituting the moment of freedom for the climactic moment of conversion. Many slave autobiographies purposely equate conversion with freedom; Fountain's data tell us as much about the conventions of a genre and of a revivalistic faith as they do about the numerical strength of Christianity. Nevertheless, historians will have difficultly refuting Fountain's claim that emancipation itself was the event that placed Christianity at the center of black cultural life. Case, *An Unpredictable Gospel*, 159–82.

59. Hood, *One Hundred Years*, 9–10.

60. *Wilmington Herald*, September 8, 1865, quoted in William McKee Evans, *Ballots and Fence Rails*, 87.

61. Andrews, *The South Since the War*, 121, 124.

62. Ibid., 122.

63. "Address of the Colored Convention to the People of Alabama," *Montgomery Daily State Sentinel*, May 21, 1867, quoted in Foner, *A Short History of Reconstruction*, 127.

64. Horace Greeley, "To the Colored People of North Carolina," *Journal of Freedom*, September 30, 1865.

65. "Mr. Greeley's Address," *Journal of Freedom*, September 30, 1865.

66. *Journal of Freedom*, October 7, 1865.

67. Cecelski, *The Waterman's Song*, 179–85; Cecelski, *Fire of Freedom*.

68. Andrews, *The South Since the War*, 124–25.

69. "Letter from Walker Pearce," *Journal of Freedom*, October 7, 1865.

70. Andrews, *The South Since the War*, 128.

71. Ibid., 128. At another time, Harris emphasized the contribution of black soldiers in emancipation to prove the political astuteness of slave populations. "Official Proceedings of the Convention," *Raleigh Weekly Standard*, February 5, 1868.

72. Hood, *The Plan of the Apocalypse*, 119.

73. *Journal of Freedom*, October 21, 1865, and October 28, 1865.

74. Quoted in *Raleigh Weekly Standard*, January 22, 1868.

75. Brundage, *The Southern Past*, 89, 94. See also Clark, *Defining Moments*.

76. Quoted in Charles Reagan Wilson, *Baptized in Blood*, 63–64.

77. Burkhead, "History of the Difficulties," 64–65.

78. See Harvey, *Moses, Jesus, and the Trickster*.

79. Edwards, *Gendered Strife and Confusion*, 194.

80. Quoted in Kachun, *Festivals of Freedom*, 238.

81. C. R. Harris, "The Negro's Mission in America," *AMEZ Quarterly* 3, no. 1 (October 1892): 48.

82. Maffly-Kipp, "Mapping the World," 618; Whitted, *A History of the Negro Baptists*, 164.

Chapter Two

1. "Address to the Colored People of North Carolina," circular, December 19, 1870.

2. Giggie, *After Redemption*, xvi–xvii.

3. Washington, *New National Era*, March 14, 1872, quoted in Harris, *The Day of the Carpetbagger*, 405.

4. For the broader impact of narratives on human culture, see Christian Smith, *Moral Believing Animals*, 63–94. The best analysis of black Americans' use of religious narrative remains Raboteau's "African-Americans, Exodus, and the American Israel."

5. Daniel Stowell, "Why Redemption?" in *Vale of Tears*, ed. Blum and Poole, 133–46. See also Emberton, *Beyond Redemption*.

6. Charles Reagan Wilson, *Baptized in Blood*, 7, 42. See also Paul Harvey, " 'Yankee Faith' and Southern Redemption: White Southern Baptist Ministers, 1850–1890," in *Religion and the American Civil War*, ed. Miller, Stout, and Wilson, 176–78.

7. Quoted in Charles Reagan Wilson, *Baptized in Blood*, 74.

8. *CR*, March 13, 1869.

9. James H. Harris, Petition to the Congress of the United States of America, July 8, 1867, James Henry Harris Papers, Record Group 1829, State Archives of North Carolina, Raleigh.

10. See William McKee Evans, *Ballots and Fence Rails*; Edwards, *Gendered Strife and Confusion*; and Hamilton, *Reconstruction in North Carolina*.

11. Quoted in Trelease, *White Terror*, 190.

12. Quoted in Snider, *Light on the Hill*, 82–83.

13. "Address to the Colored People of North Carolina," circular, December 19, 1870. For a concise account of the Klan violence of 1868–70, see Brisson, " 'Civil Government Was Crumbling around Me,' " 123–63.

14. Trelease, *White Terror*, xli.

15. *American Missionary* 6, no. 2 (February 1862): 33, quoted in Raboteau, *Slave Religion*, 320.

16. Harris, *Speech of Hon. James H. Harris*, 22.

17. Raleigh *Weekly Standard*, January 22, 1868.

18. See chapter 1.

19. Quoted in Brisson, " 'Civil Government Was Crumbling Around Me,' " 130.

20. Harris, *Speech of Hon. James Harris*, 12–13.

21. Ibid., 19.

22. Powell, *North Carolina through Four Centuries*, 397–99; Hamilton, *Reconstruction in North Carolina*, 470.

23. Bradley, *Bluecoats and Tar Heels*, 218–20.

24. One of Stephens's murderers left his recollections of the event in a sealed document in the North Carolina State Archives in Raleigh. The document was left sealed until his death, sixty-five years after Stephens's death. Escott, *Many Excellent People*, 154; Powell, *North Carolina through Four Centuries*, 397–99.

25. Powell, *North Carolina through Four Centuries*, 398–99; "Address to the Colored People of North Carolina," circular, December 19, 1870.

26. Powell, *North Carolina through Four Centuries*, 399–403; Bradley, *Bluecoats and Tar Heels*, 226–31; Brisson, " 'Civil Government Was Crumbling Around Me,' " 143–52.

27. Bradley, *Bluecoats and Tar Heels*, 230.

28. John David Smith, *Black Soldiers in Blue*, 407n68.

29. Andrews, *The South Since the War*, 124.

30. Elizabeth Davis Reid, "Stewart Ellison," in *Dictionary of North Carolina Biography*, vol. 2 (D-G), 152–53.

31. For the full list of black state representatives in 1870, see Hamilton, *Reconstruction in North Carolina*, 536. Hamilton, a Dunning School historian, listed only nineteen representatives, presumably because the North Carolina House Journal for 1870–71 identified only nineteen of its members as colored in the index. Representative Burton H. Jones, a Republican of Jackson, North Carolina, in Northampton County, likely raised the number to twenty. Jones signed the Esther circular and served as the trustee for Jackson's school for black children, two facts that point to Jones as African American, even though he was not identified as colored in the House Journal. The 1870 Federal Census records only one Burton Jones in Jackson: a forty-five-year-old mulatto carpenter who was most certainly the same Jones who served in the house and signed the circular. The three black representatives who did not sign the circular were W. Cawthorne of Warren County, T. A. Sykes of Pasquotank County, and J. H. Williamson of Franklin. Hamilton described Williamson as "the ablest representative of his race," and Williamson remained in the legislation until the late 1870s. See chapter 3, n. 49. It is unclear as to why he and the other two legislators did not join their colleagues in signing the circular. *Journal of the House of Representatives of the General Assembly of North Carolina at Its Session, 1870–1871*, 685–88; *1870 United States Federal Census* [database online] Year: *1870*; Census Place: Jackson, Northampton, North Carolina; Roll: *M593_1152*; Page: *541A*; Image: *65*; Family History Library Film: *552651*.

32. "Address to the Colored People of North Carolina," circular, December 19, 1870; Esther 2:6–7:10, KJV.

33. "Address to the Colored People of North Carolina," circular, December 19, 1870.

34. Ibid.

35. " 'Cry Mightily Unto the Lord,' " Raleigh *Daily Sentinel*, December 24, 1870.

36. Ibid.; "A Blasphemous Address," Tarboro *Southerner*, January 5, 1871.

37. "A Blasphemous Address," Tarboro *Southerner*, January 5, 1871; " 'Cry Mightily Unto the Lord,' " Raleigh *Daily Sentinel*, December 24, 1870.

38. "'Cry Mightily Unto the Lord,'" Raleigh *Daily Sentinel*, December 24, 1870.

39. Charles Reagan Wilson, *Baptized in Blood*, 89; Harvey, *Freedom's Coming*, 23.

40. "A Blasphemous Address," Tarboro *Southerner*, January 5, 1871.

41. Esther 8:11, KJV.

42. "Address to the Colored People of North Carolina," circular, December 19, 1870.

43. Matthew 17:21, KJV.

44. "Address to the Colored People of North Carolina," circular, December 19, 1870.

45. *Fayetteville Educator*, October 17, 1874.

46. Du Bois, "Border and Frontier," *Black Reconstruction in America*, 534–35; Hamilton, *Reconstruction in North Carolina*, 365.

47. Foner, *Reconstruction*, 94–95.

48. Few works on Reconstruction have given the kind of sustained attention to narrative that Eddie Glaude and Albert Raboteau have given for the nineteenth century as a whole, but since the 1990s many works have enriched our understanding of the role of religion during Reconstruction. See Stowell, *Rebuilding Zion*; Harvey, *Redeeming the South*; Blum, *Reforging the White Republic*; Blum and Poole, eds., *Vale of Tears*; and Wright and Dresser, eds., *Apocalypse and the Millennium*.

49. The general recognition of the importance of religion to black politics has carried with it a host of problematic assumptions, including those of a monolithic "Black Church" or racial predispositions to religiosity. See Curtis Evans, *The Burden of Black Religion*; Savage, *Your Spirits Walk Beside Us*; and Fountain, *Slavery, Civil War, and Salvation*.

50. See introduction, n. 2.

51. Raboteau, "African-Americans, Exodus, and the American Israel," 1, 9; Hardy, "From Exodus to Exile," 737–57; Glaude, *Exodus!*; Callahan, *The Talking Book*.

52. Stowell, *Rebuilding Zion*, 150.

Chapter Three

1. *Kinston Journal*, November 13, 1879; *Chatham Record*, January 29, 1880.

2. Berlin, *Generations of Captivity*; Williams, *Help Me to Find My People*.

3. John J. Robertson et al., to Maj.-Gen. James B. Steedman, September 27, 1865, National Archives, Bureau of Refugees, Freedmen, and Abandoned Lands, RG 105, Georgia Assistant Commissioner, Affidavits and Petitions [A-5166], quoted in Hahn, "'Extravagant Expectations,'" 122.

4. "Ex. Doc. No. 2: Message of President on condition of States lately in rebellion," in *Senate Executive Documents*, 1st Session, 39th Congress, 1865–66: 31. For detailed accounts of the Christmas Scare of 1865, see Hahn, "'Extravagant Expectations,'" and Carter, "The Anatomy of Fear," 345–64.

5. See Raboteau, "African Americans, Exodus, and the American Israel," and Glaude, *Exodus!*

6. See the book of Exodus, especially chapters 3–33, and the book of Joshua.

7. Leviticus 25:1–10, KJV. See also Dvorak, "After Apocalypse, Moses."

8. See chapter 1 for black Southerners' experience of emancipation as both Exodus and Jubilee.

9. Elizabeth Hyde Botune, *First Days Amongst the Contrabands* (Boston: Lee and Shepard, 1893), 170, quoted in Magdol, *A Right to the Land,* 139.

10. Magdol, *A Right to the Land,* 140–42; Cohen, *At Freedom's Edge,* 11; Belz, *New Birth of Freedom,* 76, 100–106.

11. Quoted in William McKee Evans, *Ballots and Fence Rails,* 69.

12. Report of the Joint Committee on Reconstruction, House Report No. 30, 39th Congress, 1st Session, part II, 192; Magdol, *A Right to the Land,* 140.

13. *New York Tribune,* September 8, 1865.

14. Samuel A. Agnew, diary entry, November 3, 1865, Southern Historical Collection, Wilson Library, University of North Carolina at Chapel Hill, quoted in Hahn, "'Extravagant Expectations,'" 122–24.

15. Litwack, *Been in the Storm So Long,* 425–26.

16. *Wilmington Daily Herald,* November 7, 1865, quoted in Carter, "The Anatomy of Fear," 357.

17. Burkhead, "History of the Difficulties," 70.

18. Quoted in Hahn, "'Extravagant Expectations,'" 136.

19. *CR,* October 1, 1864.

20. S. D. Barnes to Lieutenant E. Bamberger, December 30, 1865, cited in Magdol, *A Right to the Land,* 141.

21. Magdol, *A Right to the Land,* 142, 161, 165.

22. "Letter from Rev. J. C. Gibbs," *CR,* May 6, 1865. Chapter 1 treats black possession of church property in further detail.

23. "Letter from Rev. J. C. Gibbs," *CR,* May 6, 1865.

24. Raleigh *Journal of Freedom,* September 30, 1865. Chapter 1 includes a section on the 1865 Freedmen's Convention that explains in more detail what happened at the meeting and about the *Journal of Freedom,* the short-lived black newspaper that covered the meeting.

25. Andrews, *The South Since the War,* 122.

26. Raleigh *Journal of Freedom,* October 21, 1865.

27. Ibid.

28. Magdol, *A Right to the Land,* 142, 144; Hahn, "'Extravagant Expectations,'" 153–54.

29. *Fayetteville Educator,* November 28, 1874.

30. Campbell, *Middle Passages,* 95–96.

31. Martin Delany, "Prospects of the Freedmen of Hilton Head," in Levine, ed., *Martin R. Delany,* 397; See Delany, "Triple Alliance—The Restoration of the South—Salvation of Its Political Economy," in Levine, ed., *Martin R. Delany,* 401–2.

32. Martin Delany, "Letter to the Colored Delegation, 22 February 1866," in Levine, ed., *Martin R. Delany,* 405.

33. P. P. Erwin, Concord, N.C., to William Coppinger, August 15, 1877, Series 1A, Reel 116A, ACS Papers, Library of Congress. In the postbellum years, the ACS focused more on missionary and educational efforts in Liberia and less on transporting new colonists there. Often, the ACS asked colonists to fund their own transport, and few African Americans could afford it. From 1876 to 1894, only 318 black North Carolinians left for Liberia. See Frenise A. Logan, "The Movement of Negroes," 49.

34. Albert B. Williams, Raleigh, N.C., to ACS, February 1, 1877, Series 1A, Reel 115, ACS Papers; *Greensboro Patriot*, March 21, 1877.

35. Campbell, *Middle Passages*, 99–113; Barnes, *Journey of Hope*, 11, 13–32. By the end of the century, 600 black Arkansans had migrated to Liberia.

36. *Kinston Journal*, July 10, 1879.

37. Cohen, *At Freedom's Edge*, 187–88; Senate Report on the Exodus, part III, 381.

38. Taylor, "The Great Migration from North Carolina," 26–27, especially n. 22. There were other reasons for unrest. The political climate in post-Reconstruction North Carolina fostered pessimism in certain sectors of the black community. In a private letter to white Republican leader George W. Stanton, Ransom Howell, a black farmer from Wilson repeated a rumor circulating in his community: "The colored people are invited to go west, and to do so at once before the XVth amendment is repealed, for the purpose of returning us to a condition of slavery, if you are found South of the Ohio River." *Raleigh Signal*, January 14, 1880.

39. *Kinston Journal*, December 18, 1879.

40. Cohen, *At Freedom's Edge*, 188–91.

41. Quoted in a letter to the editor, *Kinston Journal*, November 13, 1879.

42. Painter, *Exodusters*, 195–96.

43. *Kinston Journal*, November 13, 1879.

44. Cary S. Bellamy, Battleboro, N.C., to William Coppinger, January 11, 1880, Series 1A, Reel 120, ACS Papers.

45. *Wilmington Morning Star*, January 15, 1880.

46. Senate Report on the Exodus, 314. The Senate Report on the Exodus tried to make sense of the emigration, but party politics got in the way. The majority report (Democratic) purported that the National Emigrant Aid Society was a Republican Party operation trying to ship black Republicans from solidly Democratic states like North Carolina to swing states like Indiana. The Democrats denied that the move had anything to do with conditions in North Carolina. Senate Republicans, in the minority report, pointed to the economic and political injustices black Southerners faced at home and disavowed any party connections to the failed migration to Indiana. Both reports were true. Perry and his followers had been co-opted by the members of the National Emigrant Aid Society, which was concerned more with the 1880 election than with the migrants' welfare. But the migration was not solely the work of Republican Party operatives. Unfair land practices and policies, as black witnesses testified at the hearing, prompted black North Carolinians to leave the state long before they ever met the National Emigrant Aid Society workers in D.C.

47. *Chatham Record*, January 29, 1880. This North Carolina newspaper compiled reports from Indiana newspapers without citing them.

48. Quoted in *Tarboro Southerner*, February 23, 1877.

49. *Greensboro Patriot*, February 14, 1877. John H. Williamson, a black representative from Franklin County, had put forth a resolution in the state General Assembly, calling upon the state's U.S. congressmen to work toward designating some land west of the Missouri River for the "sole occupation and colonization of the colored race." Williamson had always been both a leading black politician and an outlier; he was, for example, one of the few legislators to not sign the Esther circular in 1870. In 1877, however, he was not the only one interested in colonization, and, the day his resolution came up for debate, "the galleries and a portion of the lobbies were packed by a dense crowd of colored people of both sexes."

50. *Tarboro Southerner*, February 16, 1877.

51. *Raleigh Register*, October 4, 1877. The 1870 U.S. Census recorded the "colored population" of Tarboro at 2,094.

52. *Raleigh Register*, October 4, 1877.

53. Ibid.

54. Ibid.

55. *Raleigh Register*, October 4, 1877, and November 1, 1877.

56. *Raleigh Signal*, January 21, 1880.

57. Ibid. Those leaders also criticized recent small-scale disfranchisement moves by white Democrats. Constitutional changes took the power of electing justices of the peace away from local constituencies—many of which were majority black—and gave it the state legislature, which, as the document explained, had "no sympathy with the colored laborer."

58. Ibid.

59. *Wilmington Morning Star*, January 13, 1880.

60. *New Berne Weekly Journal*, November 21, 1889.

61. *CR*, February 11, 1884.

62. *CR*, March 13, 1890.

63. *New York Herald*, January 11, 1890, quoted in the *Lenoir Topic*, January 22, 1890.

64. *Tarboro Southerner*, December 19, 1889.

65. Ibid.

66. *New Berne Weekly Journal*, November 21, 1889.

67. *New York Herald*, January 11, 1890, quoted in the *Lenoir Topic*, January 22, 1890.

68. *Tarboro Southerner*, December 19, 1889.

69. Ibid., January 23, 1890; *New York Herald*, January 11, 1890, quoted in the *Lenoir Topic*, January 22, 1890.

70. Quoted in Frenise A. Logan, "The Movement of Negroes," 56n47.

71. Matkin-Rawn, " 'The Great Negro State,' " 1–3.

72. Frenise A. Logan, "The Movement of Negroes"; see also K. Todd Johnson, "Fences," in Powell, ed., *Encyclopedia of North Carolina*, 424–25.

73. *Tarboro Southerner*, December 19, 1889.

74. *New York Herald*, January 11, 1890, quoted in the *Lenoir Topic*, January 22, 1890.

75. NCBEMC *Proceedings*, October 1889, 14.

76. Matkin-Rawn, "'The Great Negro State,'" 14–15, 29–30.

77. *Raleigh State Chronicle*, May 3, 1889.

78. NCBEMC *Proceedings*, October 1889, 14.

79. *News & Observer*, April 27, 1889.

80. *New Berne Weekly Journal*, November 14, 1889.

81. *New York Herald*, January 11, 1890, quoted in the *Lenoir Topic*, January 22, 1890.

82. *New Berne Weekly Journal*, November 21, 1889.

83. *Tarboro Southerner*, December 26, 1889. Story Matkin-Rawn cautions historians not to overestimate the role of agents: "While planter-backed labor agents also played an important role in fostering migration to Arkansas and neighboring states, we need to appreciate the political and activist networks among African Americans that set in motion chains of migration that would continue through the turn of the century." "'The Great Negro State,'" 5.

84. *CR*, April 21, 1889.

85. *Tarboro Southerner*, December 19, 1889.

86. Ibid.

87. Ibid.

88. NCBEMC *Proceedings*, October 1889, 14.

89. Ibid., 7–8.

90. Ibid.

91. Ibid.

92. "Notes from Asheville, NC," *SOZ*, March 28, 1889.

93. "New Berne District Conference," *SOZ*, February 6, 1890.

94. *Tarboro Southerner*, December 19, 1889.

95. "Cause of the Unrest and Discontent," *SOZ*, March 28, 1889; "Exodus Movement," *SOZ*, April 25, 1889; *SOZ*, February 6, 1890.

96. *SOZ*, August 22, 1889.

97. *SOZ*, September 26, 1889; "The Facts Undisguised," *SOZ*, January 16, 1890.

98. "The Facts Undisguised," *SOZ*, January 16, 1890.

99. *Tarboro Southerner*, January 2, 1890, quoted from the *CR*, December 12, 1889.

100. *CR*, February 6, 1890.

101. Ibid.

102. Ibid.

103. Frenise A. Logan, "The Movement of Negroes," 63–65.

104. NCBEMC *Proceedings*, October 1892, 19; Isaiah 62 and 63, KJV.

105. *CR*, December 12, 1889, quoted in the *Tarboro Southerner*, January 2, 1890.

106. NCBEMC *Proceedings*, October 1892, 19; Isaac S. Grant, "The Lord Is My Rock," *CR*, February 23, 1892.

107. C. R. Harris, "The Negro's Mission in America," *AMEZ Quarterly* 3, no. 1 (October 1892): 49.

108. Ibid., 52.

109. Washington, "Atlanta Exposition Address," 583–87; Turner, "The American Negro and His Fatherland," 195.

110. *Lenoir Topic*, January 22, 1890.

111. Ibid.

Chapter Four

1. "Prof. Price's Lecture," *CR*, February 3, 1887.

2. *SOZ*, January 31, 1889.

3. *SOZ*, January 1, 1886.

4. Higginbotham, *Righteous Discontent*, 187–88, 191, 193. The only lengthy work on postemancipation Southern black temperance activism is Thompson, *A Most Stirring and Significant Episode*, which is based on his doctoral dissertation, "Race, Temperance, and Prohibition in the Post-bellum South: Black Atlanta, 1865–1890" (PhD diss., Emory University, 2005). Few scholars have addressed the role of race in Southern prohibition elections. The best work has been on the Texas Prohibition Movement of the 1880s. See Ivy, *No Saloon in the Valley*, and Cantrell, " 'Dark Tactics.' " Janette Greenwood covers the biracial coalition for the North Carolina 1881 Prohibition Referendum, a topic I return to later in this chapter; see *Bittersweet Legacy*, 80–105. For other works on prohibition elections, see Walton and Taylor, "Another Force for Disfranchisement," and "Blacks, the Prohibitionists, and Disfranchisement," 66–69. See also Herd, "Prohibition, Racism and Class Politics." There have been a few studies of antebellum black temperance activism, including Yacovone, "The Transformation of the Black Temperance Movement," 288–91, and Block, "A Revolutionary Aim," 9–24. Like Higginbotham, a number of women's historians address temperance activism within larger discussions of black reform and black religion. For North Carolina–specific studies, see Gilmore, *Gender and Jim Crow*, and Sims, *The Power of Femininity*.

5. Gaines, *Uplifting the Race*, 2, 6.

6. Thompson, "Race, Temperance, and Prohibition," 76–82; Douglass, "Temperance and Anti-Slavery," 209.

7. Thompson, "Race, Temperance, and Prohibition," 76–82.

8. American Tract Society, *The Freedman's Spelling-Book*, quoted in Morris, ed., *The Freedmen's Schools and Textbooks*, vol. 2, 13.

9. Thompson, "Race, Temperance, and Prohibition," 82–120.

10. Ibid., 68–70; Timothy Smith, "Righteousness and Hope," 21–45; Hampton, " 'The Greatest Curiosity.' "

11. *Proceedings of the State Baptist Convention* (colored) (Raleigh, N.C.: W. J. Edwards, 1872), 11.

12. Whitener, *Prohibition in North Carolina*, 55–56.

13. "Episcopal Correspondence," *Fayetteville Educator*, February 20, 1875.

14. Sims, *The Power of Femininity*, 21.

15. Historians have followed the lead of Perry Miller, who described Puritan jeremiads as "literature of self-condemnation." *Errand into the Wilderness*, 8–15. See Bercovitch, *The American Jeremiad*, 3–6.

16. Bercovitch, *The American Jeremiad*, 6–9.

17. Ibid., 11.

18. Howard-Pitney, *The African American Jeremiad*, 10–13; Moses, *Black Messiahs and Uncle Toms*, 29–32.

19. Howard-Pitney, *The African American Jeremiad*, 53–55.

20. S. F. Hamilton, "Present Times," *SOZ*, March 29, 1894; "The Age in Which We Live," *Fayetteville Educator*, March 20, 1875.

21. NCBEMC *Proceedings*, October 1890, 41.

22. Hood, *Negro in the Christian Pulpit*, 120; *Minutes of the Eighteenth Session of the North Carolina Annual Conference of the A. M. E. Zion Church in America, Held in Beaufort, N.C., November 30th to December 6th, 1881*, comp., A. B. Smyer (Salisbury, N.C.: Star of Zion Job Print, 1882), 43–44.

23. Hood, *Negro in the Christian Pulpit*, 121.

24. Ibid., 119.

25. *SOZ*, January 15, 1886.

26. Ibid., January 1, 1886.

27. C. R. Harris, "The Negro's Mission in America," *AMEZ Quarterly* 3, no. 1 (October 1892): 53.

28. NCBEMC *Proceedings*, October 1894, 18.

29. *Raleigh Register*, November 1, 1877. Williamson appears in chapter 2 as one of only three black legislators who did not sign the Esther circular in 1870; he appears in chapter 3 because in 1877 he proposed black colonization to an independent territory in the West. At the 1877 State Colored Convention, where he delivered this speech on temperance, he recanted his advocacy of colonization.

30. *Raleigh Register*, November 1, 1877.

31. *Proceedings of the State Baptist Convention* (colored), October 1872, 11.

32. Ibid.

33. *SOZ*, November 21, 1884.

34. Harris, "The Negro's Mission in America," 55–56.

35. NCBEMC *Proceedings*, November 1903, 21, 42.

36. Ibid., October 1889, 16.

37. Mitchell, *Righteous Propagation*, 80–85; Rydell, *All the World's a Fair*; Moses, *Creative Conflict*, 141–43.

38. The newspaper warned their audience of danger lurking around every corner because of the community's waywardness. The editors held out high hopes for black North Carolinians if they remained faithful to their mission yet warned of the dire

consequences that would follow if they turned astray. The jeremiads made assumptions that the editors believed their readers would share, namely that the race had a golden day ahead and that drinking alcohol was antithetical both to teachings of the Bible and to the progress of the race.

39. "For the Editors," *Fayetteville Educator*, May 8, 1875; Hornsby-Gutting, *Black Manhood*, 52–94.

40. "Our Own Boys," *Fayetteville Educator*, January 9, 1875.

41. Bederman, *Manliness and Civilization*, 18–19.

42. *Fayetteville Educator*, January 23, 1875; "Manliness," *SOZ*, January 17, 1889.

43. "A Temperance Lesson," *SOZ*, January 28, 1887.

44. W. S. Meadows, "A Warning to Preachers," *SOZ*, December 20, 1894.

45. "A Sad Blight," *SOZ*, February 20, 1885.

46. H. T. Lomax, "N. C. Conference," *SOZ*, December 26, 1884.

47. C. H. Meade, "N. C. Conference," *SOZ*, December 12, 1884.

48. W. S. Meadows, "A Warning to Preachers." See also "A Temperance Lesson," *SOZ*, January 28, 1887.

49. *The Augustinian*, December 1905: 1–3. *The Augustinian*, edited by James K. Satterwhite, was a short-lived and irregularly issued publication written by and for students and alumni of St. Augustine's College in Raleigh, a four-year African American college affiliated with the Episcopal Church.

50. See Gilmore, " 'A Melting Time,' " 153–72.

51. J. C. Price, "The Race Question in the South," *AMEZ Quarterly* 2, no. 3 (April 1892): 322–23.

52. NCBEMC *Proceedings*, October 1908, 10–11.

53. *SOZ*, November 14, 1884.

54. Whitener, "History of the Temperance Movement," 130–35.

55. Whitaker, *Whitaker's Reminiscences*, 196–98.

56. "Document No. 23," in *North Carolina Executive and Legal Documents, Session 1881*, 2–3, 4–5.

57. Whitaker, *Whitaker's Reminiscences*, 196.

58. Latta, *The History of My Life and Work*, 158–59.

59. "Prohibition in North Carolina," *CR*, July 28, 1881; "Breaking Down the Color Line," *CR*, December 8, 1887.

60. Latta, *The History of My Life and Work*, 159.

61. "Colored Prohibition," *Charlotte Observer*, July 15, 1881, quoted in Sims, *The Power of Femininity*, 21.

62. Whitener, *Prohibition in North Carolina*, 70–78.

63. Whitener, "History of the Temperance Movement," 130.

64. Ibid.; Whitaker, *Whitaker's Reminiscences*, 196–98.

65. Latta, *The History of My Life and Work*, 158–59.

66. Whitaker, *Whitaker's Reminiscences*, 196–98.

67. Latta, *The History of My Life and Work*, 155–56.

68. *Charlotte Observer*, August 5, 1881, and *Carolina Watchman*, August 11, 1881, quoted in Whitener, "History of the Temperance Movement," 153–55.

69. *Minutes of the Eighteenth Session of the North Carolina Annual Conference of the A. M. E. Zion Church* (1881), 43–44.

70. *North Carolina Presbyterian*, June 16, 1886, quoted in Whitener, *Prohibition in North Carolina*, 91.

71. *Minutes of the Eighteenth Session of the North Carolina Annual Conference of the A. M. E. Zion Church* (1881), 43–44.

72. Ibid.

73. Whitaker, *Whitaker's Reminiscences*, 198–201.

74. Ibid.

75. Ibid.

76. Whitener, *Prohibition in North Carolina*, 81–100.

77. Both newspaper reports quoted in the *North Carolina Presbyterian*, June 16, 1886; see also Whitener, *Prohibition in North Carolina*, 91.

78. "A Visit to Raleigh, N.C." *CR*, June 9, 1887.

79. *Minutes of the Eighteenth Session of the North Carolina Annual Conference of the A. M. E. Zion Church*, 43–44.

80. Interview quoted in Wells-Barnett, "A Red Record," In *On Lynchings*, 133.

81. Belle Kearney, "The Late State Convention of the W. C. T. U.," *North Carolina White Ribbon*, July 1, 1896.

82. Whitener, *Prohibition in North Carolina*, 133–35.

83. *Biblical Recorder*, December 24, 1902, quoted in Whitener, *Prohibition in North Carolina*, 134.

84. Whitener, *Prohibition in North Carolina*, 135.

85. Ibid.

86. Chapter 5 examines how black Protestant leaders reconciled their political defeats in 1898 with their hopeful eschatology.

87. C. R. Harris, "Bishop's Address: The Negro Leaves God—God Leaves the Negro," *SOZ*, December 22, 1898.

88. Ibid.

89. J. W. Hood, "Race Disturbances," *SOZ*, December 15, 1898.

90. Hood, "Race Disturbances."

91. Gaines, *Uplifting the Race*, 6.

92. Alexander Walters, "The Outlook Gloomy," *SOZ*, December 22, 1898.

Chapter Five

1. S. F. Hamilton, "Present Times," *SOZ*, March 29, 1894. I use the term "Jim Crow segregation" to mean de jure racial segregation, but I employ the term "Jim Crow" more broadly to refer to the policies of segregation, disfranchisement, intimidation,

and economic subjugation that circumscribed black Southerners' lives from the 1890s to the 1960s.

2. S. F. Hamilton, "Present Times."

3. See chapter 3, n. 20.

4. S. F. Hamilton, "Present Times."

5. Rayford Logan first identified this time period as the nadir in *The Negro in American Life and Thought*.

6. J. C. Price, "The Race Question in the South," *AMEZ Quarterly* 2, no. 3 (April 1892): 328–29.

7. NCBEMC *Proceedings*, October 1893, 9.

8. C. R. Harris, "Episcopal Dots," *SOZ*, August 4, 1898.

9. NCBEMC *Proceedings*, October 1899, 16.

10. "Anything to Get Votes," *New York Times*, July 24, 1896; Gaither, *Blacks and the Populist Movement*; Hahn, *The Roots of Southern Populism*; Creech, *Righteous Indignation*.

11. Ali, "The Making of a Black Populist."

12. Creech, *Righteous Indignation*, xvii, 139–40, 90–91; *Progressive Farmer*, September 22, 1891, quoted in Creech, *Righteous Indignation*, 91.

13. Whitted, *A History of the Negro Baptists*, 64.

14. "Nothing in It for the Negro," *SOZ*, April 5, 1894.

15. Ibid.

16. *SOZ*, September 6, 1894.

17. "Election Opinions," *SOZ*, November 15, 1894.

18. *SOZ*, November 15, 1894; Anderson, *Race and Politics*.

19. "Editorials," *AMEZ Quarterly Review* 8, no. 3 (July 1898): 76–79.

20. Ibid., 78.

21. Ibid.; Gatewood, "North Carolina's Negro Regiment"; Gleijeses, "African Americans and the War Against Spain," 184–209.

22. N. N. Bruce to the Raleigh *News & Observer*, May 22, 1898, in Gatewood, ed., "*Smoked Yankees*," 106–10. Elsa Barkeley Brown's comments at a 2005 Southern Historical Association Annual Meeting panel helped me better interpret Bruce's letter.

23. "Editorials," *AMEZ Quarterly Review* 8, no. 3 (July 1898): 78.

24. N. N. Bruce to the Raleigh *News & Observer*, May 22, 1898.

25. L. S. Slaughter, "This Present War: Should Charity Begin at Home?" *SOZ*, July 14, 1898.

26. Ibid.

27. Gatewood, *Black Americans*, 322–23.

28. The Third Regiment never left the States. Stationed in garrisons in Fort Macon, N.C., and Knoxville, Tenn., the soldiers faced increasing restlessness and declining sanitation. The soldiers wrote complaints and signed petitions, asking for

leave of garrison duty. After the war ended, they received daily letters from family, describing, as one letter did, "their suffering condition, and oh my-God, the way we are treated." Quoted in Gatewood, "North Carolina's Negro Regiment," 382.

29. See issues of the Raleigh *News & Observer*, July–November, 1898; Wooley, "Race and Politics." See also Tyson and Celeski, eds., *Democracy Betrayed*; and Anderson, *Race and Politics*.

30. NCBEMC *Proceedings*, October 1898, 40.

31. "A Race Issue Campaign," *SOZ*, October 27, 1898.

32. Ibid.

33. Ibid.

34. See chapter 2.

35. *Outlook*, November 19, 1898, quoted in John Hope Franklin, "Foreword," in Tyson and Cecelski, eds., *Democracy Betrayed*, xi; see also H. Leon Prather Sr., "We Have Taken a City," in Tyson and Cecelski, eds., *Democracy Betrayed*, 26.

36. *Wilmington Messenger*, October 21, 1898, quoted in Umfleet, *1898 Wilmington Race Riot*, 104.

37. Anderson, *Race and Politics*, 252–77.

38. *Wilmington Daily Record*, August 18, 1898, quoted in Umfleet, *1898 Wilmington Race Riot*, 98. See Prather, "We Have Taken a City," 16–23, and Gilmore, *Gender & Jim Crow*, 105–6.

39. Kirk, "A Statement of Facts," 1–3.

40. *Wilmington Messenger*, August 27, 1898, quoted in Prather, "We Have Taken a City," 23.

41. Raleigh *News & Observer*, November 1, 1898, quoted in Prather, "We Have Taken a City," 28.

42. The day following the election, an extralegal white citizens' group summoned black leaders—ministers and businessmen—to an evening meeting at the courthouse, where the group delivered an ultimatum to the city's African American community: immediately expel Manly from the city and cease the publication of the *Record*, or armed white men would do so. By that time, Manly had already fled Wilmington and ceased publication. Furthermore, none of the black leaders summoned, however willing to comply, had any direct connection with or control over the newspaper. The meeting, it seemed, was but a cover for the planned coup the next day, when the citizens' group planned to take control of the city and replace its elected biracial leadership. See Kirk, "A Statement of Facts," 5–12; Prather, "We Have Taken a City," 29–31; and Umfleet, *1898 Wilmington Race Riot*, 116.

43. Prather, "We Have Taken a City," 31–37; Umfleet, *1898 Wilmington Race Riot*, ch. 5.

44. *CR*, December 29, 1898.

45. *CR*, November 24, 1898.

46. "Bishop Gaines on the Situation in the South," *CR*, December 1, 1898, reprinted from the *Atlanta Constitution*.

47. Alexander Walters, "Outlook Gloomy," *SOZ*, December 22, 1898, and Alexander Walters, "What Must We Do to Be Saved?" *CR*, December 29, 1898.

48. W. F. Fonvielle, "Majors and Minors: Echoes from the N.C. Conference," *SOZ*, January 5, 1899.

49. James Walker Hood, "Race Disturbances, Bad Leadership the Cause of It in North Carolina: Political Extract from Bishop J. W. Hood's annual address delivered before the Central North Carolina Conference in Carthage, N.C., two weeks ago," *SOZ*, December 15, 1898.

50. Hood, "Race Disturbances."

51. "Bishop's Address," *SOZ*, December 22, 1898.

52. "Hung on Their Own Gallows," *SOZ*, January 12, 1899.

53. Anderson, *Race and Politics*, 296–312.

54. "Senator Pritchard on Guard," *AMEZ Quarterly Review* 9, no. 1–2 (January–April 1899): 89–90.

55. "Our Race Troubles: A Repeated Lesson Taught the Children of Israel," *SOZ*, January 12, 1899.

56. Gilmore, *Gender & Jim Crow*, 120.

57. Hood, "Race Disturbances."

58. J. W. Hood, "My Critic," *SOZ*, January 5, 1899.

59. Ibid.

60. C. R. Harris, "Bishop's Address," *SOZ*, December 22, 1898.

61. J. B. Small, "Our Race Troubles: A Repeated Lesson Taught the Children of Israel," *SOZ*, January 12, 1899.

62. Ibid.

63. *AME Zion Quarterly Review* 10, no. 3 (October–December 1900): 46.

64. NCBEMC *Proceedings*, October 1897, 17.

65. Ibid., 14–15.

66. *AME Zion Quarterly Review* 10, no. 3 (October–December 1900): 46.

67. "Editorial Section," *African Methodist Episcopal Zion Quarterly* 13, no. 1 (January–March 1904): 87.

68. *CR*, December 29, 1898.

69. W. M. Anderson, "Marching On," *SOZ*, July 14, 1898.

70. NCBEMC *Proceedings*, October 1908, 10–11.

71. Ibid., October 1899, 14–15.

72. The 1910 *U.S. Census of Agriculture* records the number of black-owned farms in North Carolina at 21,443 (14.75% of all farms), up from 17,520 (13.4%) in the 1900 census. Earlier censuses do not categorize North Carolina farms by the color of their owners, making it difficult to chart black land ownership rates. It is generally accepted that 1910 or 1920 was the national high point for black land ownership, and there is little reason to believe that North Carolina diverged from the national trend. For a survey of this research, see Gilbert, Sharp, and Felin, "The Decline (and Revival?) of Black Farmers"; and Mandle, *Not Slave, Not Free*.

73. George W. Clinton, "The Southern Negro: Some Evidences of His Progress Since the War," *SOZ*, October 6, 1898.

74. "Editorial Section," *AMEZ Quarterly* 13, no. 1 (January–March 1904): 87.

75. Alexander Walters, "The Outlook Gloomy," *SOZ*, December 22, 1898.

76. NCBEMC *Proceedings*, October 1899, 14–15.

77. Ibid., 24; Psalm 22:1, KJV; Matthew 27:45–46, KJV.

78. NCBEMC *Proceedings*, October 1899, 24.

79. Quoted in Edward J. Blum and Paul Harvey, *The Color of Christ*, 151.

80. Harvey, *Moses, Jesus, and the Trickster*, 115–16.

81. W. E. B. Du Bois, "The Church and the Negro," *The Crisis* 6, no. 6 (October 1913): 291; Du Bois, *Darkwater*, 25–28; Blum, *W. E. B. Du Bois*, 154–55.

82. "Thoughts for the Occasion: A Powerful Emancipation Address Delivered by Bishop G. W. Clinton, A. M., D. D., at Charlotte, N.C." *AMEZ Quarterly* 13, no. 1 (January–March 1904): 3–6.

83. Ibid., 6.

84. John C. Dancy, "Disfranchisement," *AMEZ Quarterly Review* 14, no. 4 (December 1905): 85.

85. Bruce Grit, "Don't Like the Name," *SOZ*, October 6, 1898.

86. Others, like *Christian Century* editor C. C. Morrison who in 1928 cabled home from an antiwar meeting in Paris, "Today international war was banished from civilization," held on to their optimism a bit longer. Coffman, *The Christian Century*, 116.

87. Neibuhr, "Confessions of a Tired Radical," 1046–47; Dorrien, *The Making of American Liberal Theology*.

88. Hall, "The Long Civil Rights Movement," among others.

Epilogue

1. Kachun, Festivals of Freedom, 247–54.

2. "Ex-Slaves to Celebrate Semi-Freedom," *Chicago Defender*, March 9, 1912; Kachun, *Festivals of Freedom*, 249.

3. Kachun, *Festivals of Freedom*, 256. Not all black communities abandoned the practice of commemorating emancipation. For example, African Americans in Richmond, Va., continued Emancipation Day parades into the 1930s, and black Texans never stopped celebrating Juneteenth, their version of Emancipation Day. See Brundage, *The Southern Post*, 78–88, 138–82.

4. Sernett, *Bound for the Promised Land*, 3.

5. Monroe N. Work, *Negro Year Book, 1918–1919, An Annual Encyclopedia of the Negro* (Tuskegee, Ala.: Negro Year Book, 1919), 9, quoted in Sernett, *Bound for the Promised Land*, 60.

6. Sernett, *Bound for the Promised Land*, 61.

7. Oltman, *Sacred Mission*.

8. Roll, "Garveyism and the Eschatology of African Redemption," 29; Burkett, *Garveyism as a Religious Movement.*

9. Chappell, *A Stone of Hope,* 3–5. This argument differs from saying that the institutional black churches were central to the civil rights movement or always in favor of agitation against Jim Crow segregation. See Savage, *Your Spirits Walk Beside Us.*

10. See Comstock, "Two Types of Narrative Theology," 687–717; Hauerwas and Jones, eds., *Why Narrative?*; Cullinan, *Redeeming the Story*; Loughlin, *Telling God's Story*; Sauter and Barton, eds., *Revelation and Story.*

Bibliography

Primary Sources

NEWSPAPERS AND PERIODICALS

*African Methodist Episcopal Zion
    Quarterly* (Charlotte, N.C.)
The Augustinian (Raleigh, N.C.)
The Charlotte Advertiser
Charlotte Messenger
Chatham Record (Pittsboro, N.C.)
Chicago Defender
Christian Recorder (Philadelphia)
Crisis (New York)
The Fayetteville Educator
    (Fayetteville, N.C.)
Greensboro Patriot
Journal of Freedom (Raleigh, N.C.)
Kinston Journal
Lenoir Topic
New Berne Weekly Journal
New York Times

New York Tribune
News & Observer (Raleigh, N.C.)
North Carolina Presbyterian
    (Fayetteville, N.C.)
North Carolina White Ribbon
    (High Point, N.C.)
Raleigh Register
Raleigh Signal
Raleigh State Chronicle
Southern Workman (Hampton, Va.)
The Spirit of Missions (Burlington, N.J.)
Star of Zion (Salisbury, N.C.)
Tarboro Southerner
Warrenton Gazette
The Weekly Standard (Raleigh, N.C.)
Wilmington Daily Herald
Wilmington Morning Star

MANUSCRIPT COLLECTIONS

Chapel Hill, North Carolina
    Wilson Library, University of North Carolina
        North Carolina Collection
        Southern Historical Collection
        Ransom Family Papers
Charlotte, North Carolina
    James B. Duke Memorial Library, Inez Moore Parker Archives and Research
        Center, Johnston C. Smith University
        History of Johnston C. Smith University Collection
        McCrorey Collection
        President's Gallery
Raleigh, North Carolina
    Prizell R. Robinson Library, St. Augustine's College
        Special Collections

North Carolina Divisions of Archive and History
  Adjutant General Records
  James H. Harris Papers
Salisbury, North Carolina
  Heritage Hall, Livingstone College
    Special Collections
Washington, D.C.
  Library of Congress
    American Colonization Society Papers

MINUTES AND PROCEEDINGS, RECURRING

Minutes of the Freedmen's Convention, Held in the City of Raleigh, on the 2nd, 3rd, 4th,
  and 5th of October 1866. Raleigh, N.C.: Standard Book and Job Office, 1866.
Minutes of the North Carolina Annual Conference of the A.M.E. Zion Church in
  America, variant titles, 1874–1910.
Proceedings of the Annual Session of the Central North Carolina Conference, of
  the A.M.E. Zion Church in America, variant titles, 1880–1910.
Proceedings of the Joint Sessions of the Baptist Educational and Missionary Convention,
  the Ministerial Union, the Hayes-Fleming Foreign Missionary Society, and the State
  Sunday School Convention of North Carolina, variant titles, 1889–95, 1897–99, 1901,
  1903, 1905, 1908, 1909–13.
Proceedings of the Most Worshipful Grand Lodge of Free and Accepted Ancient Masons
  for the State of North Carolina and Its Jurisdiction, variant titles, 1870, 1874–78, 1880,
  1885–87, 1890–93, 1909–13, 1916.
Proceedings of the State Baptist Convention (colored). Raleigh, N.C.: W. J. Edwards,
  1870–87.

PUBLISHED WORKS

"Address to the Colored People of North Carolina." Circular, December 19, 1870.
American Tract Society. *The Freedman's Spelling-Book.* In *The Freedmen's Schools and*
  Textbooks, vol. 2, edited by Robert C. Morris. New York: AMS Press, Inc., 1980.
"An Appeal for Help to the People of the State in Behalf of the Colored Orphan
  Children of North Carolina." Leaflet. Oxford, N.C.: Colored Orphan Asylum,
  1890.
Andrews, Sidney. *The South Since the War as Shown by Fourteen Weeks of Travel and*
  Observation in Georgia and the Carolinas. Boston: Ticknor and Fields, 1866.
Burkhead, Rev. L. S. "History of the Difficulties of the Pastorate of the Front Street
  Methodist Church, Wilmington, N.C., For the Year 1865." *An Annual Publication*
  of Historical Papers Published by the Historical Society of Trinity College, series VIII
  (1908–09): 35–118.
Burt, Mary F. *Impressions of Saint Augustine's College,* vol. 58. Hartford, Conn.:
  Church Missions Publishing Co., 1906.

Clinton, George W. *Christianity under the Searchlight.* Nashville, Tenn.: National Baptist Publishing Board, 1909.

Colored Orphan Asylum of North Carolina, Oxford, N.C. Oxford, N.C.: Public Ledger Print, 1900.

Culp, D. W., comp. *Twentieth Century Negro Literature, or, A Cyclopedia of Thought on the Vital Topics Relating to the American Negro, By One Hundred of America's Greatest Negroes.* Toronto: J. L Nichols & Co., 1902.

Delany, Martin. "Prospects of the Freedmen of Hilton Head"; "Triple Alliance—The Restoration of the South—Salvation of Its Political Economy"; "Letter to the Colored Delegation, 22 February 1866," in Robert S. Levine, ed., *Martin R. Delany: A Documentary Reader.* Chapel Hill: University of North Carolina Press, 2003.

Derby, William P. *Bearing Arms in the Twenty-Seventh Massachusetts Regiment of Volunteer Infantry during the Civil War, 1861–1865.* Boston: Wright & Potter Co., 1883.

"Document No. 23." In *North Carolina Executive and Legal Documents, Session 1881.* Raleigh, N.C.: News & Observer, State Printers and Binders, 1881.

Douglass, Frederick. "Temperance and Anti-Slavery: An Address Delivered in Paisley, Scotland, on 30 March 1846." In *The Frederick Douglass Papers,* edited by John W. Blassingame, series 1, vol. 1. New Haven, Conn.: Yale University Press, 1979.

Du Bois, W. E. B. "The Conservation of the Races." *Occasional Papers,* no. 2. Washington, D.C.: American Negro Academy, 1897.

———. *Darkwater: Voices from within the Veil.* New York: Harcourt, Brace, and Company, 1920.

"Ex. Doc. No. 2: Message of President on condition of States lately in rebellion." In *Senate Executive Documents.* 1st Session, 39th Congress, 1865–66.

Harris, James H. *Speech of Hon. James H. Harris on the Militia Bill, Delivered in the North Carolina House of Representatives Monday, January 17, 1870.* Raleigh: North Carolina Standard, 1870.

Hood, Rev. James Walker. *Negro in the Christian Pulpit, or the Two Characters and Two Destinies.* Raleigh, N.C.: Edwards & Broughton, 1884.

———. *One Hundred Years of the African Methodist Episcopal Zion Church, or the Centennial of African Methodism.* New York: AME Zion Book Concern, 1895.

———. *The Plan of the Apocalypse.* York, Pa.: P. Anstadt & Sons, 1900.

Johnson, James Weldon. *Fifty Years and Other Poems.* Boston: Cornhill Company, 1917.

Journal of the Constitutional Convention of the State of North-Carolina at Its Session 1868. Raleigh: J. W. Holden, Convention Printer, 1868.

Journal of the House of Representatives of the General Assembly of North Carolina at Its Session, 1870–1871. Raleigh: James H. Moore, State Printer and Binder, 1871.

Kirk, J. Allen. "A Statement of Facts Concerning the Bloody Riot in Wilmington, N.C. Of Interest to Every Citizen of the United States." Wilmington, N.C.: [The Author?], [1898?]. http://docsouth.unc.edu/nc/kirk/menu.html.

Latta, Morgan London. *The History of My Life and Work.* Raleigh, N.C.: Edwards and Broughton, 1903.

Lincoln, Abraham. "Second Inaugural Address of March 4, 1865." Avalon Project: Documents in Law, History, and Diplomacy. Yale Law Library, 2008. http://avalon.law.yale.edu/19th_century/lincoln2.asp.

Neibuhr, Reinhold. "Confessions of a Tired Radical." *Christian Century*, August 30, 1928: 1046–47.

Parker, Theodore. *Ten Sermons of Religion*. Boston: Crosby, Nichols, and Company, 1853.

Report of the Joint Committee on Reconstruction, House Report no. 30, 39th Congress, 1st Session, part II.

Report and Testimony of the Select Committee of the United States Senate to Investigate the Causes of the Removal of the Negroes from the Southern States to the Northern States, 3 parts, 46th Congress, 2nd Session, Senate Report no. 693.

Steward, Theophilus G. *The End of the World, or Clearing the Way for the Fullness of the Gentiles*. Philadelphia: A.M.E. Church Book Rooms, 1888.

Turner, Henry McNeal. "The American Negro and His Fatherland." In *Africa and the American Negro: Addresses and Proceedings of the Congress on Africa: Held under the Auspices of the Stewart Missionary Foundation for Africa of Gammon Theological Seminary in Connection with the Cotton States and International Exposition December 13–15, 1895*, edited by J. W. E. Bowen. Atlanta: Gammon Theological Seminary, 1896.

Waddell, Alfred Moore. *Some Memories of My Life*. Raleigh, N.C.: Edwards and Broughton, 1908.

Walker, David. *Walker's Appeal, in Four Articles; Together with a Preamble, to the Coloured Citizens of the World, but in Particular, and Very Expressly, to Those of the United States of America, Written in Boston, State of Massachusetts, September 28, 1829*. Boston: David Walker, 1830.

Washington, Booker T. "Atlanta Exposition Address." In *Booker T. Washington Papers*, edited by Louis Harlan, vol. 3, *1889–95*. Urbana: University of Illinois Press, 1974.

Wells-Barnett, Ida. "A Red Record." In *On Lynchings*. 1895. Reprint, Amherst, N.Y.: Humanity Books, 2002.

Whitaker, Rev. R. H. *Whitaker's Reminiscences, Incidents, and Anecdotes*. Raleigh, N.C.: Edwards and Broughton, 1905.

Whitted, J. A. *A History of the Negro Baptists of North Carolina*. Raleigh: Edwards & Broughton Printing Co., 1908.

Williams, James. *Narrative of James Williams, an American Slave, Who Was for Several Years a Driver on a Cotton Plantation in Alabama*. New York: American Anti-Slavery Society, 1838.

Wright, Richard R., Jr., ed. *Centennial Encyclopedia of the African Methodist Episcopal Church*. Philadelphia: Book Concern of the A.M.E. Church, 1916.

Secondary Sources

Alexander, Roberta Sue. *North Carolina Faces the Freedmen: Race Relations During Presidential Reconstruction, 1865–67*. Durham, N.C.: Duke University Press, 1985.

Ali, Omar H. "The Making of a Black Populist: A Tribute to the Rev. Walter A. Pattillo." *Oxford (North Carolina) Public Ledger* 121, no. 25 (March 28, 2002).

Anderson, Eric. *Race and Politics in North Carolina, 1877–1901: The Black Second*. Baton Rouge: Louisiana State University Press, 1981.

Ash, Steven. *Middle Tennessee Society Transformed, 1860–70: War and Peace in the Upper South*. Knoxville: University of Tennessee Press, 2006.

Athearn, Robert G. *In Search of Canaan: Black Migration to Kansas, 1877–80*. Lawrence: Regents Press of Kansas, 1978.

Ayers, Edward L. *The Promise of the New South: Life after Reconstruction*. New York: Oxford University Press, 1992.

Barnes, Kenneth C. *Journey of Hope: The Back-to-Africa Movement in Arkansas in the Late 1800s*. Chapel Hill: University of North Carolina Press, 2004.

Bay, Mia. *To Tell the Truth Freely: The Life of Ida B. Wells*. New York: Hill and Wang, 2010.

Bederman, Gail. *Manliness and Civilization: A Cultural History of Gender and Race in the United States, 1880–1917*. Chicago: University of Chicago Press, 1995.

Belz, Herman. *New Birth of Freedom: the Republican Party and Freedmen's Rights, 1861 to 1866*. Westport, Conn.: Greenwood Press, 1976.

Bennett, James B. *Religion and the Rise of Jim Crow in New Orleans*. Princeton, N.J.: Princeton University Press, 2005.

Bercovitch, Sacvan. *The American Jeremiad*. Madison: University of Wisconsin Press, 1978.

Berlin, Ira. *Generations of Captivity: a History of African-American Slaves*. Cambridge, Mass.: Belknap Press of Harvard University Press, 2004.

Block, Shelley. "A Revolutionary Aim: The Rhetoric of Temperance in the Anglo-African Magazine." *American Periodicals* 12 (2002): 9–24.

Blum, Edward J. *Reforging the White Republic: Race, Religion, and American Nationalism*. Baton Rouge: Louisiana State University, 2005.

———. *W. E. B. Du Bois, American Prophet*. Philadelphia: University of Pennsylvania Press, 2007.

Blum, Edward J., and Paul Harvey. *The Color of Christ: The Son of God and the Saga of Race in America*. Chapel Hill: University of North Carolina Press, 2012.

Blum, Edward J., and W. Scott Poole, eds. *Vale of Tears: New Essays on Religion and Reconstruction*. Macon, Ga.: Mercer University Press, 2005.

Boles, John B., and Bethany L. Johnson, eds. *Origins of the New South Fifty Years Later: The Continuing Influence of a Historical Classic*. Baton Rouge: Louisiana State University Press, 2003.

Bradley, Mark L. *Bluecoats and Tar Heels: Soldiers and Civilians in Reconstruction North Carolina.* Lexington: University Press of Kentucky, 2009.

Brisson, Jim D. " 'Civil Government Was Crumbling around Me': The Kirk-Holden War of 1870." *North Carolina Historical Quarterly* 88, no. 2 (April 2011): 123–63.

Browning, Judkin. "Visions of Freedom and Civilization Opening before Them: African Americans Search for Autonomy during Military Occupation in North Carolina." In *North Carolinians in the Era of Civil War and Reconstruction*, edited by Paul D. Escott. Chapel Hill: University of North Carolina Press, 2008.

Brundage, W. Fitzhugh. *The Southern Past: A Clash of Race and Memory.* Cambridge, Mass.: Belknap Press of Harvard University Press, 2005.

Burkett, Randall K. *Garveyism as a Religious Movement: The Institutionalization of a Black Civil Religion.* Metuchen, N.J.: Scarecrow Press, 1978.

Caird, G. B. *Jesus and the Jewish Nation.* London: Athlone Press, 1965.

———. "The One and the Many in Mark and John." In *Studies of the Church in History: Essays Honoring Robert S. Paul on His Sixty-Fifth Birthday*, edited by Horton Davies. Allison Park, Pa.: Pickwick, 1983.

Callahan, Allen Dwight. *The Talking Book: African Americans and the Bible.* New Haven, Conn.: Yale University Press, 2006.

Campbell, James T. *Middle Passages: African American Journeys to Africa, 1787–2005.* New York: Penguin Books, 2006.

Cantrell, Gregg. " 'Dark Tactics': Black Politics in the 1887 Texas Prohibition Campaign." *Journal of American Studies* 25 (1991): 85–93.

———. *Kenneth and John B. Rayner and the Limits of Southern Dissent.* Urbana: University of Illinois Press, 1993.

Carter, Dan T. "The Anatomy of Fear: The Christmas Day Insurrection Scare of 1865." *Journal of Southern History* 42, no. 3 (1976): 345–64.

Case, Jay. *An Unpredictable Gospel: American Evangelicals and World Christianity, 1812–1920.* New York: Oxford University Press, 2012.

Cecelski, David. *The Fire of Freedom: Abraham Galloway and the Slaves' Civil War.* Chapel Hill: University of North Carolina Press, 2012.

———. *The Waterman's Song: Slavery and Freedom in Maritime North Carolina.* Chapel Hill: University of North Carolina Press, 2001.

Chappell, David. *A Stone of Hope: Prophetic Religion and the Death of Jim Crow.* Chapel Hill: University of North Carolina Press, 2004.

Cimbala, Paul A., and Barton C. Shaw. *Making a New South: Race, Leadership, and Community after the Civil War.* Gainesville: University Press of Florida, 2007.

Clark, Kathleen. *Defining Moments: African American Commemoration & Political Culture in the South, 1863–1913.* Chapel Hill: University of North Carolina Press, 2005.

Coffman, Elesha J. *The Christian Century and the Rise of the Protestant Mainline.* New York: Oxford University Press, 2013.

Cohen, William. *At Freedom's Edge: Black Mobility and the Southern White Quest for Racial Control, 1861–1915*. Baton Rouge: Louisiana State University Press, 1991.

Coker, Joe L. *Liquor in the Land of the Lost Cause: Southern White Evangelicals and the Prohibition Movement*. Lexington: University Press of Kentucky, 2007.

Comstock, Gary. "Two Types of Narrative Theology." *Journal of the American Academy of Religion* 55, no. 4 (1987): 687–717.

Concise Oxford Dictionary of the Christian Church, s.v. "Eschatology." http://www .oxfordreference.com/views/ENTRY.html?entry=t95.e1976.

Cone, James H. *God of the Oppressed*. Maryknoll, N.Y.: Orbis Books, 1997.

Creech, Joe. *Righteous Indignation: Religion and the Populist Revolution*. Urbana: University of Illinois Press, 2006.

Crow, Jeffrey. *Black Experience in Revolutionary North Carolina*. Raleigh, N.C.: Division of Archives and History, 1977.

Cullinan, Colleen Carpenter. *Redeeming the Story: Women, Suffering, and Christ*. New York: Continuum, 2004.

Curtis, Susan. *Consuming Faith: The Social Gospel and Modern American Culture*. Columbia: University of Missouri Press, 2001.

Davidson, James West. *The Logic of Millennial Thought: Eighteenth-Century New England*. New Haven, Conn.: Yale University Press, 1977.

Davis, David Brion. *The Problem of Slavery in the Age of Emancipation*. New York: Knopf, 2014.

Devlin, George Alfred. "South Carolina and Black Migration 1865–1940: In Search of the Promised Land." PhD diss., University of South Carolina, 1984.

Dickerson, Dennis C. "Liberation, Wesleyan Theology and Early African Methodism, 1766–1840." *Wesley and Methodist Studies* 3 (2011): 109–20.

Dictionary of North Carolina Biography, vol. 2 (D-G), ed. William S. Powell, s.v. "Stewart Ellison," by Elizabeth Davis Reid. Chapel Hill: University of North Carolina Press, 1986.

Dorrien, Gary. *The Making of American Liberal Theology: Idealism, Realism, and Modernity, 1900–1950*. Louisville: Westminster John Knox Press, 2003.

Du Bois, W. E. B. *Black Reconstruction in America: An Essay toward a History of the Part which Black Folk Played in the Attempt to Reconstruct Democracy in America, 1860–1880*. New York: Harcourt, Brace, 1935.

Dunlap, Leslie Kathrin. "In the Name of the Home: Temperance Women and Southern Grass-Roots Politics, 1873–1933." PhD diss., Northwestern University, 2001.

Dvorak, Katherine. *An African-American Exodus: the Segregation of Southern Churches*. Brooklyn: Carlson Publishing, 1991.

———. "After Apocalypse, Moses." In *Masters and Slaves in the House of the Lord: Race and Religion in the American South, 1740–1870*, edited by John Boles. Lexington: University Press of Kentucky, 1988.

Edwards, Laura. *Gendered Strife and Confusion: The Political Culture of Reconstruction*. Urbana: University of Illinois Press, 1997.

Emberton, Carole. *Beyond Redemption: Race, Violence, and the American South after the Civil War*. Chicago: University of Chicago Press, 2013.

Escott, Paul. *Many Excellent People: Power and Privilege in North Carolina, 1850–1900*. Chapel Hill: University of North Carolina Press, 1985.

Evans, Curtis. *The Burden of Black Religion*. New York: Oxford University Press, 2008.

Evans, William McKee. *Ballots and Fence Rails: Reconstruction on the Lower Cape Fear*. Athens: University of Georgia Press, 1995.

Fahey, David M. *Temperance and Racism: John Bull, Johnny Reb, and the Good Templars*. Lexington: University Press of Kentucky, 1996.

Foner, Eric. *Reconstruction: America's Unfinished Revolution, 1863–77*. New York: Harper and Row, 1988.

———. "Reconstruction and the Black Political Tradition." In *Political Parties and the Modern State*, edited by Richard L. McCormick. New Brunswick, N.J.: Rutgers University Press, 1984.

———. *A Short History of Reconstruction, 1863–1877*. New York: Harper Collins, 1990.

Fountain, Daniel L. *Slavery, Civil War, and Salvation: African American Slaves and Christianity, 1830–1870*. Baton Rouge: Louisiana State University Press, 2010.

Frazier, Edward Franklin. *The Negro Church in America*. New York: Schocken Books, 1964.

Fulop, Timothy. "The Future Golden Day of the Race: Millennialism and Black Americans in the Nadir, 1877–1901." *Harvard Theological Review* 84, no. 1 (1991): 75–99.

Gaines, Kevin. *Uplifting the Race: Black Leadership, Politics, and Culture in the Twentieth Century*. Chapel Hill: University of North Carolina Press, 1996.

Gaither, Gerald H. *Blacks and the Populist Movement: Ballots and Bigotry in the "New South."* Tuscaloosa: University of Alabama Press, 2005.

Gatewood, Willard, Jr. *Black Americans and the White Man's Burden, 1898–1903*. Urbana: University of Illinois Press, 1975.

———. "North Carolina's Negro Regiment in the Spanish-American War." *North Carolina Historical Review* 48, no. 4 (October 1971): 370–87.

———, ed. *"Smoked Yankees" and the Struggle for Empire: Letters from Negro Soldiers, 1898–1902*. Urbana: University of Illinois Press, 1971.

Genovese, Eugene. *From Rebellion to Revolution: Afro-American Slave Revolts in the Making of the Modern World*. Baton Rouge: Louisiana State University Press, 1979.

———. *Roll, Jordan, Roll: The World the Slaves Made*. New York: Pantheon Books, 1974.

Giggie, John. *After Redemption: Jim Crow and the Transformation of Religion in the Delta, 1875–1915*. New York: Oxford University Press, 2008.

Gilbert, Jess, Gwen Sharp, and M. Sindy Felin. "The Decline (and Revival?) of Black Farmers and Rural Landowners: A Review of Research Literature." University of Wisconsin-Madison Land Tenure Center Working Paper no. 44 (May 2001). North America Series. http://minds.wisconsin.edu/bitstream/1793 /21927/1/31_wp44.pdf.

Gilkes, Cheryl. *If It Wasn't for the Women: Black Women's Experience and Womanist Culture in Church and Community*. Maryknoll, N.Y.: Orbis Books, 2001.

Gilmore, Glenda. *Gender & Jim Crow: Women and the Politics of White Supremacy in North Carolina, 1896–1920*. Chapel Hill: University of North Carolina Press, 1996.

———. "'A Melting Time': Black Women, White Women, and the WCTU in North Carolina, 1880–1900." In *Hidden Histories of Women in the New South*, edited by Virginia Bernhard, Betty Brandon, Elizabeth Fox-Genovese, Theda Perdue, and Elizabeth H. Turner, 153–72. Columbia: University of Missouri Press, 1994.

Glaude, Eddie. *Exodus!: Religion, Race, and Nation in Early Nineteenth-Century Black America*. Chicago: University of Chicago Press, 2000.

Gleijeses, Peiro. "African Americans and the War against Spain." *North Carolina Historical Review* 74, no. 2 (1996): 184–209.

Gravely, Will. "African Methodisms and the Rise of Black Denominationalism." In *Reimagining Denominationalism: Interpretative Essays*, edited by Robert Bruce Mullin and Russell E. Richey, 239–263. New York: Oxford University Press, 1994.

Greenwood, Janette. *Bittersweet Legacy: The Black and White "Better Classes" in Charlotte, 1850–1910*. Chapel Hill: University of North Carolina Press, 1994.

Hahn, Steven. "'Extravagant Expectations' of Freedom: Rumour, Political Struggle, and the Christmas Insurrection Scare of 1865 in the American South." *Past and Present* 157 (1997): 122–58.

———. *A Nation under Our Feet: Black Political Struggles in the Rural South, from Slavery to the Great Migration*. Cambridge, Mass.: Belknap Press of Harvard University Press, 2003.

———. *The Roots of Southern Populism: Yeoman Farmers and the Transformation of the Georgia Upcountry, 1850–1890*. New York: Oxford University Press, 2006.

Hall, Gwendolyn Midlo. *Slavery and African Ethnicities in the Americas: Restoring the Links*. Chapel Hill: University of North Carolina Press, 2005.

Hall, Jacquelyn. "The Long Civil Rights Movement and the Political Uses of the Past." *Journal of American History* 91, no. 4 (2005): 1233–63.

Hamilton, Joseph Gregoire de Roulhac. *Reconstruction in North Carolina*. 1914. Reprint, Freeport, N.Y.: Books for Libraries Press, 1971.

Hampton, Monte. "'The Greatest Curiosity': Race, Religion, and Politics in Henry Evans' Methodist Church, 1758–1858." Paper delivered at the Southern Historical Association Annual Meeting, Richmond, Va., November 2007.

Hardy, Clarence. "From Exodus to Exile: Black Pentecostals, Migrating Pilgrims, and Imagined Internationalism," *American Quarterly* 59 3 (2007): 737–57.

Harris, William C. *The Day of the Carpetbagger: Republican Reconstruction in Mississippi*. Baton Rouge: Louisiana State University Press, 1979.

Harvey, Paul. *Freedom's Coming: Religious Culture and the Shaping of the South from the Civil War through the Civil Rights Era*. Chapel Hill: University of North Carolina Press, 2005.

———. *Moses, Jesus, and the Trickster in the Evangelical South*. Macon, Ga.: Mercer University Press, 2010.

———. *Redeeming the South: Religious Cultures and Racial Identities among Southern Baptists*. Chapel Hill: University of North Carolina Press, 1997.

Hauerwas, Stanley, and L. Gregory Jones, eds. *Why Narrative? Readings in Narrative Theology*. Grand Rapids, Mich.: W. B. Eerdmans, 1989.

Herd, Denise. "Prohibition, Racism and Class Politics in the Post-Reconstruction South." *Journal of Drug Issues* 13 (1983): 77–94.

Higginbotham, Evelyn Brooks. *Righteous Discontent: The Women's Movement in the Black Baptist Church, 1880–1920*. Cambridge, Mass.: Harvard University Press, 1993.

Hildebrand, Reginald. " 'Brother, Religion Is a Good Thing in Time of War': The Theology of U.S. Colored Troops." Paper presented at the 96th Annual Convention of the Association for the Study of African American Life and History, Richmond, Va., 2011.

———. *The Times Were Strange and Stirring: Methodist Preachers and the Crisis of Emancipation*. Durham, N.C.: Duke University Press, 1995.

Hilkey, Judy Arlene. *Character Is Capital: Success Manuals and Manhood in Gilded Age America*. Chapel Hill: University of North Carolina Press, 1997.

Hobson, Christopher Z. *The Mount of Vision: African American Prophetic Tradition, 1800–1950*. New York: Oxford University Press, 2012.

Hornsby-Gutting, Angela. *Black Manhood and Community Building in North Carolina, 1900–1930*. Gainesville: University Press of Florida, 2009.

Howard-Pitney, David. *The African American Jeremiad: Appeals for Justice in America*. Philadelphia: Temple University Press, 2005.

Hull, Gloria T., Patricia Bell-Scott, and Barbara Smith. *All the Women Are White, All the Blacks Are Men, but Some of Us Are Brave: Black Women's Studies*. Old Westbury, N.Y.: Feminist Press, 1982.

Ivy, James D. *No Saloon in the Valley: The Southern Strategy of Texas Prohibitionists in the 1880s*. Waco, Tex.: Baylor University Press, 2003.

Johnson, K. Todd. "Fences." In *Encyclopedia of North Carolina*, edited by William S. Powell, 424–25. Chapel Hill: University of North Carolina Press, 2006.

Jones, Lawrence N. "The Black Churches: A New Agenda." In *Afro-American Religious History: A Documentary Witness*, edited by Milton Sernett, 491. Durham, N.C.: Duke University Press, 1985.

Kachun, Mitch. *Festivals of Freedom: Memory and Meaning in African American Emancipation Celebrations, 1809–1915.* Amherst: University of Massachusetts Press, 2003.

Lincoln, C. Eric, and Lawrence H. Mamiya. *The Black Church in the African-American Experience.* Durham, N.C.: Duke University Press, 1990.

Litwack, Leon. *Been in the Storm So Long: the Aftermath of Slavery.* New York: Alfred A. Knopf, 1981.

Logan, Frenise A. "The Movement of Negroes from North Carolina, 1876–1894." *North Carolina Historical Review* 33, no. 1 (1956): 45–65.

Logan, Rayford. *The Negro in American Life and Thought: The Nadir, 1877–1901.* New York: Dial Press, 1954.

Loughlin, Gerard. *Telling God's Story: Bible, Church, and Narrative Theology.* New York: Cambridge University Press, 1996.

Maffly-Kipp, Laurie F. "Denominationalism and the Black Church." In *Reimagining Denominationalism: Interpretive Essays,* edited by Robert Mullin and Russell E. Richey, 59–62. New York: Oxford University Press, 1994.

———. "Mapping the World, Mapping the Race: The Negro Race History, 1874–1915." *Church History* 64, no. 4 (1995): 610–26.

———. "Redeeming Southern Memory: The Negro Race History, 1874–1915." In *Where These Memories Grow: History Memory, and Southern Identity,* edited by W. Fitzhugh Brundage, 169–90. Chapel Hill: University of North Carolina Press, 2000.

———. Setting Down the Sacred Past: African-American Race Histories. Cambridge, Mass: Belknap Press of Harvard University Press, 2010.

Magdol, Edward. *A Right to the Land: Essays on the Freedmen's Community.* Westport, Conn: Greenwood Press, 1977.

Mandle, Jay R. *Not Slave, Not Free: The African-American Economic Experience since the Civil War.* Durham, N.C.: Duke University Press, 1992.

Maslowski, James Joseph. "North Carolina Migration, 1870–1950." PhD diss., University of North Carolina at Chapel Hill, 1953.

Matkin-Rawn, Story. "'The Great Negro State of the Country': Arkansas's Reconstruction and the Other Great Migration." *Arkansas Historical Quarterly* 72, no. 1 (Spring 2013): 2–41.

Mays, Benjamin E., and Joseph William Nicholson. *The Negro's Church.* New York: Russell and Russell, 1969.

Meier, August. *Negro Thought in America, 1880–1915: Racial Ideologies in the Age of Booker T. Washington.* Ann Arbor: University of Michigan Press, 1963.

Melton, J. Gordon Melton. *A Will to Choose: The Origins of African-American Methodism.* Lanham, Md.: Rowman and Littlefield, 2007.

Metzger, Bruce M., and Michael D. Coogan, eds. *Oxford Companion to the Bible,* s.v. "Eschatology." Oxford: Oxford University Press, 1994. http://www.oxfordreference.com/views/ENTRY.html?entry=t120.e0229.

Miller, Perry. *Errand into the Wilderness.* Cambridge, Mass.: Belknap Press of Harvard University Press, 1956.

Miller, Randall, C. R. Wilson, and Harry Stout, eds. *Religion in the American Civil War.* New York: Oxford University Press, 1998.

Miller, Timothy. *Revivalism and Social Reform: American Protestantism on the Eve of the Civil War.* 1957. Reprint, Gloucester, Mass.: Peter Smith, 1976.

Mitchell, Michele. *Righteous Propagation: African Americans and the Politics of Racial Destiny after Reconstruction.* Chapel Hill: University of North Carolina Press, 2004.

Mobley, Joe A. *James City: A Black Community in North Carolina, 1863–1900.* Raleigh: N.C. Division of Archives and History, 1981.

Moltmann, Jürgen. *Theology of Hope: On the Ground and the Implications of a Christian Eschatology,* translated by James W. Leitch. New York: Harper and Row, 1967.

Montgomery, William. *Under Their Own Vine and Fig Tree: The African-American Church in the South, 1865–1900.* Baton Rouge: Louisiana State University Press, 1993.

Morehead, James H. *World without End: Mainstream American Protestant Visions of the Last Things, 1880–1925.* Bloomington: University of Indiana Press, 1999.

Morgan, Philip D. *Slave Counterpoint: Black Culture in the Eighteenth-Century Chesapeake & Lowcountry.* Chapel Hill: University of North Carolina Press, 1998.

Moses, Wilson. *Black Messiahs and Uncle Toms: Social and Literary Manipulations of a Religious Myth.* University Park: Pennsylvania State University Press, 1993.

———. *Classic Black Nationalism: From the American Revolution to Marcus Garvey.* New York: New York University Press, 1996.

———. *Creative Conflict in African American Thought: Frederick Douglass, Alexander Crummell, Booker T. Washington, W. E. B. Du Bois, and Marcus Garvey.* New York: Cambridge University Press, 2004.

Mullin, Robert Bruce, and Russell E. Richey, eds. *Reimagining Denominationalism: Interpretative Essays.* New York: Oxford University Press, 1994.

Murray, Andrew E. *Presbyterians and the Negro: A History.* Philadelphia: Presbyterian Historical Society, 1966.

Nieman, Donald G. *The Day of the Jubilee: The Civil War Experience of Black Southerners.* New York: Garland, 1994.

Noll, Mark A. *America's God: From Jonathan Edwards to Abraham Lincoln.* New York: Oxford University Press, 2002.

———. *The Civil War as a Theological Crisis.* Chapel Hill: University of North Carolina Press, 2006.

Nowaczyk, Elaine Joan. "The North Carolina Negro in Politics, 1865–1876." Master's thesis, University of North Carolina at Chapel Hill, 1957.

Numbers, Ronald, and Jon Butler, eds. *The Disappointed: Millerism and Millenarianism in the Nineteenth Century.* Knoxville: University of Tennessee Press, 1993.

Oltman, Adele. *Sacred Mission, Worldly Ambition: Black Christian Nationalism in the Age of Jim Crow*. Athens: University of Georgia Press, 2008.

Painter, Nell. *Exodusters: The Black Migration to Kansas after Reconstruction*. New York: W. W. Norton, 1977.

Perman, Michael. *Struggle for Mastery: Disfranchisement in the South, 1888–1908*. Chapel Hill: University of North Carolina Press, 2001.

Powell, William S. *North Carolina through Four Centuries*. Chapel Hill: University of North Carolina Press, 1989.

Raboteau, Albert J. "African-Americans, Exodus, and the American Israel." In *African-American Christianity: Essays in History*, edited by Paul E. Johnson, 1–17. Berkeley: University of California Press, 1994.

———. " 'Ethiopia Shall Soon Stretch Forth Her Hands to God': Black Destiny in Nineteenth-Century America." In *African American Religious Thought: An Anthology*, edited by Cornel West and Eddie S. Glaude Jr., 397–413. Louisville, Ky.: Westminster John Knox Press, 2003.

———. *A Fire in the Bones: Reflections on African-American Religious History*. Boston: Beacon Press, 1995.

———. *Slave Religion: The "Invisible Institution" in the Antebellum South*. New York: Oxford University Press, 1978.

Raboteau, Albert J., et al. "Retelling Carter Woodson's Story: Archival Sources for Afro-American Church History." *Journal of American History* 77 (June 1990): 183–99.

Reaves, William. *"Strength Through Struggle": The Chronological and Historical Record of the African American Community in Wilmington, North Carolina, 1865–1950*. Wilmington, N.C.: New Hanover County Public Library, 1998.

Redkey, Edwin S., ed. *A Grand Army of Black Men: Letters from African-American Soldiers in the Union Army, 1861–1865*. Cambridge Studies in American Literature and Culture 63. Cambridge: Cambridge University Press, 1992.

Richardson, Harry V. *Dark Salvation: The Story of Methodism as It Developed Among Blacks in America*. Garden City, N.Y.: Anchor Press, 1976.

Roediger, David. *Seizing Freedom: Slave Emancipation and Liberty for All*. London: Verso, 2014.

Roll, Jared. "Garveyism and the Eschatology of African Redemption in the Rural South, 1920–1936." *Religion and American Culture* 20, no. 1 (2010): 27–56.

Rydell, Robert W. *All the World's a Fair: Visions of Empire at American International Expositions, 1876–1916*. Chicago: University of Chicago Press, 1984.

Sauter, Gerhard, and John Barton, eds. *Revelation and Story: Narrative Theology and the Centrality of Story*. Burlington, Vt.: Ashgate Press, 2000.

Savage, Barbara Diane. *Your Spirits Walk Beside Us: The Politics of Black Religion*. Cambridge, Mass.: Belknap Press of Harvard University Press, 2008.

Sernett, Milton C. *Bound for the Promised Land: African American Religion and the Great Migration*. Durham, N.C.: Durham University Press, 1997.

Sims, Anastatia. *The Power of Femininity in the New South: Women's Organizations and Politics in North Carolina, 1880–1930.* Columbia: University of South Carolina Press, 1997.

Smith, Christian. *Moral Believing Animals: Human Personhood and Culture.* New York: Oxford University Press, 2003.

Smith, John David. *Black Soldiers in Blue: African American Soldiers in the Civil War Era.* Chapel Hill: University of North Carolina Press, 2002.

Smith, Theophus Harold. *Conjuring Culture: Biblical Formations of Black America.* New York: Oxford University Press, 1994.

Smith, Timothy. "Righteousness and Hope: Christian Holiness and the Millennial Vision in America, 1800–1900." *American Quarterly* 31 (1979): 21–45.

Snider, William D. *Light on the Hill: A History of the University of North Carolina at Chapel Hill.* Chapel Hill: University of North Carolina Press, 1992.

Stowell, Daniel W. *Rebuilding Zion: The Religious Reconstruction of the South, 1863–77.* New York: Oxford University Press, 1998.

Taylor, Joseph H. "The Great Migration from North Carolina in 1879." *North Carolina Historical Review* 31, no. 1 (1954): 18–33.

Teed, Paul E. "Loyalty and Liturgy: Union Occupation and Religious Liberty in Wilmington, North Carolina, 1865." *American Nineteenth Century History* 15, no. 1 (2014): 43–65.

Thompson, H. Paul. *A Most Stirring and Significant Episode: Religion and the Rise and Fall of Prohibition in Black Atlanta, 1865–1887.* DeKalb: Northern Illinois University Press, 2013.

———. "Race, Temperance, and Prohibition in the Postbellum South: Black Atlanta, 1865–1890." PhD diss., Emory University, 2005.

Trelease, Allen. *White Terror: The Ku Klux Klan Conspiracy and Southern Redemption.* New York: Harper & Row, 1971.

Trulear, Harold Dean. "Sociology of Afro-American Religion: An Appraisal of C. Eric Lincoln's Contributions." *Journal of Religious Thought* 42, no. 2 (1985): 44–55.

Tucker, David M. *Black Pastors and Leaders: Memphis, 1819–1972.* Memphis: Memphis State University Press, 1975.

Tyson, Timothy, and David S. Celeski, eds. *Democracy Betrayed: The Wilmington Race Riot of 1898 and Its Legacy.* Chapel Hill: University of North Carolina Press, 1998.

Umfleet, LeRae, and the 1898 Wilmington Race Riot Commission. *1898 Wilmington Race Riot.* Office of Archives and History, North Carolina Department of Cultural Resources, 2006. http://www.ah.dcr.state.nc.us/1898-wrrc/report/report.htm.

Wagner, Clarence M. *History of the National Baptist Convention, U.S.A., Inc.* Decatur, Ga.: Tru-Faith Publishing, 1993.

Walls, William J. *The African Methodist Episcopal Zion Church: Reality of the Black Church.* Charlotte, N.C.: A.M.E. Zion Publishing House, 1974.

Walton, Hanes, Jr., and James E. Taylor. "Another Force for Disfranchisement: Blacks and the Southern Prohibition Movement." *Phylon* 32 (3rd Quarter 1971): 247–59.

———. "Blacks, the Prohibitionists, and Disfranchisement." *Quarterly Review of Higher Education among Negroes* (April 1969): 66–69.

Washington, James Melvin. *Frustrated Fellowship: The Black Baptist Quest for Social Power*. Macon, Ga.: Mercer University Press, 1986.

Washington, Joseph R. *Black Religion: The Negro and Christianity in the United States*. Boston: Beacon Press, 1964.

Weber, Timothy. *Living in the Shadow of the Second Coming: American Premillennialism, 1875–1925*. New York: Oxford University Press, 1979.

Wheeler, Edward L. *Uplifting the Race: The Black Minister in the New South, 1865–1902*. Lanham, Md.: University Press of America, 1986.

Whitener, Daniel Jay. "History of the Temperance Movement in North Carolina, 1715 to 1908." PhD diss., University of North Carolina at Chapel Hill, 1932.

———. *Prohibition in North Carolina, 1715–1945*. Chapel Hill: University of North Carolina Press, 1945.

Williams, Heather. *Help Me to Find My People: the African American Search for Family Lost in Slavery*. Chapel Hill: University of North Carolina Press, 2012.

Williamson, Joel. *The Crucible of Race: Black/White Relations in the South Since Emancipation*. New York: Oxford University Press, 1984.

Wills, David W. "Introduction." In *Black Apostles at Home and Abroad: Afro-Americans and the Christian Mission from the Revolution to Reconstruction*, edited by David Wills and Richard Newman. Boston: G. K. Hall & Co., 1982.

Wilmore, Gayraud. *Black Religion and Black Radicalism: An Interpretation of the Religious History of African Americans*. Maryknoll, N.Y.: Orbis Books, 1998.

———. *Last Things First*. 1st ed. Library of Living Faith. Philadelphia: Westminster Press, 1982.

Wilson, Bryan R. *Magic and the Millennium: A Sociological Study of Religious Movements of Protest Among Tribal and Third-world Peoples*. London: Heinemann, 1973.

Wilson, Charles Reagan. *Baptized in Blood: the Religion of the Lost Cause, 1865–1920*. Athens: University of Georgia Press, 1980.

Wilson, Keith P. *Campfires of Freedom: The Camp Life of Black Soldiers during the Civil War*. Kent, Ohio: Kent State University Press, 2002.

Wimbush, Vincent L. "The Bible and African Americans: An Outline of an Interpretive History." In *Stony the Road We Trod: African American Biblical Interpretation*, edited by Felder Cain Hope. Minneapolis: Fortress Press, 1991.

Woodson, Carter Godwin. *The History of the Negro Church*. 3rd ed. Washington, D.C.: Associated Publishers, 1985.

Woodward, C. Vann. *Origins of the New South, 1877–1913*. Baton Rouge: Louisiana State University Press, 1951.

———. *The Strange Career of Jim Crow.* 2nd rev. ed. New York: Oxford University Press, 1966.

Wooley, Robert H. "*Race and Politics: The Evolution of the White Supremacy Campaign of 1898 in North Carolina.*" PhD diss., University of North Carolina at Chapel Hill, 1977.

Wright, Ben, and Zachary W. Dresser, eds. *Apocalypse and the Millennium in the American Civil War Era.* Baton Rouge: Louisiana State University Press, 2013.

Yacovone, Donald. "The Transformation of the Black Temperance Movement, 1827–1854: An Interpretation." *Journal of the Early Republic* 8 (Fall 1988): 288–91.

Index

MIX
Paper from
responsible sources
FSC® C013483